COUNTERSTRIKE

To Gerry —

COUNTERSTRIKE

THE UNTOLD STORY OF AMERICA'S SECRET CAMPAIGN AGAINST AL QAEDA

Best Wishes —

ERIC SCHMITT AND **THOM SHANKER**

TIMES BOOKS   HENRY HOLT AND COMPANY   NEW YORK

Times Books
Henry Holt and Company, LLC
Publishers since 1866
175 Fifth Avenue
New York, New York 10010
www.henryholt.com

Library of Congress Cataloging-in-Publication Data
Schmitt, Eric, 1959–
  Counterstrike : the untold story of America's secret campaign against al Qaeda / Eric
Schmitt and Thom Shanker.—1st ed.
     p. cm.
  Includes bibliographical references and index.
  ISBN 978-0-8050-9103-8
  1. Qaida (Organization)   2. Terrorism—United States—Prevention.   3. War on
Terrorism, 2001–2009.   4. United States—Military policy—21st century.   I. Shanker,
Thom.   II. Title.
  HV6432.5.Q2S34 2011
  973.931—dc22   2011010294

Henry Holt books are available for special promotions and
premiums. For details contact: Director, Special Markets.

Designed by Kelly S. Too

Printed in the United States of America
3   5   7   9   10   8   6   4   2

To Mom and Dad, for providing so many opportunities;
To Felice, for all your loving support;
And to Talia and Alexa, follow your dreams!
—E.S.

To Shirley and Ben, who set me on the right path;
To the lovely Lisa G., on the journey with me every day;
And to Sam and Daniel, onward, with your father's blessing!
—T.S.

CONTENTS

PROLOGUE

IN THE BEGINNING . . .

> One of the lamentable principles of human productivity is
> that it is easier to destroy than to create.
>
> —Thomas C. Schelling, *Arms and Influence* (1966)

Nearly a decade of frustration, false hopes, and faulty leads had
come to an end. A thirty-eight-minute raid by a secret Navy assault
team dropping into a walled, three-story compound in Abbottabad,
Pakistan, marked the culmination of months of painstaking intelligence work, military planning, and political risk assessment.

"Justice has been done," President Barack Obama declared to
the world on May 1, 2011. Osama bin Laden was dead.

The mission that successfully took Al Qaeda's founder forever
off the battlefield would not have been possible for the American
government to organize and execute in the years immediately after
the terror attacks of September 11, 2001. The national security
bureaucracy was divided, almost tribal. Information on threats
was hoarded by individual departments and agencies; planning
was walled off. Surveillance technologies that supplied details critical for the bin Laden raid were just being tested or did not even

exist. The military resisted incursions into its missions by the intelligence community. The spies didn't trust the soldiers. Members of the nation's most highly trained counterterrorism and hostage-rescue units could go their entire careers and never deploy on a real mission. Now, these teams carry out dozens of strikes and counterstrikes every night in places like Afghanistan and Iraq, with commandos and intelligence analysts teamed up throughout the operations. It once would have been unthinkable, but the raid by the Pentagon's top-tier force of commandos that killed bin Laden was under the overall command of the CIA director.

But it was more than just bigger and better tools, more than just hard-learned experience. The campaign against violent, religious extremism has required the United States to develop a new mind-set, including new principles, new doctrines, and even a new strategy to guide America's counterterrorism campaign. On 9/11, there was no playbook comparable to the doctrine of containment and the strategy of deterrence that characterized the long, cold war against the Communist threat. And it took years after 9/11 for policy makers to understand that the key to divining this new way forward would require them to reach back in time to the old lines of thought on how to protect America from its global enemies.

He is the last of them.

Tom Schelling is the last of the founding fathers of deterrence, the final survivor of an elite circle of strategic analysts and game-theory economists who pondered the impenetrable, planned for the horrific, dreamed up the nightmare scenarios, and plotted how nuclear weapons could kill millions, all in the hope that this very threat would prevent it from ever happening. The other cardinals of Cold War deterrence have passed: Bernard Brodie, Herman Kahn, Klaus Knorr, Albert Wohlstetter. Schelling is the last of them.

He already was eighty years old when terrorists converted a quartet of passenger airliners into cruise missiles for the September 11, 2001, attacks on New York City and Washington. In the aftermath of America's second Pearl Harbor, Schelling began pondering whether an updated system of coercion and inducement might be found to influence the behavior of a new generation of adversaries. Deterrence strategies had kept a tense nuclear peace with the Communist leadership of the Kremlin for more than four grim decades of the Cold War. Might they not offer guidance for how America could protect itself and its allies during this long war against violent religious extremists?

As the tenth anniversary of the 9/11 attacks approached, and as Schelling prepared to enter his tenth decade of life, he also began another major effort: a complete gutting and remodeling of his kitchen. He juggled discussions of deterrence and the installation of drywall one afternoon in his home in Bethesda, Maryland, just beyond the northwest boundary of Washington, D.C. He scurried about the construction site with puckish good humor, a sparkle in his eye, and a lilt in his speech, looking like Einstein by way of Yoda.

How does a Nobel laureate in economics rationalize a six-figure kitchen upgrade at age ninety? How does someone at that point in life amortize the experience of the remaining meals to be prepared and savored with a whopping contractor's bill? Was this healthy optimism or simple delusion? Perhaps that is the essence of Schelling's deterrence analysis, of his conflict-prevention strategies, on a most individual and human scale. For the professor whose essays helped inspire Stanley Kubrick to make his cinema classic *Dr. Strangelove*, it is obvious there are no guarantees. When every day is a potential Doomsday, don't you have to try everything you possibly can to make life better?

The central problem in attempting to apply Cold War deterrence theories to the age of violent religious extremism is that terrorists hold no territory and thus hold no territory dear. They offer no large and obvious high-value targets for American attack comparable to the national treasures the Soviets knew were at risk: populous cities, critical factories, dachas of the elite, military bases, or silos protecting the Kremlin's own nuclear force.

Then there is the question of attribution: A nuclear warhead hurled toward American soil by intercontinental ballistic missile has a return address. The attacking nation and its leaders can be identified and held responsible, and with certainty. Not so with a weapon of mass destruction smuggled into America and set off by a shadowy, stateless terrorist organization.

Finally, there are the millennial, aspirational, otherworldly goals of the jihadists. The Politburo pursued its clear self-interest, which required the survival of the Kremlin leadership. What can you threaten that will deter a suicide terrorist so obviously willing to give up his life in pursuit of holy war against the United States? This new threat may be wholly irrational, with no identifiable self-interest to which appeals can be made. Negotiations may be impossible, deterrence questionable. The future, then, holds little but a long war until one side is beaten into submission or eliminated; the only course is a fight to the death—or at least to exhaustion.

In fact, the 2002 National Security Strategy, signed by President George W. Bush one year after the September 11 attacks, stated that "traditional concepts of deterrence will not work against a terrorist enemy whose avowed tactics are wanton destruction and the targeting of innocents." Combating terrorists, then, can be done only by picking them up or picking them off.

"I don't believe that. I just don't believe that," Schelling said that day in his half-finished kitchen. "I think that there may be a lot of jihadists who are happy to immolate themselves as suicide bombers." Schelling advocated fashioning a campaign of inducements and pressures to alter the behavior of terrorist leaders, rather than relying on a continuing effort to kill them all.

Even the Bush administration, before leaving office, acknowledged the value of combining traditional national-security thinking with an evolving, broader, and more nuanced approach to combating terrorism. It would include capture-and-kill missions, to be sure. But it would also create a broader set of policies that included increased defenses to deny terrorists certainty of success; disruption of their fund-raising, recruiting, and planning networks; campaigns to dissuade those who may support extremist ideology but who would not want to sacrifice their own lives to the cause; and, yes, even deterrence strategies to prevent an attack with weapons of mass destruction, whether nuclear, radiological, biological, or chemical.

"A new deterrence calculus combines the need to deter terrorists and supporters from contemplating a WMD [weapons of mass destruction] attack and, failing that, to dissuade them from actually conducting an attack," the Bush administration wrote in its 2006 National Strategy for Combating Terrorism, just four years after declaring that deterrence "will not work."

In applying the term *deterrence* to counterterrorism policy, had the administration found a new strategy or just a new slogan? Deterrence in the strictest Cold War sense refers to the idea that you induce, even compel, an adversary not to do something by credibly threatening terrible pain and suffering in retaliation. From the beginning, American officials conceded that their evolving strategy included a more elastic set of concepts, in particular deterrence by denial (of the opportunity to attack) and deterrence by disruption as well as deterrence by punishment. As the debate spread across the government and military, some national security experts sought to create something new by recapturing the concept's meaning from an older literature of criminal law. Criminal deterrence puts cops on the street and bars over windows—and prisons in our communities—to force potential lawbreakers to weigh costs and benefits before deciding whether or not to engage in illegal activity. When we lock up a bad guy, we are preventing him from committing more crimes, with the added benefit of perhaps deterring others from the same actions.

President Barack Obama, who inherited a Bush administration counterterrorism strategy that was still evolving, moved rapidly to put his own imprint on a still-maturing policy. "The single biggest threat to U.S. security, short-term, medium-term and long-term, would be the possibility of a terrorist organization obtaining a nuclear weapon," he told world leaders in the spring of 2010 at a summit he convened in Washington to discuss exactly this threat. The president expressed certainty that Al Qaeda's leadership was unwavering in "trying to secure a nuclear weapon—a weapon of mass destruction that they have no compunction at using."

There are no guarantees. That's why the United States during the Cold War spent hundreds of billions of dollars to research, develop, test, and deploy a nuclear arsenal of intercontinental reach and ever-increasing accuracy and destructive power even as deterrence theories became more refined and nuanced, and targeting strategies grew more complicated and precise. Show the Kremlin it had nothing to gain by nuclear war, and maybe you prevent nuclear war, argued Schelling and the other high priests of deterrence theory. And they were proved right.

Schelling argues that while all of these steps are prudent and that it is the government's obligation to do all it can, it would nonetheless be difficult for a terrorist organization to obtain a nuclear weapon. "First, it is not easy to smuggle out of the country where it was stolen," he said. "Second, if you wanted to buy a nuclear bomb on the black market, you'd have to recognize that nobody can tell the difference between a live bomb and a dummy. That means that if somebody shows up on the black market to buy what is alleged to be a nuclear bomb, they don't know whether it's a CIA agent, or a Mossad agent or a KGB agent or it could simply be an entrepreneur who makes something that looks like a bomb and says something like: 'You know if you hit the trigger, it will explode.'" But in a world of increasing proliferation, when it is not beyond the realm of possibility that nuclear components might enter the black market from North Korea or some other rogue power, or even from an increasingly unstable ally like Pakistan, verification of the weapon's functionality may not be a concern.

Even President Obama's own terrorism adviser, John Brennan, has confirmed that Al Qaeda appears to have been hoodwinked in the past on the global radiological black market. "There have been numerous reports over the years, over the past eight or nine years, about attempts throughout the world to obtain various types of purported material that is nuclear-related," said Brennan, who is in charge of counterterrorism issues on the National Security Council. "We know that Al Qaeda has been involved in a number of these efforts to acquire it. Fortunately, I think they've been scammed a number of times."

But there is no evidence that Al Qaeda has been deterred. "We know that they have continued to pursue that," Brennan said. "We know individuals within the organization that have been given that responsibility."

A stocky man with a craggy face and close-cropped hair, Brennan rose through the ranks of the CIA, becoming the agency's station chief in Saudi Arabia in the late 1990s, then chief of staff to CIA director George Tenet, and later the agency's deputy executive director. After the September 11 attacks, Brennan helped establish the Terrorism Threat Integration Center. When that became the National Counterterrorism Center, he was its interim director, but he was passed over for the permanent job and left government. Brought in to advise Obama's 2008 presidential campaign, he and the candidate hit it off. After Obama was elected, Brennan's name was on the short list for the post of CIA director, but his ties to the Bush administration's war on terror, specifically the secret interrogations program, drew criticism from liberal Democrats. Instead, Obama named Brennan to a White House staff position, deputy national security adviser for homeland security and counterterrorism, a job that does not require Senate confirmation. From his windowless West Wing basement office, Brennan became the president's point man on cyberthreats, homegrown extremism, and threats from Al Qaeda and its affiliates. Brennan visited Yemen, where an Al Qaeda affiliate is especially active and worrisome, four times in the administration's first two years. He spoke frequently by phone with the country's mercurial leader, Ali Abdullah Saleh, whose regime was tottering on the brink of collapse by May 2011.

For senior intelligence analysts like John Brennan—skeptics by nature—the proof that terrorists have not yet gained access to a weapon of mass destruction is that no such weapons have been used or threatened. "I don't think anybody would argue that if Al Qaeda had the opportunity, that they wouldn't use them," said one senior defense intelligence analyst. "That is why they don't have it: They would have used it."

That brought Tom Schelling to ponder the undesirable, the "what-if?" of Al Qaeda acquiring a horror weapon. "My hunch is that by the time they have a bomb, they will have spent more hours thinking and talking about what it is good for than any head of state, any minister of defense, any foreign minister," he said. "Probably only a few people in think tanks have spent so many hundreds of thousands of hours thinking about what you would do if you were a terrorist and had a bomb. I think they might decide that this bomb is much too valuable to waste killing people."

Schelling postulated that Al Qaeda with the bomb could think, "We're the world's tenth nuclear power. It's the U.S., Russia, China, France, Britain, India, Israel, Pakistan, North Korea—and us. Why go kill one million people in Los Angeles or Hamburg when we can maybe establish diplomatic relations and start negotiating?" Warming to the subject, he continued, "I think that if they are ingenious they would say: 'We have already planted a nuclear weapon in one of the following ten American cities.' Then Al Qaeda would start making its demands." This, of course, requires an assessment that Al Qaeda would, indeed, engage in a cost-benefit analysis the way a rational nation-state would.

The next question comes quickly: Is it possible to reach out to terrorists and to teach them the rules that responsible nations have followed since becoming nuclear powers? "Should I be out there trying to educate them that if you do get a nuclear weapon there are better things to do than killing people in Baltimore or Boston?" Schelling said. "I've been trying to think for a few years, how to reach the Iranians or North Koreans, to explain to them that getting the bomb may be very useful as long as they don't plan to use it. Then, how do I reach, whoever it is, the terrorist organization? I tend to believe that proving you've got one doesn't require that you detonate one someplace."

Although the Bush administration, like all of its predecessors, swore never to negotiate with terrorists, it did undertake an extraordinary, and extraordinarily secret, effort to open a line of communication with bin Laden and Al Qaeda's senior leadership. It was an attempt to replicate how the United States tried to sustain a dialogue with the Soviet Union, even during the darkest days of the Cold War, when White House and Kremlin leaders described in private and in public a set of acceptable behaviors—and described with equal clarity the swift, vicious, even nuclear punishment for gross violations. In the months after the September 11 attacks, Bush's national security staff made several attempts to get a private message to bin Laden and his inner circle. The messages were sent through business associates of the bin Laden family's vast financial empire as well as through some of bin Laden's closest relatives, a number of whom were receptive to opening a secret dialogue to restrain and contain their terrorist kinsman, whom they viewed as a blot on their name. (Other relatives were openly hostile to the American entreaties.) According to a senior American intelligence officer with first-hand knowledge of the effort, the response from Osama bin Laden was silence.

Schelling points out that the United States exploded the first atomic device in the New Mexico desert on July 16, 1945, with the bombing of Hiroshima following three weeks later. But theories of how to deter the use of nightmare weapons evolved slowly.

His own landmark work on deterrence theory, *Arms and Influence*, was not published until more than two decades after the attacks on Hiroshima and Nagasaki. And nuclear deterrence theories continued to evolve long after that.

It has been said that America's failure on September 11, 2001, was a failure of imagination, the consequence of America's inability to anticipate how a sophisticated terrorist network could infiltrate its operatives into the United States, train them how to fly—but not take off or land—commercial airliners, and use those passenger planes in a fiery assault on national landmarks. But the failures went beyond imagination to gaps in intelligence, in capability, in technology.

In the first years after 9/11, America was lucky and good, and the terrorists were unlucky and not particularly good. Al Qaeda was unable to replicate the success of a simultaneous, mass-casualty attack, but the public must understand that the United States— its military, its intelligence community, and its law enforcement personnel—cannot count on being lucky all the time. Terrorism and counterterrorism are the new Darwinism; both species are evolving. And it is certain that despite improvements in tactical American counterterrorism skills, in time a determined terrorist plot is certain to get through again.

The United States could move from tactical success to tactical success against extremists and still end in stalemate against terrorism. An evolution in strategic thinking was called for in counterterrorism, much as the Cold War necessitated the rise of thinkers like Tom Schelling. This evolution would be carried out over the better portion of a decade after the attacks on the World Trade Center and the Pentagon.

1

KNOW THINE ENEMY

At the U.S. Embassy in Kuwait City, Brigadier General Jeffrey Schloesser watched in horror—but not surprise—the sickening images from 6,500 miles away that flickered from the television screen. It was Tuesday afternoon, September 11, 2001.

Schloesser, a forty-seven-year-old former Army Special Operations helicopter pilot from Kansas, was one of a small number of counterterrorism experts in the military's ranks. He spoke fluent Arabic and was steeped in Middle East politics and history, having earned a master's degree from Georgetown University's School of Foreign Service and served a yearlong tour in Jordan. He was now serving as the embassy's liaison to the Kuwaiti military.

For Schloesser and for many of his uniformed and civilian colleagues serving in the Middle East, the United States had been in an undeclared war with Al Qaeda long before this day. Eleven months earlier, on October 12, 2000, Al Qaeda operatives in a small skiff had detonated a one-thousand-pound suicide bomb alongside the Navy destroyer USS *Cole* as it refueled in the port of Aden, on Yemen's southern coast. Seventeen American sailors were killed, and thirty-nine others injured in the blast that ripped a forty-by-forty-foot blackened gash in the ship's port side. The gloves are coming off now, Schloesser had thought then. But the deadly strike failed to outrage the American public.

After the *Cole* bombing, the movements and travel of American embassy employees and their families in Kuwait were sharply restricted. Al Qaeda had failed in an eerily similar but less publicized attack against the Navy destroyer USS *The Sullivans* earlier that January as part of the 2000 millennium plots. The terrorists' plan had been to load a boat full of explosives and blow it up near the warship during a port call in Yemen. But the plotters overloaded the skiff, causing it to sink to the bottom of Aden harbor. Months later, after leaving Kuwait, Schloesser would learn that an Al Qaeda operative had been captured carrying a chilling set of blueprints, plans of the house next door to where he and his wife, Patty, had lived. Years later, it gave Patty Schloesser the creeps just thinking about it.

Now, as the searing Kuwaiti summer afternoon gave way to a hazy evening, Schloesser and the CIA station chief looked away from the television images and locked glances with their boss, Ambassador James A. Larocco, a career foreign service officer who had served tours in Egypt, Israel, and Saudi Arabia. "Guys, we've got to take immediate steps right here," Larocco said. As the three men rushed out of the station chief's office to report to superiors in Washington, coordinate with Kuwaiti security forces going on alert, and check in with a spider web of informants and spies for clues to a possible next wave of attacks, each man felt it in his gut: Al Qaeda. For Schloesser, who was already preparing to leave for a new assignment at the Pentagon, a decade of planning and carrying out a secretive counterterrorism campaign against Al Qaeda was just beginning.

Juan Zarate stood at the window of his new fourth-floor office at the Treasury Department in Washington looking south toward the Pentagon. Clouds of billowing black smoke smeared the early morning sky. "Jim, I can tell you right now, the Pentagon's been hit!" Zarate yelled over the phone to his former boss at the Justice Department, James S. Reynolds, whom he had called to alert to the strikes. "We're under attack!"

Three weeks earlier, Zarate had been a rising star in the Justice Department's terrorism and violent crimes section. With degrees from Harvard College and Harvard Law School, Zarate had been a young federal prosecutor assisting on some of the biggest cases in the burgeoning field of counterterrorism.

The son of immigrants—his mother from Cuba; his father, a physician, from Mexico—Zarate had already lived a life that was a classic all-American success story. Raised in Orange County, California, in a politically conservative family, he showed an interest in security conflicts at a precocious age. As a fifth grader, he wrote a term paper on the war in Angola in the 1970s and the role of Cuban forces there. Zarate, balding, with rimless glasses, looked older than his thirty years. As a junior-level attorney, he had already participated in the prosecutions of the bombers of the U.S. embassies in Kenya and Tanzania in August 1998, attacks organized by Al Qaeda that killed 224 people and wounded thousands. Later, his superiors assigned him to cases involving Hamas, the FARC insurgent group in Colombia, and the attack on the USS *Cole*. The *Cole* bombing, in particular, was seared in his mind after he pored over the graphic photos of damage to the ship and the sailors killed on board. "If the American people saw what we're seeing, they'd demand war," Zarate said.

When the Treasury Department came calling in August 2001 and offered to make him part of a senior team running its international financial enforcement and sanctions branch, Zarate jumped at the chance to broaden his counterterrorism credentials and delve into the murky world of illicit financing. Three weeks later, on September 11, Zarate could barely find his new office in the cavernous Treasury Department building, much less know which levers to pull and which people to call in a crisis. It left him feeling momentarily helpless. "If I were back at DOJ, I'd know what to do, who to call," he said. "I didn't really know what to do here yet." Zarate followed his instincts, which were screaming, "Al Qaeda, Al Qaeda," and called his former colleagues at Justice to offer his assistance.

As a Californian, Zarate was quick to remind federal investigators to watch for aircraft flying from the West Coast, not just the East Coast. Zarate had a flashback to an earlier failed Al Qaeda plan: the so-called Bojinka plot, hatched in the Philippines in 1995, to bomb twelve American commercial jets as they flew over the Pacific. That scheme unraveled only after extensive planning and even some trial runs. One of the conspirators in that plot was a man named Khalid Shaikh Mohammed, whom authorities would later identify as the mastermind of the September 11 attacks. "Bojinka animated a lot of our thinking," Zarate said. "We expected more attacks. We anticipated more attacks. The only question in my mind was size and scope."

Soon after the strike on the Pentagon, Zarate and a handful of senior Treasury officials rushed from their offices to the Secret Service headquarters six blocks away, where they watched the day's events unfold from the service's command center. Within months, Zarate would become the point man for the Treasury—and for much of the U.S. government—tracking the movement of money through the murky channels of terrorist financing, dissecting the sophisticated and shadowy networks of donors, illicit activities, and other sources that filled terrorist and insurgent coffers. From Justice to Treasury and ultimately to the upper echelons of the White House's National Security Council, Zarate would over the next decade employ his keen intellect, near-photographic memory, and deft ability to bring together disparate players in the government's bruising internal bureaucratic battles over how to carry out the Bush administration's global war on terror.

■ ■ ■

On the morning of September 11, Michael G. Vickers was immersed
in the details of plans to help transform the Pentagon by creating
lighter, faster, and more lethal forces to deal with emerging threats.
Vickers directed strategic studies at the Center for Strategic and
Budgetary Assessments, one of the leading independent defense
research organizations in Washington. Restructuring the armed
forces was one of the Pentagon's top priorities in the early days of
the Bush administration. Defense Secretary Donald H. Rumsfeld
was in the midst of setting strategy and budgets under a process
called the Quadrennial Defense Review, which was mandated by
statute. The Pentagon's new leadership was assessing which weapons systems it ought to buy, how much money ought to be requested,
and whether the number of soldiers, sailors, airmen, and marines
should be changed.

But in the midafternoon, one of Rumsfeld's top aides franti-
cally called Vickers, telling him that the secretary urgently needed
him for a different assignment, one that drew on his storied terror-
fighting career from his Cold War days. Soft-spoken and wearing
thick glasses, Vickers was the Pentagon's own version of Clark Kent,
an unassuming figure whose spare but unusually impressive official
Pentagon biography only hinted at the extraordinary life he had
lived in the 1970s and 1980s: "His operational experience spans
covert action and espionage, unconventional warfare, counterterrorism (including hostage rescue operations), counterinsurgency, and
foreign internal defense." Mild manner notwithstanding, Vickers
was one of the nation's most experienced counterterrorism operatives and planners.

In 1973, when he was twenty years old, Vickers had enlisted
directly into the Green Berets, taking advantage of a rarely offered
program that admitted qualified civilians straight out of college or
private life into the Special Forces. In Germany, with the 10th Special Forces Group, he learned how to operate behind Soviet lines
to link up with partisan forces. The Soviet Union and its Warsaw
Pact allies had positioned a vastly greater number of tanks and

armored troop carriers along the Fulda Gap in central Germany, across from American and NATO forces. If it came to war, one of his unit's most sensitive missions would be to infiltrate behind Soviet lines, each four-man team armed with a backpack-size nuclear bomb. Vickers and his comrades were to plant these miniature nuclear warheads near massed Warsaw Pact forces and along their lines of attack to blunt their overmatched numbers. But, given the sensitivity of the nuclear technology, the orders were not to drop and run but to maintain "positive control" over the nukes until the detonate directives were broadcast via coded message. Vickers and his men had spoken with the weapons designers and knew the detonation sequence. There was much gallows humor about whether they would have time to get away.

Fortunately, Vickers never had to carry out these orders. Instead, he took advance training and became a Special Forces officer and shifted to Central America, where he combated Salvadoran rebels and helped resolve an airline hijacking and another hostage situation involving Honduran government ministers. Vickers loved the dangerous, fast-paced missions, and when advancement in the Army hierarchy threatened to limit his opportunities to conduct field operations, he packed his rucksack and transferred to the CIA in 1983. By now Vickers spoke Spanish, Czech, and some Russian and was qualified to plan and lead the most sensitive covert operations. In his first year at the agency he was quickly dispatched to the Caribbean island of Grenada to fight alongside Army airborne forces sent to help restore a pro-Western government that had been overthrown by Cuban-backed insurgents.

No sooner had Vickers finished in Grenada when the agency sent him to Beirut in the aftermath of the suicide truck bombings there in October 1983 that killed 241 American service members and 58 French paratroopers. It was Vickers's first brush with Hezbollah, the Iranian-backed, anti-American terrorist organization. But his most heralded mission was yet to come. In late 1984, he was tapped to be the principal strategist for the largest covert action program in the CIA's history: the paramilitary operation to funnel guns, antiaircraft missiles, and money to the Afghan mujahideen that in time would drive the Soviet Army out of Afghanistan. Vickers was featured in the book *Charlie Wilson's War* and was introduced to film audiences in the Hollywood version as the whiz kid playing chess against three opponents at once in a park across from the White House. But that was artistic license: Vickers does not play chess, at least not the kind on a board with sixty-four black and white squares. From the late summer of 1984 to the spring of 1986, Vickers worked with the Afghan resistance and came to know dozens of Afghan commanders, many of whom on 9/11 were allied with the Taliban or fighting against it.

Few if any American officials understood Afghanistan's history, rugged terrain, and complicated set of warring personalities on 9/11 better than Michael Vickers. And, now more than a decade after his greatest professional triumph, Vickers was being summoned back to help combat a threat in Afghanistan, this time as a civilian adviser to the secretary of defense—a role that would open a second major chapter in his counterterrorism career. But he was still a little out of date in his knowledge, having left the CIA in the spring of 1986 to attend Wharton Business School and having spent the 1990s in academia, the private sector, and the think-tank community. "My view of terrorism was shaped by my experiences in the '80s, which were hijackings, largely Palestinian terrorism," Vickers said. "On 9/12, I had a lot of catching up to do in a hurry."

The day began at 3:30 a.m. for the thirty-year-old Defense Intelligence Agency (DIA) analyst who, just a few years out of a prestigious midwestern graduate school, had already earned a spot within a tiny, elite cadre of Al Qaeda specialists in the U.S. government. September 11 had started auspiciously for the analyst, who will be identified in this book as John Tyson because of the highly sensitive nature of his intelligence work. He was in early that day to brief his boss, Rear Admiral Lowell E. Jacoby, the Joint Staff's top uniformed intelligence officer, on a complicated stream of information about a terrorist threat that Tyson and some other analysts were tracking. The Joint Staff is made up of 1,300 uniformed officers, enlisted troops, and civilians who work grueling hours in the Pentagon to support the chairman of the Joint Chiefs of Staff, the military's top officer and senior military adviser to the president and secretary of defense.

Shortly after 5:30 a.m., as the briefing wrapped up, the admiral summoned him for a private word. The National Security Council's top counterterrorism official, Richard A. Clarke, had asked for Tyson to join his staff at the White House. Tyson was pleased. During graduate school, he had studied briefly in Egypt and had researched terrorism under the tutelage of a retired police detective who had migrated into academia and specialized in international criminal justice. Tyson joined the DIA in 1997 as the agency's first analyst dedicated solely to assessing the threat posed by a little-known Saudi radical "with a lot of money and a big mouth"—a man named Osama bin Laden. He became a member of a small, eclectic group of bin Laden experts whose ranks included a gruff National Security Agency code breaker; a church-going, cat-loving CIA terrorism specialist; and a mother of six who in her day job at the State Department drew on lessons from child rearing to help master the understanding of an emerging terrorist organization called Al Qaeda. Tyson, with his earnest enthusiasm, close-cropped military haircut, and athletic build, was the rookie of the group. Now, he would be working at the White House, the pinnacle of decision making in the government. But the events of that morning would cancel those plans; Tyson was too valuable for the DIA to spare.

At 8:46 a.m., American Airlines Flight 11 plowed into the North Tower of the World Trade Center, and Tyson's world turned upside down. He and other American intelligence analysts had worked through Al Qaeda's attacks on the U.S. embassies in Kenya and Tanzania in 1998. They had worked through the bombing of the USS *Cole* in 2000. "The *Cole* attack, where they tried to kill our guys—you take that pretty personal, because we are the Department of Defense," Tyson said. Now 9/11. "They tried to kill me here in this building—you take that personal a little bit, too," he added. "There's something in the pit of your stomach because we'd been waiting for something like this."

Trained for this kind of emergency, one group of DIA analysts immediately began assessing what had happened; another group started going back through classified intelligence reports searching for previously undetected clues about how the attack was planned and conducted; and yet another group reached out to colleagues at the CIA and other intelligence agencies to swap information. That's what Tyson was doing when the Pentagon was hit at 9:37 a.m. "Biggest office building in the world. It is all made of concrete. And to feel it shift, almost like it went up and then back down again, was pretty jolting," Tyson said. After the attack, Tyson drove across the Potomac to the DIA's main headquarters at Bolling Air Force Base in Washington. A few hours later, he was summoned back to the Pentagon. Armed military personnel had to come from a Pentagon command center to vouch for him at the heavily guarded entrance and to escort him back into the building, where he worked and slept that night. "The next year was basically a blur," he recalls.

These four individuals—Schloesser, Zarate, Vickers, and Tyson—are largely unknown to the general public, toiling one or more levels below the most senior officials in the Bush and Obama administrations. But they represent a cadre of counterterrorism specialists from a variety of backgrounds in the military, law enforcement, intelligence services, and other government agencies who found themselves playing key roles after the 9/11 attacks. Over the past decade, they and others like them have struggled to devise—and sometimes improvise—policies and strategies to fight a persistent and ever-changing, but not always very effective, terrorist foe. Often these were the people who had a first glimmer of a more expansive approach to combating the terrorists and their guiding ideology but were frustrated until some piece of insight broke through and took hold. Their personal experiences over the past ten years offer a glimpse into the evolution of America's fight against Al Qaeda and affiliated terrorist groups.

With skill and luck, the United States was able to avert another large-scale, high-casualty attack in the first years after 9/11. Yet the fact remains that even with improved defenses and increasingly effective tactical success, in the faraway safe havens of Pakistan and Yemen a determined and creative terrorist plot is certain to succeed sooner or later. America cannot be good enough and lucky forever. Had a young Nigerian man been more adept in detonating an explosive sewn into his underwear on Christmas Day 2009, an American commercial jetliner would likely have crashed in Detroit, killing hundreds of people. Had a Pakistani American honed his bomb-making skills just a bit better, his SUV packed with explosives would have detonated in Times Square in May 2010. Had that plot, hatched in Pakistan's tribal areas, succeeded, it likely would have forced the Obama administration to attack targets in Pakistan in ways that would have had exceedingly negative and enduring ripple effects on American policy in the Muslim world.

In many ways, the best the United States can now do is to push that day of reckoning farther down the road, reduce the possible damage inflicted by a strike, and build a national resilience akin to what the British and the Israelis have developed over time and through grim experience: to recover quickly and confidently from the terrorist attack that is sure to come. But to make this happen, the American public needs to know more about what those in our counterterrorism structure know—and what they fear.

■ ■ ■

The memory remains strong throughout the U.S. government of how ill-prepared it was on 9/11 to cope with the threats of modern terrorism. The commander in chief, President George W. Bush, was aboard his vaunted flying command post, Air Force One, for most of the day, but its Cold War command-and-control capability made it virtually useless for the requirements of this twenty-first-century threat.

Air Force One was built to protect the president and broadcast launch codes in the event of a nuclear war, not to operate as an airborne information hub and media center. Getting live television and Internet aboard the aircraft had never been a priority and was not possible on September 11. Bush, who had begun the day in Florida and was fuming that he could not return immediately to Washington, was infuriated that he could not receive a live feed from Fox News, CNN, or any other cable television network. The president, his aides, and reporters on board were left squinting at soundless, fuzzy images skimmed from weak ground signals of local television channels below as the presidential plane passed overhead. Despite the investment of hundreds of billions of dollars in the country's military arsenal and spy networks, Bush was largely blind to the vivid images of destruction and disarray that were seen by millions of Americans live on television.

To protect the president after the attacks in New York and Washington, Air Force One zigzagged west on a secret route from Florida to Barksdale Air Force Base in Louisiana to refuel. On the tarmac, Bush was unnerved by what he saw outside his window: rows of B-52 nuclear bombers were on the runway in scramble mode, and air crews were running around in battle-dress uniforms. The airmen were not gearing up in response to the terrorist attacks, it turned out, but were part of a previously scheduled annual drill by the U.S. Strategic Command, simulating a nuclear attack against the homeland. Barksdale did not possess the technology to connect the president by secure videoconference with his top advisers in Washington, so Air Force One was quickly airborne again, this time bound for Offutt Air Force Base outside of Omaha,

Nebraska, the headquarters of the Strategic Command, or "Strat-com." Deliberately located in the middle of the country during the Cold War—at that time out of reach of Soviet long-range missiles and bombers—Stratcom and its subterranean war room were built to transmit a president's orders to launch a nuclear strike.

Stratcom had been engaged for more than a week in a high-level exercise called Global Guardian, which posited that a rogue nation called Slumonia would attack the United States with nuclear weapons. The State Department insists that countries cast as adversaries in war games not be identified, but Slumonia was a small nuclear power in northeast Asia—obviously, North Korea. With the cancellation of constant high alerts at the end of the Cold War, American bomber crews did not have extensive experience in load-ing nuclear weapons, so this exercise was a way to keep their skills up to date. That is why on the morning of 9/11 air crews were pulling nuclear bombs and missiles out of their heavily guarded storage sites and loading them aboard B-52s and B-2s in Louisi-ana and Missouri—precisely the scene that startled Bush at Barks-dale. The nuclear weapons were real, but their triggers were not armed.

By the time Bush landed at Offutt, Admiral Richard W. Mies, Stratcom's commanding officer, had cancelled the training exercise and ordered the nuclear warheads returned to secure storage bun-kers and the bombers dispersed, lest either pose a target of oppor-tunity for an unforeseen follow-on terrorist attack. "We are not under pretend attack," Mies told his assembled staff. "We are really being attacked."

Even as Stratcom was rehearsing for old-school threats, the military's elite counterterrorism force, the Joint Special Operations Command at Fort Bragg, North Carolina, was preparing to con-duct an exercise against the growing threat of a nuclear, chemi-cal, or biological terrorist attack against the United States or against American interests. On September 11, about 1,800 Special Operations forces and a handful of other secret government operators were preparing to launch a sixteen-day exercise in six European and Mediterranean countries and on a ship at sea. The goal of the classified drill was to find and thwart terrorists who had captured an unconventional weapon and threatened to use it against the United States. The exercise, overseen by the U.S. European Command and code-named Ellipse Charlie, was called off that day during its final planning stages, and the commandos rushed back to their real-world bases.

The European Command and the Special Operations forces had identified the right kind of threat. Because they were trained in hostage-rescue operations and counterterrorism missions, it also made sense that the Special Operations troops were rehearsing a complicated mock attack from a foe like Al Qaeda. But the American commandos and the rest of the U.S. government were still several steps behind Al Qaeda in piecing together the critical intelligence and threat information that could have helped prevent the attacks. Now the race was on to learn everything possible about Al Qaeda before it could strike the homeland again.

On Monday, October 15, Jeff Schloesser steered his dark green BMW onto Interstate 95 and started the thirty-minute trip from his home in Springfield, Virginia, to the Pentagon. At 5:30 a.m., the crushing Washington morning commute had not yet turned the eight-lane freeway into a parking lot, and Schloesser made good time on this crisp morning, the first day of his new job and a world away from the Middle East.

In the five weeks since 9/11, Schloesser had returned from his fifteen-month assignment in Kuwait, expecting to go to Washington to punch the next ticket in his climb up the Army's leadership ladder: a stint working European policy issues on the military's Joint Staff. Schloesser had served in Kosovo in the late 1990s, giving him some exposure to the bedeviling intricacies of Balkan politics. But Schloesser's boss, Lieutenant General John Abizaid, had other ideas for him. Abizaid directed political-military affairs for the Joint Staff and was one of the Army's most intelligent officers. A Lebanese American with small-town roots in northern California—and the only Arabic speaker to advance to four-star rank in the Army (he would get his fourth star in 2003)—Abizaid had served in Jordan and had spent a year as a member of a UN observer force in southern Lebanon. In between those assignments, Abizaid had commanded a 120-man Ranger company that parachuted into Grenada as part of the 1983 invasion. At one point in the operation, Abizaid ordered a soldier to hot-wire a bulldozer at the airfield and charge at Cuban troops with blade raised, giving cover to himself and his men (an incident that was immortalized in the 1986 Clint Eastwood film *Heartbreak Ridge*). Schloesser reported to Abizaid's office early that morning, not knowing exactly what was in store for him. "Forget Europe," Abizaid said. "You're going to stand up a brand-new office here, the Strategic Planning Cell for the War on Terror."

In wartime, the responsibility for planning and waging specific campaigns falls to the regional military commander assigned to oversee that slice of the globe. In this case, responsibility for Afghanistan fell to the U.S. Central Command, based in Tampa, Florida, and led by General Tommy R. Franks. The broader strategic military planning that cuts across different regional commands is the domain of the Joint Staff. On September 11, the Joint Staff had no office or staff specifically assigned to thinking about fighting terrorists around the world. Jeff Schloesser and his new team would be filling a crucial void.

At the end of the week, Abizaid convened his crisis-action team and singled out his newest chief terrorist hunter. "Have we killed any Al Qaeda yet?" Abizaid demanded, staring at Schloesser. Schloesser, still trying to find his way around the labyrinthine halls of the Pentagon, wrote that night in one of the small, green notebooks that he kept for every assignment since he was a young captain: "Not sure, too much focus on the Taliban in Afghanistan and not enough on our global fight against Al Qaeda." Schloesser was not alone in grappling with America's newest Public Enemy Number One.

Within the U.S. government on September 11, 2001, there were peaks and valleys in terms of understanding Al Qaeda, but mostly valleys. The Clinton administration had reacted with increasing alarm after Al Qaeda's attacks in 1998 against the U.S. embassies in Kenya and Tanzania as well as the strike on the *Cole* two years later. But President Clinton never ordered more than cruise missile strikes against Al Qaeda targets. When George W. Bush took office in January 2001, few of his advisers had any detailed understanding of how Al Qaeda was organized, how it was equipped, and how it could train its operatives to carry out the worst attack on American soil since Pearl Harbor. As one senior White House official who closely monitored terrorist intelligence reports recalled, "There were people up and down the hallways who couldn't spell Al Qaeda. Literally they didn't know a thing. I remember being asked, 'Is it all one word or two?'"

The new administration's greater national security concerns centered on building antimissile defenses against a rogue state like North Korea or countering the growing military influence of China throughout Asia. After September 11, there was a mad scramble to catch up. Within the inner circles of the Bush administration, officials vented frustration at the lack of clear understanding about the nature of this new enemy. At the same time, intense debates involving senior policy makers and intelligence officials centered on how precisely to define the enemy beyond Al Qaeda. "Pretend it's a box," explained one participating intelligence official, recounting a primer he gave to senior White House aides. "Who is inside the box and who is outside the box with this enemy? Is it Hezbollah? Is it Hamas? There is a lot of debate about how big this box is and what you put in it."

In the months after the 9/11 attacks, government officials arrived at a tentative consensus about transnational threats with global reach. Al Qaeda and its associated groups became the main target. But intelligence officials and policy makers struggled with how to define the nature of the enemy, where it resided, and its nexus to state actors, including Iran, Sudan, and Iraq. It was a question that grew increasingly politically charged beginning in early 2002, as senior Bush administration officials sought to draw links between Al Qaeda and the government of Saddam Hussein in Baghdad.

In the initial weeks after the attack, the more than fifty organizations that make up the U.S. government's intelligence and law enforcement agencies scrambled to try to answer these questions. But often they found they spoke past each other, had different priorities, and played diverging and uncoordinated roles in combating the new threat.

At the National Security Agency, the supersecret eavesdropping agency at Fort Meade, Maryland, a call went out from its director, Lieutenant General Michael V. Hayden of the Air Force, to open the spigots and provide as much information as possible to the FBI, which was responsible for tracking terrorists inside the United States. Little of the NSA's technical wizardry had been aimed at Al Qaeda before 9/11. As FBI agents chased tips culled from telephone, e-mail, and other communications intercepts, many of them complained that the NSA's information was nothing but a series of dry holes that wasted critical manpower and resources. The NSA fired back that the FBI had misused and misunderstood the valuable clues they had been provided. It didn't help that the FBI lagged woefully behind in updating its outmoded computer systems. "We in no way thought we were giving them leads," Hayden said. "We thought we were giving them raw data that they would put into a larger database. It took us a period of time to go, 'Oh, hell, that's not working. Tighten it up here,' because they just didn't have the ability to absorb what was coming down."

But the nation was on edge, fearing another wave of attacks. In this heightened threat environment, the CIA began dumping its in-box of raw intelligence reports of plots, sightings, and potential attacks on Bush's desk every morning as part of his top-secret Presidential Daily Briefing. The data came in a neatly printed spreadsheet called the Threat Matrix, the top two or three dozen of the most disturbing pieces of intelligence and suspected plots that American and allied spy agencies had dug up in the previous twenty-four hours. "In those early days, believe me, we saw them all—nuclear, biological, chemical [NBC]," said a former senior staff member of the National Security Council. "There were compelling reports of NBC being developed, smuggled in, and planned for use in the U.S. None of them panned out, but it all affected the psyche of policymakers after 9/11."

As the FBI and NSA crossed signals early on, the FBI and the CIA also operated at cross-purposes, sometimes unwittingly. In order to avoid being shunted aside in advising the president on threats to the nation, the FBI soon came up with its own version of a threat matrix for the president. At one point in early 2002, both agencies were tracking what American analysts said were growing preparations for a major "wedding" somewhere in the Midwest. In terrorist parlance, the word *wedding* is often code for a major attack. Dribs and drabs on this "wedding" planning made their way to the president from both agencies, independent of each other, of course. Finally, over the Easter holiday, during a video-teleconference with top aides in Washington from his ranch in Crawford, Texas, Bush halted the briefing, exasperated by the discrepancies in the rival agencies' reporting about the suspected threat. "George, Bob, get together and sort this out," he told his CIA director, George J. Tenet, and FBI director, Robert S. Mueller III.

Bush's instincts were right. When the analysts finally untangled their clues, it turned out that the ominous "wedding" really was just that: the matrimony of a young man and a young woman from two prominent Pakistani American families. There was no threat. There was no plot. Until the president personally intervened, however, the FBI and CIA had jealously guarded their sources and assessments without collaborating to resolve what turned out to be a time-consuming dead end.

Within three months of the 9/11 attacks, the Taliban had been routed and had fled Afghanistan. Osama bin Laden had escaped the bombing of Tora Bora and slipped across the border into Pakistan. Mindful of the lessons of the Soviet occupation in Afghanistan, the Americans maintained a light footprint there: small groups of CIA paramilitary officers supported by Special Operations forces that worked closely with the indigenous Northern Alliance troops. At the Pentagon and at the CIA, analysts and operatives watched as militants spilled out of Afghanistan and scurried for refuge elsewhere, plotting to fight another day. Yet the outlines of what constituted Al Qaeda and its affiliates were still vague. A fear of when and where the next attack might take place continued to grip official Washington. With little information or understanding of how extremist networks like Al Qaeda work, some proposed responses by various agencies were driven by overreaction or worse.

Some planners proposed that if Al Qaeda appeared ready to attack America again, the United States should publicly threaten to bomb the city of Mecca in Saudi Arabia, the holiest site in all of Islam, in retaliation. "Just nuts!" one sensible Pentagon aide wrote to himself when he heard the proposal. This plan, while farfetched, copied traditional Cold War deterrence in laying out punishment in advance to deter an attack. While this proposal was quickly rejected, more refined and realistic versions would come along in its place.

Also in the Pentagon, Jeff Schloesser and other planners used the visceral image of cutting off the head of the snake to describe their goal. Kill or capture the leaders of Al Qaeda, the strategy dictated, and the organization would wither and die or at least be seriously disrupted and less able to launch major attacks against the homeland. In those early days after 9/11, the government struggled to coordinate the disparate counterterrorism efforts, from CIA clandestine missions to NSA electronic eavesdropping. The Pentagon, with its vast budgets and ability to marshal manpower around the globe, sought a leading role. By early December 2001, the Pentagon's top policy official, Undersecretary of Defense Douglas J. Feith, had directed Schloesser and his team to prepare a highly classified plan, called Next Steps. The briefing, culled from the recommendations of combatant commanders around the world, outlined a series of secret military operations against Al Qaeda and its affiliates in more than a dozen countries, including Yemen, Somalia, and Sudan.

Feith, a Georgetown University–trained lawyer and self-acclaimed big thinker, was drilling down into the nitty-gritty details of military and intelligence operations against Al Qaeda cells worldwide. Schloesser and other military planners on the Joint Staff were early and ardent advocates for a longer-term strategic plan for the military to combat terrorism, a project normally expected to flow from the Pentagon's top civilian policy maker. But in this case the call for strategy flowed in the opposite direction. Feith supported the idea, but feeling pressure from Rumsfeld, he was focused on the immediate threat and specific missions to counter it.

"When we would go up and do an early conceptual brief on what we thought the national military strategic plan would be, Feith would say okay, that's fine, but let's talk about what we're going to do next month," Schloesser recalled. "What are we going to do in Indonesia? What are we going to do in Mali? What are we going to do in the tri-border area of South America? He was very tactically oriented."

The Next Steps planning quickly took shape. In Somalia and Yemen, countries with weak or virtually no effective central governments capable of identifying and attacking Al Qaeda cells, plans were set in motion to deny safe havens to Al Qaeda and other terrorists. Teams of Special Operations forces and CIA paramilitary officers would target militants with nighttime raids throughout the world. In the Mediterranean, Navy warships would step up patrols to disrupt terrorists' logistics and snatch militants at sea.

In the Philippines, a new program was envisioned to help train and equip the Philippine military and security force to combat the Abu Sayyaf group, an Islamic militant group linked to Al Qaeda in the southern part of a country made up of over seven thousand islands. In Bosnia and Kosovo, commanders proposed combining an ongoing mission to hunt war criminals from the Balkan wars with a new plan to track Islamic extremists.

Deputy Secretary of Defense Paul D. Wolfowitz sounded a warning note to nations that might be harboring or otherwise helping terrorists, echoing the "with us or against us" theme that President Bush had articulated in the days after 9/11. At the same time, a handful of influential commanders and analysts began expressing concerns that this strategy would not be enough to slay the terrorist organization and keep its ideology and appeal from spreading. Top commanders like John Abizaid acknowledged that these first series of steps after 9/11 to isolate terrorists in a handful of kill zones in other countries were unrealistic, because of a lack of precise intelligence, a lack of trained forces on the ground, and little understanding of how emerging terrorist cells operated. "We thought we could take our counterterrorist forces, move them decisively to the right place and kill the right people at the right time," Abizaid explained. "We started to understand very quickly that the intelligence wasn't good enough to allow us to have a campaign like that. So people are looking for a method to be able to engage, disrupt, defeat terrorist actions."

"Our ideas about this enemy were very rudimentary at the time," said Abizaid. "It wasn't because the professionals that were working on them were bad guys or they were incompetent. It had nothing to do with that. There were very, very few people in the government that were dedicated to the problem, and all of a sudden the shift in our focus showed there were huge intelligence gaps."

One example illustrates both the bold thinking and wildly unrealistic aims of the military's initial approach. The plan called for hunting eight to ten senior Al Qaeda leaders and operatives, including at least one of Osama bin Laden's sons, who had sought refuge in Chalus, an Iranian resort town on the Caspian Sea. In the chaotic days leading up to the fall of Kabul, Afghanistan, in November 2001, Osama bin Laden and Al Qaeda's top leadership made a pivotal decision about its future. Al Qaeda's leadership had been divided into management and consultative councils, or *shuras*, both of which reported to bin Laden. The management arm, the most important element in the terrorist group's continued operations, which included bin Laden and his top deputy, Ayman al-Zawahri, would flee east into Pakistan's rugged tribal areas and teeming cities.

The consultative arm, which included the son, Saad bin Laden, would go west, to northern Iran, where American troops could not pursue them and the Iranians would likely not detain them. The younger bin Laden was a member of Al Qaeda and had been part of a small group of Al Qaeda operatives who fled from Afghanistan and would later become involved in managing the terrorist organization from Iran. But the Shiite clerics running the country placed the Al Qaeda operatives and their family members under virtual house arrest, and they became a shield against possible future attack from the Sunni-based terrorist organization.

At the Joint Special Operations Command (JSOC) at Fort Bragg, military planners drew up schemes for Navy SEALs to sneak ashore under the cloak of darkness using state-of-the-art mini-submarines called submersibles. Once they landed, the SEALs would slip past Iranian guards to snatch the Al Qaeda leaders. Another option called for Special Operations helicopters to spirit American commandos into the town and whisk them out again with their quarry. The American commandos went as far as conducting two or three rehearsals of a clandestine kill-or-capture mission into Chalus at an undisclosed location along the Gulf Coast of the United States in early 2002. They conducted small-boat insertion exercises involving about thirty Special Operations personnel, mostly SEALs, and eventually concluded the mission was feasible if they were provided with more detailed intelligence on the location of the Al Qaeda members and the security around them.

The logistics of the mission were daunting. Chalus sits at the edge of the Elburz coastal mountain range about seventy miles north of Tehran, and the failed rescue of the American hostages in Iran in April 1980 loomed large in commanders' memories. Eventually, General Richard B. Myers, the chairman of the Joint Chiefs of Staff, rejected the missions as too risky and too politically volatile. In the end, even the JSOC commanders seemed relieved they would not be tasked with such a long-shot operation.

By March 2002, as the fight in Afghanistan wound down and policy makers in Washington secretly began shifting their attention to Iraq, General Myers was worried that the country was losing sight of the larger global threat posed by Al Qaeda, an enemy that intelligence analysts concluded had the patience, will, and resolve to outlast its Western adversaries. Myers was also deeply frustrated that the early fight against Al Qaeda had been dominated by the military. Myers, a fighter pilot in Vietnam and a student of history, knew that military power alone could not defeat a committed terrorist organization. "You learn very quickly that most insurgencies are not brought to heel through military power alone," Myers said. "It is using political and diplomatic power and economic power. In my view, they have to be applied simultaneously."

But in National Security Council meetings, it was easier to talk about deploying another brigade of the 82nd Airborne Division or a squadron of fighter-bombers than mapping out a coherent political and economic recovery plan for a destitute country like Afghanistan. "It is made harder yet, because other departments and agencies are not as well resourced," Myers said. "And maybe their heart is not in it. Maybe they do not feel the same sense of urgency as the military does because we are dying and we have injured. That was the frustration. It led to the thought that we do not really have a strategy. We do not have an overarching strategy." Myers and his allies in the Pentagon set about exploring a new strategy that built off Next Steps but also called for more involvement by other parts of the government.

In early March 2002, Myers convened a Saturday meeting of his top staff directors. He looked around the table at some of the military's best and brightest officers. "Who in this room thinks we have a strategy to defeat Al Qaeda?" he asked. Not a hand went up. Myers assigned his team to come up with a plan by the following Saturday. When the group reassembled a week later, the officers recommended, as a first step, an all-of-government effort to eliminate Al Qaeda's top leaders and planners, specifically Osama bin Laden and Ayman al-Zawahri as well as seven leading planners and operational commanders. The plan was dubbed Two + Seven and was drafted by John Tyson and his fellow DIA analysts before going to Schloesser, General Myers, and, ultimately, all the way to President Bush's desk. (The original plan was actually called Two + Nine, but two of the Al Qaeda leaders were killed before Tyson could brief senior officials on the new concept.) "Two + Seven was pretty crude," Myers acknowledged later. "It was trying to bring a strategy to what we were doing."

Myers consulted closely with CIA director George Tenet on the list and on how to carry out the goal of crippling or seriously disrupting Al Qaeda's planning and operations. Both sides brought strengths and abilities to the plan. The CIA had skilled linguists, experienced case officers with networks of informants on the ground, and finely honed analytical skills. The military had firepower, unparalleled reconnaissance and surveillance abilities from satellites to spy planes, and seasoned teams of Special Operations forces. The Treasury Department, armed with Juan Zarate's financial sleuths expert at tracking terrorists' financing, weighed in with critical information that helped diagram the web of connections between terrorists and their suppliers, recruiters, and financiers.

Tyson and the other DIA analysts warned their bosses against getting overly enamored of the new plan to wipe out Al Qaeda's leadership. Al Qaeda, they pointed out, had already proved surprisingly adept at replacing its fallen leaders. "If you get these guys simultaneously or in quick order, you're going to have a major impact on the organization," Tyson said. "If you don't, it is going to have an effect, but it will be considerably less."

Senior Pentagon officials brushed the warnings aside. Over the next weeks, Two + Seven became Two + Seven + Thirty, adding another ring of lethal Al Qaeda planners and subcommanders around the world. Each time informants provided enough solid or "actionable" intelligence to target one of the militants on the list, executive orders were drafted and signed by Rumsfeld, sometimes going all the way to the White House for Bush's approval. The president kept an updated copy of the list in his desk and crossed out each name and photograph after a militant was killed or captured. But this case-by-case approach took time, often time the covert forces didn't have before an Al Qaeda commander might slip away. Under Myers's direction, Jeff Schloesser and his Pentagon team looked for ways to speed up the process. They began shepherding through the senior levels of the military, CIA, and National Security Council a list of more than a dozen countries where high-level militants were believed to be operating as well as the preapproved decisions and legal authorities to kill those militants. These authorities were translated into a color-coded matrix that made it clear the military had approval in advance from the president and secretary of defense to attack fleeting targets in countries like Afghanistan. Where more covert means were required, as in Pakistan, the CIA would take the lead. In some countries, such as Iran, there were no preapproved targets. "In the end, it was asking for pre-approval rather than having to go back to the president at three o'clock in the morning," Schloesser said.

Much of the early effort called for mounting continuous counterterrorism operations on both sides of the border with Pakistan. Handfuls of American military intelligence and communications specialists joined Pakistani forces searching for fugitive fighters in the mountainous tribal border areas traditionally outside the control of the government in Islamabad. In addition, small numbers of Special Operations commandos conducted cross-border reconnaissance missions into Pakistan, ready to strike at Al Qaeda fighters. The Pakistani and American forces were treading gingerly, however, since they were operating for the first time in the Pakistani tribal zones and sought to avoid provoking resistance from Pashtun tribesmen who shared ethnic ties with Taliban fighters.

In Pakistani cities, FBI agents helped the local police and provided information—in rare instances even personnel—to break up what senior American intelligence and law enforcement officials regarded at the time as a depleted but still dangerous network. The traditionally independent American military and law enforcement organizations were now working more closely together than they ever had prior to 9/11, sharing information and expertise as Al Qaeda tried to reconstitute itself in Pakistan. The presence of Al Qaeda in the cities was confirmed by intercepts of cell phone, Internet, and e-mail traffic. The commitment of American troops was relatively light, with no more than two dozen Special Operations forces working in the tribal areas at any given time. The operations, including day-and-night raids and methodical sweeps, were carried out by rapidly moving, highly trained allied soldiers with intensive intelligence-gathering elements to kill or capture specific militants.

The strategy of targeting Al Qaeda's senior leaders paid early dividends. In March 2002, the key Al Qaeda planner, Abu Zubaydah, was one of the first terrorists captured by Pakistani authorities and turned over to the CIA for interrogation. In September, Pakistani police raided an apartment in Karachi and captured Ramzi bin al-Shibh, a senior Al Qaeda member, in a gun battle. On November 4, a Hellfire missile fired from a CIA Predator drone in the Yemeni desert killed Qaed Senyan al-Harthi, also known as Abu Ali, one of the planners of the *Cole* bombing two years earlier. The Yemen strike was the first time an armed Predator drone had been used to attack suspected terrorists outside of Afghanistan. It also signaled a more aggressive phase in the campaign against terrorism, with the United States relying less on the cooperation of other nations to arrest and detain suspected terrorists when they were discovered overseas. But the most important Al Qaeda leader on the Two + Seven list to be seized was Khalid Shaikh Mohammed, generally recognized as the third-ranking official in Al Qaeda and one of the principal planners of the East Africa embassy attacks, the *Cole* bombing, and 9/11 itself. Pakistani forces seized him during a raid on a house in Rawalpindi on March 1, 2003.

As time went on, the seven terrorists initially linked with bin Laden and al-Zawahri on the Two + Seven chart were killed or captured, and new names turned up on President Bush's scorecard. The initial strategy was chipping away at the enemy's leadership, but an approach broader than kill-or-capture was clearly needed.

Another problem remained unresolved: Who would lead that effort? The president, of course, was ultimately in charge of what he called the "war on terror." But day-to-day, who would take the lead and have the responsibility and authority? "Who was in charge of the war on terror from 9/11 to now?" Myers would later reflect. "I'd say there was probably nobody in charge." The military was still locked in a kill-or-capture mentality, but elsewhere in the government new thinking on combating terrorists was emerging.

In the months after 9/11, the FBI was undergoing a seismic shift in combating terrorism at home and abroad. From the days of J. Edgar Hoover's G-men, FBI agents had risen through the ranks by arresting bank robbers, kidnappers, and white-collar criminals. But the bureau was transforming fitfully after the 9/11 attacks and now ranked fighting terrorism as its number-one priority. It doubled the number of agents assigned to counterterrorism duties to roughly five thousand and created new squads across the country that focused more on deterring and disrupting terrorism than on solving crimes.

The FBI was no stranger to domestic terrorism. The bombing of the Alfred P. Murrah Federal Building in Oklahoma City on April 19, 1995, by Timothy McVeigh killed 168 people. And the first World Trade Center bombing on February 26, 1993, by Ramzi Yousef, the nephew of Khalid Shaikh Mohammed, killed six people and injured more than a thousand others. But counterterrorism remained a highly specialized backwater at the bureau. On September 11, fewer than one hundred agents had the know-how, field experience, and background running national programs to coordinate a multidistrict, multiagency, international operation like the investigation after 9/11.

A major lesson from the first World Trade Center bombing was
to keep the terrorists off balance and disrupt their plots before they
could carry out the next big one. In the initial weeks and months
after 9/11, with government experts concerned about a second wave
of terrorist strikes, there was a full-court press to anticipate and
interdict any follow-up attacks.

As top FBI counterterrorism officials saw it, if they did not detect
a plot unfolding and identify the potential plotters, they needed
"to shake the trees hard and make sure that anybody that looks
like or smells like or breathes like a terrorist is not given the opportunity to execute on an operation that we don't see." That strategy came at a cost. By 2003, some counterterrorism experts within
the FBI began challenging whether disruption alone was the best
strategy to combat terrorists. "What we began to realize pretty
rapidly was that there was a lot at stake when you disrupt somebody and you really don't have a clear picture of what their involvement is or what the network is," said Arthur M. Cummings II, a
top FBI counterterrorism official.

Cummings, a stocky former Navy SEAL, worried that while
arresting a suspected or known terrorist would remove that particular threat, it might also leave authorities blind to a larger terrorist network and its ongoing operations. "When we have somebody
who is a terrorist come to American borders, the question always
should be asked: Are we losing more than we're gaining in this
disruption strategy?" he said. "Do we have a view into the genuine
nature of the enemy and what they plan to do and what their network is and what facilitation capacities they have within the
United States? Does that exist? Do we have that knowledge?"

In 1995, when American and Pakistani authorities arrested
Ramzi Yousef in Islamabad, the federal agents who brought him
back to the United States for trial questioned him for six hours on
the flight. Most of the questions focused on Yousef's culpability
and building a body of evidence that would hold up in court. "He

was proud of what he did, he gave us a ton of evidence, all of which was Mirandized and all of which we could use in court," Cummings said. "What we didn't understand about Ramzi Yousef was that basically he could have told us what the future of Al Qaeda was going to be, what the leadership of Al Qaeda was going to be, what their aims were, where their aims were going to focus, what was the future of this organization." Before 9/11, the FBI focused on the individual and building a case against him. "If you take that paradigm and you completely turn it around, and you take a saw and buzz around his head and peer in, that is your new objective," Cummings said. "I don't care about the man. Ramzi Yousef is of no interest to me except that he is a means to my understanding of the broader network."

By late 2002 and 2003, FBI counterterrorism officials were pressing state, local, and federal law enforcement authorities to answer a series of questions before making any arrests. For Cummings and a growing cadre of counterterrorism specialists in the bureau, teasing out the contours of a potential terrorist network became more important than making an immediate arrest. "Do you know everything there is to know about this individual and his network and his area of influence? And if you don't, and if he is not an imminent threat, why are you taking him off the street and why are you effectively going blind?" Cummings said. "And that blindness is going to hurt us in the long run."

With some resistance from old-guard agents, the new paradigm began to take hold and have a pivotal impact on the daily morning intelligence briefings convened by FBI director Mueller and on special briefings with Attorney General John Ashcroft. Cummings and other champions of the strategy called it risk management. Once the FBI, through electronic surveillance, informants, or information from foreign partners, realized that a known or suspected terrorist was operating in the United States, the question became: How long do you track him in order to identify his contacts and map his "pattern of life," all the while risking that the suspect might slip his surveillance, before arresting him and possibly closing whatever window authorities had into an emerging plot? "Before, it would be that our focus was only on developing evidence, facts that were admissible in a courtroom," Mueller said. "Yes, you have to identify those that may end up in a courtroom but beyond that you have to paint a full picture of what is going on."

Local authorities were also engaged in taking steps to interdict terrorist attacks. New York City beefed up its intelligence and counterterrorism capability after 9/11. In March 2003 the New York Police Department (NYPD) dealt with a plot to severely damage the Brooklyn Bridge involving Iyman Faris, a thirty-four-year-old naturalized American citizen from Kashmir living in Columbus, Ohio. Faris had been under federal surveillance, and when the police were informed of the potential threat, they increased marine and land security coverage around the bridge. Faris concluded that the plot was unlikely to succeed—apparently because of increased security—and aborted it. He was arrested shortly after that. "We made a very visible presence there, and that may have contributed to it," said Paul J. Browne, the chief spokesman for the NYPD. "Deterrence is part and parcel of our entire effort."

In New York City today, as many as one hundred police officers in squad cars from every precinct converge twice daily at randomly selected times and selected sites, like Times Square or the financial district, to rehearse their response to a terrorist attack. Police officials say the operations are a crucial tactic to keep extremists guessing as to when and where a large police presence may materialize at any hour. Borrowing a page from the playbook of authorities in London, the police in New York are working on a plan to track every vehicle that enters Manhattan to intensify the city's vigilance against a potential terror attack. Data on each vehicle—its time-stamped image, license plate imprint, and information on whether it is releasing radio waves or even radiation—

would be sent to a command center in Lower Manhattan, where it would be indexed and stored for at least a month as part of a broad security plan that emphasizes protecting the city's financial district.

Federal agencies were also realigning their focus on counterterrorism, expanding beyond the military's kill-capture focus to hone new measures to deter terrorist activity. At the Treasury Department, Juan Zarate was piecing together the remaining law enforcement components after the Secret Service and the Customs Service were incorporated into the new Department of Homeland Security in 2002. Zarate laid out an ambitious plan to make Treasury a pivotal player in the government's post-9/11 counterterrorism arena, leading the global effort to track down Saddam Hussein's assets; working with important Middle East allies such as Saudi Arabia, Pakistan, and the United Arab Emirates to crack down on terrorists' use of financial networks in those countries; and with David Aufhauser, Treasury's general counsel, creating the Office of Terrorism and Financial Intelligence in 2004, with the first intelligence shop inside any finance ministry in the world.

By the middle of 2002, the focus of political leaders in Washington and military commanders in the field was shifting dramatically toward Iraq. Scarce military resources like reconnaissance and surveillance planes, Predator drones, and Special Operations forces were being readied for the invasion to come.

For many policy makers, including Vice President Dick Cheney and Deputy Secretary of Defense Wolfowitz, the various threats often had tantalizing though vague connections to Iraq, a threat they saw as larger than the one posed by Al Qaeda. By late November, Jeff Schloesser had been assigned to write a classified internal assessment, entitled "Leveraging Iraq," that sought to forecast how toppling Saddam Hussein's government would influence the behavior of state sponsors of terrorism, notably Iran, Syria, Libya, and Sudan. When Schloesser questioned the timing of a potential military campaign against Iraq, Myers snapped at him, "Get with the team."

Schloesser's frustration, however, was understandable. The Two + Seven chart that Bush kept in his desk kept acquiring new names and mug shots in addition to those of the maddeningly elusive top two leaders. There seemed to be an endless supply of replacements to plot new attacks. Schloesser's concern was prescient. Seven months later, on May 16, 2003, a series of suicide bombings ripped through Casablanca, Morocco, killing forty-four people. On March 11, 2004, bombs exploded on four trains at three stations in Madrid, killing 192 people and wounding about 1,800.

Efforts to rouse a "whole-of-government" approach were gaining little traction, despite the growing evidence that the administration needed to devise a more creative strategy to enlist popular support in places like Iraq, Afghanistan, and the broader Middle East to dry up the seemingly endless stream of young recruits and money flowing to the terrorist networks. While the president spoke of "a nation at war," it was really a military at war, along with its partners in the intelligence community. Efforts to combat Al Qaeda's ideology and narrative that the West was at war with Islam—the so-called war of ideas—got short shrift in the meetings of Bush's top national security aides.

After a White House meeting on December 13, 2002, Myers returned to the Pentagon in a foul mood. Bush had made it clear to him and to his other top national security officials that the way to victory was killing and capturing the enemy. "He doesn't have much patience for the battle of ideas," Myers told his aides after the meeting. Bush's edict to his top military and civilian advisers came just a week after Donald Rumsfeld had written a memo to the president, warning him that the United States was losing the pivotal ideological war of ideas against Al Qaeda. It would be several more years before Bush changed his thinking, losing critical time and focus on what ultimately became one of the U.S. government's main efforts to combat terrorists.

By the summer of 2003, just a few short months after the giddy early days of battlefield success in Iraq and Bush's declaration of "Mission Accomplished," any aura of victory was beginning to fade as a shadowy insurgency in Iraq stepped up its attacks on American forces. At first, Rumsfeld denied that the American forces were facing any kind of guerrilla force in Iraq. But on July 16, John Abizaid, now a four-star general who had just taken over the Central Command from Tommy Franks, acknowledged for the first time that American troops were, indeed, in a "classical guerrilla-type" war against the remnants of former Iraqi president Saddam Hussein's Baath Party. These fighters had organized cells at a regional level and demonstrated the ability to attack American personnel with homemade bombs and tactical maneuvers. Abizaid warned that the Baathist attacks were growing in organization and sophistication, and he also cited a resurgence of Ansar al-Islam, a fundamentalist group the State Department said was tied to Al Qaeda, and the appearance of both Al Qaeda and Al Qaeda look-alike fighters on the battlefield.

The Bush administration's justification for the war in Iraq at first hinged on fears that Saddam Hussein was developing and stockpiling weapons of mass destruction, possibly to share with terrorists. When no such weapons were found, the administration's rationale for toppling the Iraqi government shifted toward bringing democracy to the Middle East. But now, foreign fighters were being drawn to Iraq to fight the Americans. Iraq may not have been the central front in the war on terror immediately after 9/11, but it was now. Two months later, Abizaid briefed senior administration officials, allies, and lawmakers on what he called the Long War, which extended far beyond Iraq. "Despite remarkable victories, the fight against terrorism is far from over," Abizaid told the Senate Armed Services Committee on September 25. "The enemy's ideological base, financial networks and information networks remain strong. Indeed, the demographic and economic conditions that breed terrorists may be worsening and those conditions are heightening the ideological fervor associated with radical Islamic extremism." Abizaid told the lawmakers that the Pentagon recognized that the spreading war was not against Islam. "It is not a war against religion," he said. "It is a war against irreligious murderers."

The gloomy message was sinking in. On October 16, 2003, Rumsfeld sent a two-page memo to Wolfowitz, Feith, Myers, and General Peter Pace, the vice chairman of the Joint Chiefs. "Are we capturing, killing or deterring and dissuading more terrorists every day than the madrassas and the radical clerics are recruiting, training and deploying against them?" Rumsfeld asked in the note. "Does the U.S. need to fashion a broad, integrated plan to stop the next generation of terrorists? The U.S. is putting relatively little effort into a long-range plan, but we are putting a great deal of effort into trying to stop terrorists. The cost-benefit ratio is against us! Our cost is billions against the terrorists' costs of millions. It is pretty clear that the coalition can win in Afghanistan and Iraq in one way or another, but it will be a long, hard slog."

Two years after 9/11, the U.S. government's counterterrorism efforts had made great strides. Teams of Special Operations forces and CIA paramilitary officers were coordinating more closely in the field than ever before. The FBI had scored several successes with allied law enforcement agencies, including Pakistani authorities, to kill or capture top Al Qaeda leaders. Treasury Department analysts were cracking terrorists' financial networks. Slowly, barriers to intelligence sharing were crumbling. But two years into the fight, it was dawning on Rumsfeld and Myers at the highest levels of government as well as on people like Jeff Schloesser, Juan Zarate, and Art Cummings on the front lines just how little the U.S. government knew about Al Qaeda and other militant organizations, and how they attracted a growing following in the Muslim world. Bush remained the self-declared "war-on-terror president." But military commanders, senior intelligence officers, and law enforcement officials squared off every day against violent extremists while they also confronted unresolved questions within their own government about competing interests, competing strategies, and a competition for financial resources, personnel, and information. It left many of them wondering who was really in charge of the war on terror.

2

THE NEW DETERRENCE

It was the late summer of 2005, and the fourth anniversary of the 9/11 attacks was fast approaching. The invasion in Afghanistan had drifted into a forgotten war, becoming what the military called an economy-of-force mission, where the military did just what it was able to. Only in Iraq was the military doing everything it had to, but still things were not going well. The strategy and focus of the war against terrorism was about to undergo a significant rethinking.

Donald Rumsfeld was en route to Crawford, Texas, for his annual summer sojourn and sharing of private concerns with President Bush at his ranch. Rumsfeld carried in his battered leather briefcase a series of briefing papers, actual hard copies of Power-Point slides, on a half-dozen critically pressing national security themes. Each of those briefings for the president was spare. Rumsfeld was known to scold officers who showed up with rainbow-hued printouts of the slides full of tridents and spiderwebs and coiled ropes to depict the complex mix of threats to the nation. And knowing he was about to sit with the commander in chief, Rumsfeld had demanded this time that his staff "really neck down the number of words," recalled one aide who helped in the preparation. Rumsfeld ordered that these slides for the president be conceived as a briskly paced visual guide to a verbal presentation and a follow-up discussion. No Technicolor. No fabric design. Brief. Blunt. Black-and-white bullet points.

The staff had paid particular attention to preparing an update on missile defense, which was a passion of the president. But nestled among the handful of sensitive themes for Bush's consideration that day was a radical new concept for counterterrorism. The secret briefing by Rumsfeld bore the prosaic title "A Concept for Deterring and Dissuading Terrorist Networks." But its half-dozen pages, distilled from a thirty-one-page master briefing, contained radical new thinking. The briefing laid out a truly new strategy that would apply the lessons of Cold War–era deterrence to a wholly new effort to counter shadowy, stateless terrorist networks.

For two years, Rumsfeld had been demanding answers to the blunt question he had put to his top aides in his October 2003 memo: "Are we capturing, killing or deterring and dissuading more terrorists every day than the madrassas and the radical clerics are recruiting, training and deploying against us?" And as Al Qaeda grew stronger and new affiliates sprang up, his grim-faced lieutenants had but one reply: "No." But now, from a completely unexpected quarter, came the kind of creative, even counterintuitive thinking that Rumsfeld had all but given up eliciting. As he prepared for the flight to Crawford and his crucial meeting with the president, Rumsfeld was convinced that he now possessed something that offered the new answers the United States needed in its "long war" against global terrorism, and his usual supreme confidence was mixed with a certain apprehension.

Rumsfeld's brief grew out of work by Douglas Feith, a champion of thinking about what had come to be described as "the new deterrence" in his role as the Pentagon's top policy official. Feith had told confidants that, with unusual brashness, he had politely, respectfully, scolded Bush in May 2004, saying that while senior administration officials met frequently on Afghanistan or Iraq or outreach to the Muslim world or terrorist financing, there had been absolutely no meetings to look systematically at the administration's marquee national security issue: the "global war on terror." No National Security Council meeting of the president, his cabinet, and his top-level advisers to assess the broader strategy of combating Al Qaeda and other terrorist groups.

"I said, 'Mr. President, you never have a meeting on the war on terrorism,'" Feith recalled. "If we're serious about the war on terrorism being a war with multiple elements and campaigns, one would think that at some point, you'd ask how we're doing in the larger effort."

The briefing Rumsfeld gave President Bush on August 11, 2005, might not have happened were it not for a veteran Cold Warrior toiling deep inside the Pentagon's policy bureaucracy who mentored a young Ph.D. candidate from the University of California at Berkeley assigned to the Defense Department as a summer fellow in June 2005. As was often the case with the impatient defense secretary known for his "wire-brush treatment" of subordinates, even four-star officers, it was an angry Rumsfeld outburst that spawned an important internal debate. That discussion yielded results that were eventually condensed into the PowerPoint briefing for President Bush, a forecast of what has since become a pillar of the new counterterrorism strategy.

The veteran Cold Warrior was Barry Pavel, one of those highly respected, long-serving civilian policy planners who can spend an entire career moving around from one place to another—the Pentagon, the National Security Council, the State Department, and the intelligence community—without their names ever surfacing in the media. That's how they like it. The idea for applying principles of deterrence to terrorists? "It came from my head because I am a longtime nuclear deterrence/nuclear arms control guy," he said. "Everybody was saying it can't be done, it can't be done. I just thought about it—and, well, terrorists are human beings and they have various incentive structures and it is not like they don't value anything—they value something."

One of Pavel's subordinates in the Pentagon policy shop was a summer intern from Berkeley, Matthew Kroenig, a graduate student with the credentials to be one of Pavel's counterterrorist Jedi trainees. A native of St. Louis and the son of an environmental engineer and a stay-at-home mom, Kroenig had spent a semester during his junior year at the University of Missouri aboard a research vessel at sea, traveling to twelve countries over four months. The experience sparked an intense interest in foreign affairs. Kroenig had gone on to study the proliferation of nuclear weapons and Cold War nuclear-deterrence theory while pursuing his doctorate at the University of California at Berkeley. He is Hollywood handsome, which runs in the family. His younger brother has been ranked as one of the world's top models and his sister is a regional TV news anchor. Later, during a stint as an assistant professor at Georgetown University's School of Foreign Service, Kroenig would rate a "chili pepper" at *ratemyprofessors.com* not for his lecture style but for being a "hot" teacher, as voted by the university's students.

Atop the Pentagon policy organization was Feith, in his role as undersecretary of defense. A self-proclaimed hard-core neoconservative, Feith was placed in the Pentagon's senior policy spot by the Bush administration as a favor to Richard Perle, a Reagan-era hawk who was one of the first—and continually most vocal—advocates of war with Iraq well before 9/11. Feith began pushing like Perle for an Iraq-first strategy in the early hours after the 9/11 attacks and soon was put in charge of the Office of Special Plans, a shadowy Pentagon-within-the-Pentagon to begin war planning even before invading Iraq became official U.S. policy. Feith and his boss, Paul Wolfowitz, also created a small intelligence unit deeper within the Pentagon policy shop to search for bits of information on Iraq's links to terrorists, which antagonized the main intelligence agencies. Wolfowitz and Feith defended the team's work data mining for raw files—in other words, reports completely without analysis or evaluation—that they suspected held leads to Saddam Hussein's ties to Al Qaeda that the intelligence community had missed or deliberately ignored. But any suggestions of Saddam's close ties to Al Qaeda were proved spurious or inconsequential at best. The Feith team's effort was denounced by intelligence professionals as "politicization" and "cherry picking." Rumsfeld, according to his senior aides, was embarrassed by the disclosure.

While Feith was criticized by his foes within the national security establishment and within the military's top ranks for being doctrinaire, in his leadership of the large policy directorate at the Pentagon he encouraged nondoctrinaire thinkers. He created a number of working groups to analyze the terrorist threat and to seek new methods for combating those who might attack the United States with unconventional weapons. The groups' papers, full of ideas and recommendations, were adopted throughout the Bush administration and in time would be sustained by the Obama administration despite their parentage.

Pavel's thinking during the summer of 2005 about whether Cold War deterrence could be applied to twenty-first-century threats appealed to Feith: If deterrence had kept the Kremlin leadership in line and eventually helped topple the Soviet giant, might there be tools from the Cold War arsenal of threat, bluff, and guaranteed nuclear punishment that similarly could be used to corner, combat, and conquer America's present-day adversaries? Early in the summer of 2005, Feith had ordered one group to tackle how to deter peer competitors like China from attempting nuclear blackmail—let alone nuclear attack—against the United States. Another group would address how deterrence theory could be updated to manage unpredictable rogue states, like Iran or North Korea, with emerging nuclear capabilities. Matt Kroenig was assigned to lead the effort that colleagues told him was the least likely to succeed: how to deter terrorist networks from attacking the United States or its allies.

It was a widely accepted premise in President Bush's war cabinet that it would be impossible to deter the most fervent extremists from carrying out deadly terrorist missions with weapons of mass destruction or of mass disruption. To the president's top national security advisers, the answer was a matter of military action solely, of capturing or killing terrorist leaders and their foot soldiers. There was no middle ground and no interest in finding one.

But Kroenig was undaunted. If the only tool you have is a hammer, then of course every problem looks like a nail. Kroenig had planned to stay at the Pentagon for just a few months before returning to California to write his dissertation, so why not take on this complex assignment and view the terrorist threat through fresh eyes? Working in a windowless cubicle in a nondescript office, in a few days he completed a draft that combined his studies on classic deterrence theory with his growing knowledge of global terrorism, gleaned from highly classified assessments by the CIA, the NSA, and the rest of the American intelligence community. Kroenig and Pavel crafted a briefing to make the case that a combination of efforts—economic, diplomatic, military, political, and psychological, some highly classified and some carried out in the broad daylight of public debate—could in fact establish a new strategy and create a new and effective posture of deterrence against terrorist groups.

"People at the time thought that terrorists weren't deterrable, that they were irrational, that we had no control over the things they valued, so we couldn't threaten to hold it at risk," Kroenig said. "But terrorists are deterrable. While they may have a preference structure that's different than ours, they do value things—things that we could hold at risk—and we can, therefore, influence their decisions."

Kroenig argued that terrorists value operational success, personal glory, their reputation and honor, and their support in the broader Muslim population. Undermining or sowing doubt among those motivated by any one of those values, or a combination of them, could help dissuade terrorists, or the people helping them, from carrying out an attack. But the efforts to advocate for such strategies encountered several roadblocks. Skeptical midlevel Pentagon bureaucrats refused to pass the "new deterrence" concept up the chain of command. Partly, it was fear of the new; it was also obvious that this proposed strategy contradicted the Bush administration's public line, that is, until Rumsfeld exploded one day. In the midsummer of 2005, the defense secretary had received a briefing from top military commanders on how many megatons of nuclear bombs they could drop on an array of targets. Rumsfeld, furious at what he said was Cold War thinking, cut short the briefing and threw the generals out of his office. "Isn't anyone doing anything relevant, like thinking about deterring terrorists?" Rumsfeld bellowed at his aides.

The next morning, Feith, who was aware of Pavel and Kroenig's work but had not read the latest drafts, asked to see the current version. He liked it and ordered the briefing, with a few changes, sent to Rumsfeld as soon as possible. "I just remember it intellectually being a very good piece of work—creative, well presented, rigorous, just good stuff," Feith said.

Perhaps he was pleased because the work followed a path that Feith himself had started to explore three years earlier in a speech in April 2002 to the American Israel Public Affairs Committee, the nation's major pro-Israel lobby. In that address, Feith spoke of what terrorists hold dear and what they hope for: "a perverse form of religious hope," "earthly glory and reward," and "political hope" for the creation of a greater Palestinian state. Within that toxic mix, Feith saw the potential to exploit an unusual opportunity: "This suggests a strategic course for us: attack the sources of these malignant hopes."

Reviewing the Pavel-Kroenig brief, Feith suggested a few

changes to tighten and polish the new deterrence proposal, putting it into one-paragraph briefing slides, the way Rumsfeld liked to digest new ideas. Seven weeks after walking in the door of the Pentagon, Kroenig had completed a PowerPoint briefing that was on its way to the secretary of defense.

Rumsfeld could be a hard man to read, but Feith surely knew that the briefing had a good chance of appealing to him. One of Rumsfeld's favorite axioms is "When you can't solve a problem, expand it." He describes his most-favored posture as "forward leaning." As secretary of defense, he terrorized those who came to staff meetings unprepared but was impressed by those who stood up to him. Rumsfeld truly had hoped to be a "change agent" within the ossified Pentagon, so he appreciated those with fresh, transformational ideas. It was therefore no surprise that he was pleased by the presentation of a "new deterrence" against terrorism. Pavel and Kroenig had identified the specific "territory," physical and virtual, that terrorists hold dear:

- Calculus of chances for success of their attacks
- Personal glory
- Personal reputation
- Support among Muslim populations
- Publicity
- Network cohesion and dependability
- Trust in fellow cell members
- Well-being of their family
- Enhancement of the Muslim community
- Material assets
- Growing membership for the movement
- Strategic success

The United States needed to impose costs on that "territory," put it at risk, and deny terrorists the benefits they expect to receive—that was the essence of the "new deterrence." As was the case with traditional deterrence, the idea was to take steps to alter the behavior and thinking of your adversary while simultaneously taking steps to reduce his ability to alter your behavior and thinking.

The challenge to the new deterrence became one of cracking the organizational DNA of constantly evolving militant networks, especially as Al Qaeda adopted a new business model, franchising out activities and becoming as big a threat as an inspirational idea as in its operations. That would require the U.S. government to focus not solely on bin Laden and Al Qaeda's senior leadership but also on a proliferating network of cells in Afghanistan, Iraq, and the rest of the Middle East, along with much of Africa, Indonesia, and the Philippines. The original slides for the Pavel-Kroenig concept for deterring and dissuading terrorist networks listed nine functions required by militant networks to survive, thrive, and operate. Here is the air and water and land of terrorism:

- Leadership
- Safe havens
- Intelligence
- Communications
- Movement
- Weapons
- Personnel
- Ideology
- Finances

This was the presentation that Rumsfeld took to his meeting with President Bush at Crawford. According to participants at the session, the president was not exactly dismissive of the concept, but he was openly skeptical. Kill or capture—those were the tactics of the Bush war on terror, and the concept briefed by Rumsfeld did not resonate. "Bush listened to it," said one senior official. "He was reflective. But it was clear he was not really buying into it."

In an opportune coincidence, also present at Crawford was

General James E. Cartwright, the top officer of the Strategic Command, which has custody and control of the traditional tools of nuclear retaliation: the long-range bombers and the warhead-carrying missiles in land-based silos and aboard submarines. Cartwright was on hand to brief the president on missile defense. Bush turned to him and asked his opinion of applying Cold War deterrence theories to counterterrorism. Cartwright had not been briefed on the Feith-Pavel-Kroenig proposal but had been thinking through these issues in parallel. He discussed how if one believes missile defense adds to deterrence—and Bush was a huge advocate of that—then the application to counterterrorism followed naturally. In missile defense, you hope to inject a high level of doubt into the mind of a potential attacker that a first strike will be successful and certainty that it will provoke retaliation. Ditto with deterrence and terrorism. "If you can remove a certainty of success in striking an objective, if you make the price too high, then you increase the opportunity the adversary will not strike," Cartwright said. "Ambiguity and uncertainty: That is the calculus of missile defense as contributing to an overall deterrence strategy." He applied it to terrorism: "If you can convince a suicide bomber that he most likely will only kill himself, then you have increased chances you can influence his thinking to not strap on the vest. Applying deterrence theories to terrorism may not eliminate the threat, but you can increase your chances of influencing an adversary's behavior, his cost-benefit analysis—and perhaps deter an attack."

Bush was the most important skeptic but hardly the only one. Pavel and Kroenig had to crack institutional resistance throughout the Pentagon. Some initial push-back came from the community of traditional deterrence strategists, who argued that Pavel and Kroenig were misappropriating a powerful historical term simply because it resonated and was a persuasive bumper sticker. "Don't define deterrence so narrowly," Kroenig said to these skeptics as he shopped around the new concept. "During the Cold War, deterrence meant threatening unacceptable damage on an adversary. No other use was allowed. But an expansive concept of deterrence can be used today to restrict an enemy's actions in the world of counterterrorism. It contributes to a national objective."

In March 2006, Bush signed the twelve-page National Security Presidential Directive 46; an accompanying strategy document was released with great fanfare six months later. The work by Barry Pavel and Matt Kroenig, under Feith's leadership, was incorporated into the final documents. During the review process overseen by the National Security Council, the following text was approved: "A new deterrence calculus combines the need to deter terrorists and supporters from contemplating a WMD attack and, failing that, to dissuade them from actually conducting an attack." The emerging belief that terrorists could be swayed and dissuaded from action by various forms of deterrence marked a stunning change of direction in the government's thinking on dealing with terrorists.

A new notion of deterrence was finding its way into the daily business of the Pentagon and the rest of the national security agencies. On February 3, 2006, a month before NSPD-46 was formally approved, the Pentagon briefed reporters on another significant planning effort, the Defense Department's quadrennial review of defense priorities and policies. In his opening statement, Ryan Henry, one of Feith's top deputies, explained, "We will selectively be able to enhance our deterrence anywhere of our choosing around the globe, but that deterrence will not be a one-size-fits-all of massive retaliation that we've built up over the last fifty years. It'll also be augmented by an ability to deter rogue powers and also terrorists and their networks."

Al Qaeda soon responded to the new American strategy of deterrence but in an unexpected way. In September 2007, Sheik Abu Yahya al-Libi, a top Al Qaeda official, released a videotape offering the United States several unsolicited tips on how to defeat the terrorist organization. Abu Yahya recommended that the United States fabricate stories about jihadist mistakes and exaggerate real Al Qaeda missteps. He advised the West to discredit prominent Islamic clerics who back Al Qaeda's goals in their Friday prayers. In short, he said the best way to defeat Al Qaeda was to tie it in knots and degrade its appeal and legitimacy among Muslims. Although the narrative fit perfectly with the concepts emerging from Pavel and Kroenig, American counterterrorism officials were at first puzzled. Why would a senior Al Qaeda leader hand his enemies the very means to destroy the group? Was this a disinformation campaign? American officials now believe that Abu Yahya's effort was a clever attempt to inoculate Al Qaeda and the terrorist movement from the very criticisms they were already encountering from within their own ranks and to attribute anything that came from such criticisms as the handiwork of American propaganda. It was a concrete sign that the information war between the terrorists and the terrorist hunters was heating up.

A growing number of influential Islamic clerics and imams who once supported bin Laden were indeed denouncing Al Qaeda's violence, particularly its killing of civilians. Saudi Arabia's top cleric, Grand Mufti Sheik Abdul Aziz al-Asheik, gave a speech in October 2007 warning Saudis not to join unauthorized jihadist activities, a statement directed mainly at those considering going to Iraq to fight American troops. Al Qaeda relies on public support within the Islamic world to recruit new fighters to dispatch to the battlefields of Afghanistan, Pakistan, and Iraq, and to help finance a network of new franchises, from the deserts of North Africa to the far reaches of northern Iraq. Terrorism experts know that splits within the jihadist world threaten to undermine the terrorists' power and incline more moderate Muslims to speak out against their tactics.

■ ■ ■

It is one thing to disrupt terrorists' messages, but it is another to dissuade insurgents from even considering an attack with unconventional weapons. Counterterrorism specialists agree that for the "new deterrence" strategy to succeed, it is crucial to counteract the militant and fatalistic culture of martyrdom of terrorist leaders. To do so, they are examining aspects of the militants' culture, families, and religion. Jeff Schloesser, the general tapped to lead a new counterterrorism planning cell in the Pentagon, said that soon after 9/11, American officials considered whether seizing some or all of Osama bin Laden's wives and other extended family members, many of whom lived in Saudi Arabia, would deter him from plotting other attacks, possibly with unconventional weapons. "We decided that wouldn't change him one bit," Schloesser said. "It'd just cause him to be more brutal."

Suicide bombers believe they will enjoy seductive "heavenly delights" as a reward for martyrdom, and so the U.S. government is seeking ways to amplify the voices of respected Muslim religious leaders who warn that suicide bombers will not enjoy the heavenly rewards promised by terrorist literature and that their families will be dishonored by such attacks. Those efforts are aimed at undermining a terrorist's will, since without foot soldiers willing to die, there is little for an organization like Al Qaeda to do.

Terrorists hold no obvious targets for American retaliation—targets like Soviet cities, factories, military bases, and missile silos—so it is harder to deter terrorists than it was to deter a Soviet attack. The U.S. government and the American military knew exactly where the offices of the Politburo were in those years. It is all but impossible to deter attacks by credibly threatening a retaliatory strike when you cannot pinpoint the location of a terrorist group's leadership. And they know it.

The "new deterrence" strategy identified other kinds of "territory" that extremists hold dear: psychological and public relations territory that matters more to terrorists than actual physical land.

What matters most to terrorists is their reputation and credibility with other Muslims. If a seed of doubt can be planted in the mind of Al Qaeda's strategic leadership that an attack would be viewed as a shameful murder of innocents or, even more effectively, that it would be an embarrassing failure, then the order may not be given. During the months of debate, many government officials said these "new deterrence" efforts represent a second-best solution. Their preferred way to combat terrorism remained to capture or kill extremists. But killing extremists just puts new extremists in their place since it creates more glory for the terrorists. If the wars in Iraq and Afghanistan have proved one thing, it is that America cannot kill its way to victory.

Critics in the Bush administration who clung to this strategy of capture or kill derided talk of a "new deterrence" as irrelevant, even naïve. They preferred to discuss Cold War strategies of massive retaliation, since the "new deterrence" is not about massive retaliation but about small steps and a relentless effort at persuasion. Such critics are lost in a misreading of the past, Pavel and Kroenig argued. After the tragedy of 9/11, the United States copied Cold War strategy by punishing those who organized the attacks and their benefactors—surprising any who thought the United States was a paper tiger—by invading Afghanistan to rout Al Qaeda and the Taliban. It was a textbook example of retaliation, and for a time it knocked Al Qaeda completely into remission. That the swift victory in Afghanistan was not rapidly followed by an implementation of these new counterterrorism strategies only argues for their value as Al Qaeda and Taliban have regrouped in sanctuaries in the Federally Administered Tribal Areas (FATA) of Pakistan along the Afghan border, where they continue to train new recruits, including Europeans and Americans, and plot new attacks.

Part of deterrence strategy is to make sure that the other side knows that America will stop at nothing to punish it. Senior Bush administration and military officials said that if a terrorist group were to execute an attack on the United States, its allies, or interests with biological, chemical, or nuclear weapons, then the president had the option of massive retaliation against those terrorists, those they hold dear, and any who assisted them. Ironically, the most difficult part of this top-secret planning was how to communicate to terrorists that the United States actually had been restrained in its actions against certain terrorists out of respect for the sovereign territory of the countries in which they resided, notably Pakistan. But those restraints would be cast aside after a catastrophic attack, top officials insisted.

And no longer is it the case that the U.S. government might not know whom to blame in a terrorist attack. Much effort is being spent on perfecting technical systems that can identify the source of unconventional weapons or their components regardless of where they are found or detonated—and on letting nations around the world know that America has this ability. Every batch of nuclear materials has a specific chemical identity that it picks up in production, as unique a marker as a fingerprint or DNA. Using records held at the UN or gathered by American intelligence, the United States is very confident that it can identify the source of radioactive materials in an attack, even if carried out by a stateless group. Thus, it is argued, a dictator with a nuclear arsenal will not be able to hide behind an anonymous terrorist organization if he aids the attack by supplying nuclear materials.

The first public indication that the Bush administration was expanding the traditional view of nuclear deterrence came in a brief statement by President Bush in October 2006, following a test detonation of a nuclear device by North Korea. Bush said North Korea would be held "fully accountable" for the transfer of nuclear weapons or materials to any nation or terrorist organization. Over the next months, work continued across the government, focused in the National Security Council, until the president had formally approved an expanded deterrence policy. Stephen J. Hadley, who had succeeded Condoleezza Rice as national security advisor, wanted to trumpet the decision and openly define this more detailed and nuanced version of the strategy, but he chose to do so in a speech on the West Coast, at Stanford University, on February 8, 2008, with no mainstream media in attendance. The Hadley address generated no significant press coverage and therefore went unnoticed by America's allies and adversaries.

So later that year, in October 2008, the task fell to Rumsfeld's successor as secretary of defense, Robert M. Gates, to put America's adversaries on notice that the United States would hold "fully accountable" any country or group that helped terrorists to acquire or use nuclear, chemical, or biological weapons. Gates's speech before the Carnegie Endowment for International Peace in Washington was the Bush administration's most expansive in trying to articulate a vision of deterrence for the post-9/11 world. It went beyond the Cold War notion that a president could respond with overwhelming force against a country that directly attacked the United States or its allies with unconventional weapons. "Today we also make clear that the United States will hold any state, terrorist group or other non-state actor or individual fully accountable for supporting or enabling terrorist efforts to obtain or use weapons of mass destruction—whether by facilitating, financing or providing expertise or safe haven for such efforts," Gates said. To be sure, Gates left the door open to diplomatic and economic responses as well as military ones in this expanded concept of deterrence, but he was far more explicit than the president had been in 2006 in saying that the administration would extend the threat of reprisal for the transfer of nuclear weapons or materials to all countries, not just North Korea, and he also expanded the threat to nations or groups that provide a broader range of support to terrorists.

Gates's speech was viewed as a landmark in America's "declaratory" policy of a new concept of deterrence. But the secret history proved the odd machinations of government. Gates had intended the speech to focus on nuclear modernization and the obligation of the military to secure and safely handle the nuclear arsenal as a sacred trust, but when the White House heard of his proposed topic, he was ordered to rewrite the address to include a section that finally and formally and publicly broadcast the new deterrence concepts, which had expanded since the Bush statement and had gone unheard in the Hadley speech.

In the years since Matt Kroenig's initial briefing in July 2005, the new strategy to deter terrorist attacks has been incorporated into a new, broader counterterrorism strategy that includes muting Al Qaeda's message, turning the jihadist movement's own weaknesses against itself, and illuminating Al Qaeda's missteps whenever possible. A bombing of a hotel in Jordan in which the victims were Muslims at a wedding party? Publicizing this attack from November 2005 played perfectly into the strategy. Strapping suicide vests to teenagers lured away from a Baghdad mental asylum to kill Iraqi police and shoppers in an outdoor market? What Muslim could support that? Statistics that showed Al Qaeda's post-9/11 attacks had killed and wounded far more Muslims than Christians. What sort of jihad could that be?

"The artful presentation of Al Qaeda as an international movement with groups acting in concert all over the world—that, too, has deteriorated," said Richard Barrett, a former member of the British spy agency MI6, who is now the coordinator of the Al Qaeda/Taliban sanctions monitoring team for the UN. "Al Qaeda has not been able to sustain that image in the short term, if only because most of the targets that terrorist groups attack are now essentially local, and are no longer so clearly linked to some sort of global agenda. And the environment within which Al Qaeda is operating is far less friendly both towards Al Qaeda as an organization and towards its stated goals and objectives, and even in some ways it has become hostile to Al Qaeda. Public opinion seems definitely to have turned against it."

The emerging belief that terrorists may be dissuaded from action by various forms of deterrence underscores the shift in the nation's thinking since Bush's 2002 national security strategy document asserted that traditional aspects of deterrence would fail against a committed terrorist. "What we've developed since 9/11 is a better understanding of the support that is necessary for terrorists, the network which provides that support, whether it's financial or material or expertise," said Michael E. Leiter, a top counterterrorism official in the Bush and Obama administrations. "We've now begun to develop more sophisticated thoughts about deterrence looking at each one of those individually. Terrorists don't operate in a vacuum."

Leiter is an outstanding example of the nation's newest generation of terrorist fighters, many of whom took unusual paths into the counterterrorism world. He grew up in Englewood, New Jersey, the son of a Holocaust survivor, and once considered becoming a New York City police officer. Leiter's academic career mirrors President Obama's own: he graduated from Columbia University (the president's alma mater) and Harvard Law School, where he followed in Obama's footsteps as president of the *Harvard Law Review*. He spent six years in the Navy between college and law school, flying E-6B "Prowler" radar-jamming planes for the Navy over Bosnia and Iraq. After law school, Leiter was a clerk for Supreme Court Justice Stephen Breyer and was at the court on 9/11, watching on television as the World Trade Center collapsed. "It hit very close to home for me," he once told National Public Radio, noting that he had attended his senior prom at the twin towers and was sworn into the Navy there. Leiter went on to become a lawyer for the International Criminal Tribunal at The Hague, playing a key role in bringing Bosnian war criminals to justice. He also served as a federal prosecutor in northern Virginia, handling a wide variety of federal crimes, including narcotics offenses, organized crime, racketeering, and money laundering.

Since November 2007, Leiter has led the National Counterterrorism Center, the government's central clearinghouse and analytical hub for intelligence on terrorist threats. He is one of a handful of influential counterterrorism figures who carried over to the Obama administration from the Bush administration, and he likes to tell a story that illustrates how political affiliations are buried in his line of work.

At the end of President George W. Bush's final intelligence briefing in January 2009, the discussion turned to who was staying on in the Obama administration and who was leaving. "Someone asked me what I thought about going to work for the Democrats and Obama," Leiter recalled, "and I said, 'Sir, I am not a Republican.'"

President Bush looked at him and asked, "Well, you voted for me, right?"

Leiter was in a jam: "I was stuck and had to say, 'Well, I voted for your dad once.'"

As the analysts walked out of the Oval Office, Bush pulled Leiter aside. "He put his arm on my shoulder," Leiter recalled, "and said, 'Keep up the fight.'"

3

THE EXPLOITATION OF INTELLIGENCE

Sunset in the badlands of modern terrorism, the Sunni Triangle north of Baghdad.

A red mist matching the crimson sky at twilight floated toward First Lieutenant Garry Owen Flanders. Except this was not the fine grit of the typical Iraqi sandstorm, the kind that inflamed your eyeballs, crusted your throat until your voice dropped half an octave, locked up computers, blinded radars, grounded helicopters, and made a mystical palette of light filtered through pastel crud. This red mist was blood and bile and body parts Osterized by an explosive suicide vest detonated just seconds before by a man captured by Flanders and his platoon.

Flanders was just twenty-three years old and only a couple of weeks into platoon command on the ground in Iraq. Before deploying with the Cavalry, he had time to get used to the kidding about his name: Garry Owen Flanders. "The Garryowen" is the title of the whistle-and-drum-and-fiddle drinking song, an Irish quick-step really, adopted by Lieutenant Colonel George Armstrong Custer as the marching cadence of his 7th Cavalry Regiment. Flanders's father, Joseph, who served in the Cavalry in Vietnam, chose the one hundredth anniversary of Custer's Last Stand as his wedding day.

When he and his wife had a son, his name was an obvious choice and one of pride. "The epitome of the word 'cavalry'? That would be my father," Flanders said. He followed his dad into the Army and into the Cav, and his first assignment after commissioning was with the 1st Battalion, 12th Cavalry Regiment. In the lottery of fate and the dictates of Army planning, his unit was reassigned as the 1st Battalion of the legendary 7th Cavalry Regiment, Custer's heir. And the battalion adopted the historic regimental flag of the 7th Cav as well as "The Garryowen" melody as its anthem. "Everybody said, 'You have got to go over to the battalion headquarters now. You just got to go over and see it.' My name was written all over everything," Flanders recalled. Patches now bore his name, as did signposts all over the headquarters. Jokes about the coincidence of name and unit followed him to Iraq when he deployed as part of the 1st Cavalry Division out of Fort Hood, Texas. "In this whole big Army, this had to happen to me," he said. "But it was a wonderful icebreaker."

As the sun was setting at about 6:00 p.m., Flanders set off in a convoy of four up-armored Humvees moving west out of Taji, a focus of terrorist and insurgent violence about twenty miles north of Baghdad. The percussion of homemade land mines—known as improvised explosive devices (IEDs)—had set the tempo. "We were hit by an IED, a small IED," Flanders thought, going down his mental checklist, ticking off the enemy's successes—a soldier's disciplined method used to stay sharp. "A route clearance team in same vicinity, hit with an IED and one Killed in Action. Just to the north: found several IEDs, one booby trapped. Horribly injured explosive ordnance disposal team trying to defuse. Unit to our north, Charlie Troop, 1st of the 7th Cav, their vehicle hit a deep-buried IED. Four killed." All in just seventy-two hours, all in a patrol area no bigger than six miles by six miles.

The enemy's goal was not just to kill and maim American soldiers but also to imperil all traffic on Highway 1, known by the troops as MSR Tampa (Major Supply Route Tampa), which carried ammunition, food, fuel, and personnel through Flanders's patrol area. The IED campaign was also meant to knock back the American military presence along the terror network's own critical supply lines, coming from Syria and crossing the deserts of Anbar and Nineveh provinces, then pushing all the way through to Diyala Province and other terror and insurgent havens surrounding Baghdad, their ultimate prize.

A sunset-to-dawn curfew had done little to prevent the terrorists from planting IEDs. For two nights straight, Flanders and his soldiers of 1st Platoon, Delta Troop, had seen no traffic at all from their checkpoint, but the IEDs kept detonating—and kept killing. He bet he could get straight to the root of the problem. The enemy's informal intelligence network was relaying the exact location as the Army set up its static traffic control roadblocks. "We have to 'out-G' the 'G,' " Flanders decided and told his soldiers so. "We have to 'out-guerrilla' the guerrilla. The best way to do that is being unpredictable and not falling into a pattern set." So Flanders ordered his roadblock force to hit the road, to operate as an all-night mobile checkpoint that might surprise anybody out past curfew but clever enough to try and skirt the stationary patrol posts.

Over the course of any tour of duty, missions blur together into a jumble of fragmentary memories, since a soldier's life most days is the numbing routine of patrol, eat, patrol, exercise, patrol, sleep, shower, eat, patrol. Some missions end in victory, large or small; some end in great tragedy. And some, like Flanders's operation of December 19, 2006, change the very course of a war, in this case the war against Al Qaeda in Iraq.

The convoy was moving west out of Taji on a narrow paved road just wider than a single Humvee. Flanders scanned the open terrain, the occasional clump of trees among thick reeds growing along canals separated from the roadway by a low berm. "We almost ran head-on into them," Flanders said. "We caught them by surprise. And they caught us by surprise." It was a dark Mercedes 300-series sedan, the vehicle of choice of Baathist diehards and the transportation adopted by the insurgent and terrorist network's top officers. The Mercedes tried to pull a quick U-turn but was boxed in by the quartet of Humvees in front and the parallel berms that defined the narrow strip of pavement on both sides.

Flanders and the troops in his platoon jumped out of their Humvees, except for the soldiers operating the heavy machine guns poking out of the turrets on top. An Iraqi interpreter told the driver to step out of the Mercedes. The driver was in his midthirties, with a beard and black hair, wearing a jacket, an open-collared shirt, and dress pants. Flanders noted right away that the driver wouldn't look him in the eye and was shuffling—nervous tics he had been taught to notice during his training for deployment to Iraq. "He was acting like we weren't there," Flanders said. The soldiers noticed two more things at once. That the driver had a large bulge under his shirt, and that there was a passenger in the backseat. They ordered the passenger to step out of the car. And that was when the driver made a run down the road and made ready to leap into the reeds. The soldiers on the ground raised their weapons and shouted; the machine gunners spun in their turrets.

Then came the red mist. "There was this explosion. A cloud. Red mist," Flanders recalled. "He self-detonated. A suicide vest." The soldiers could see individual body parts thrown in the air. As sometimes happens with suicide vests, shoes and shins still stood on the roadway, disconnected for eternity from their owner.

The soldiers pounced on the passenger, a man in his late thirties to forties, wearing a shirt and pants but no jacket, curly hair, and no beard. He said through the interpreter that he had been taken hostage by the local terrorist cell and was being held for ransom to subsidize the bombing network. He said the terrorists were going to kill him. He begged for help. Flanders noticed, however, that he wasn't tied or gagged, but for the moment, his identity was not the big question. The soldiers knew terrorist standard operating procedures and feared the entire car was rigged with explosives. The passenger was moved a safe distance from the car and held at gunpoint. An explosive-ordnance disposal team was called, and it sent a small robot on wheels to check the car, which was clean.

It was then that Flanders and his soldiers were able to inspect the Mercedes, where they found a black satchel briefcase, a laptop computer, a half-dozen hard drives, smaller thumb drives, and sheaves of documents. Flanders had been trained not to boot up the computer; a favorite terrorist trick was to booby-trap their laptops with explosives in case they were seized and someone tried to turn them on without putting in a pass code. Even so, he was beginning to suspect that this was a major intelligence find. It was almost 2:00 a.m. as Flanders and his soldiers finished inspecting the car, photographing the seizure, turning the confiscated material over to the battalion intelligence officer, and passing the detainee to a medical team who would examine him before turning him over to Army interrogators.

The day after the sunset encounter with the dark Mercedes, Flanders told his soldiers it was time to get back out there and "out-G the G." Another patrol, another mobile checkpoint. But over the next few months, they heard the rumors. Their detainee was a major Al Qaeda courier. He proved too well trained at countering interrogation techniques to be cracked even at the central "high-value detainee" facility in Iraq at Camp Cropper and eventually was separated from the run-of-the-mill detainees and sent for higher-level interrogation by the CIA. Their cache—the computer and drives—was a treasure trove of valuable data. Four-star generals were briefed on their find. Even the president knew about it. Or so the soldiers of 1st Platoon told themselves over a steady diet of PowerBars and Red Bull.

At the headquarters of the 1st Cavalry Division's 1st Brigade Combat Team, Colonel Paul E. Funk II, in command of Flanders's unit, sat looking at the map of the huge area of responsibility he had inherited a month before. He had to exercise control over more than 350 square miles of Iraq, from Tarmiyah through Taji, around to the western deserts and down to Abu Ghraib. Every commander knew this was to be one of the lines of attack into Baghdad by the antigovernment forces. The IEDs told him that. But he had more to worry about. An Air Force F-16 had just gone down, and his troops were securing the area to ensure that its high technology was not scavenged. The intelligence bonanza secured by Flanders's platoon was being examined; the brigade's intelligence-exploitation teams had been poring over the maps, translating the documents, and cracking open the computer for about ten days. Their ace in the hole was an analytical team on loan from the National Security Agency, the nation's premier electronic intelligence-espionage organization, but one that had never before assigned its experts down to the brigade level, where they get a fingertip sense of the threat in a combat zone. The analysis is painstakingly detailed work, carried out in the midst of a war.

Funk had already alerted his boss, the 1st Cavalry's assistant division commander, Brigadier General John Campbell, who had come to the division by way of Army Special Forces and then a stint as executive officer to the Army's chief of staff. Campbell was eager to move on the platoon's find. He pushed the trove up to his commander, Lieutenant General Ray Odierno, in charge of the day-to-day fight as the top officer of Multinational Corps–Iraq. From there, it went to the intelligence community in Washington and back to Central Command at MacDill Air Force Base in Tampa. (The troops assigned there call the headquarters Tampa-stan.)

It took weeks to crack the computer and thumb drives and translate all the documents. It would have taken even longer, but the military headquarters in Baghdad was able to send digital files of all the data and images over a secure forty-megabyte transmission line that had been installed to connect a number of bases across Iraq and Afghanistan earlier that year. This was a major change in operations. "They did an initial triage and sensitive-site exploitation downrange—phones, e-mails, signatures for guys they knew to be emirs," said a military intelligence officer who worked the trove. "There are automated systems for analyzing and exploiting cell phone numbers. Same with GPS and mini flash drives. We can get data off of anything."

Another important change was in personnel. As the war in Iraq became more intelligence driven, the number of analysts assigned to the sensitive-site exploitation mission grew from a mere fifty in 2003 to four hundred by the time of the Taji coup at the end of 2006.

While senior military officers and intelligence officials say the working relationship between the troops and analysts is a good and productive one today, the pressure to find new and better ways for analysts to support the war-fighters produced an unanticipated clash of cultures in the early years of the Iraq War. When the scandal at the Abu Ghraib prison was breaking in the spring of 2004, tensions were rising between the Special Operations troops and civilian interrogators and case officers from the Defense Intelligence Agency's (DIA) Defense Human Intelligence Service at another secret detention facility in Iraq, Camp Nama. The dispute centered on the harsh treatment of detainees as well as restrictions the Special Operations troops placed on their civilian colleagues, which included monitoring their e-mail messages and phone calls. Vice Admiral Lowell E. Jacoby, the DIA's director, wrote a two-page memo to Stephen Cambone, a close adviser to Secretary Rumsfeld, in which he described a series of complaints from DIA personnel. The most disturbing was a May 2004 incident in which a DIA interrogator said he witnessed soldiers punch a detainee hard enough to require medical attention. The DIA officer took photos of the injuries, but a supervisor confiscated them, Jacoby wrote.

The military-versus-civilians conflict could not be ignored. "These guys wanted results, and our debriefers were used to a civil environment," said one Defense Department official who was briefed on the task-force operations, speaking of the soldiers. Within days after Admiral Jacoby sent his memo, the DIA took the extraordinary step of temporarily withdrawing its personnel from Camp Nama. Admiral Jacoby's memo also provoked an angry reaction from Cambone. "Get to the bottom of this immediately. This is not acceptable," Cambone said in a handwritten note on June 26, 2004, to his top deputy, Lieutenant General William G. Boykin. "In particular, I want to know if this is part of a pattern of behavior."

John Tyson, the DIA's top Al Qaeda tracker, recalls the painful birth of this new, intensive relationship between the intelligence community and the soldiers on the ground. "That was a situation where we were building the airplane as we were flying it," he said. "It was anything but smooth sailing. After 9/11, we had our troops pouring into Afghanistan. These are guys we have worked with for several years. And, they need a lot of intel support. We had to create a mechanism, a process, product lines that supported them, that got to the finite level of detail they needed and that was timely enough for their requirements. That was one of the biggest changes immediately after 9/11."

There had been spikes in tempo before, of course: The East Africa embassy bombings. The *Cole*. But as the military moved into the Afghanistan offensive, with bin Laden as their target, there were daily, hourly, even minute-by-minute demands for analysis and targets. "Literally you were talking to the guys who were going to be knocking down doors that night on whatever objective it was going to be," Tyson recalls. "There was this learning process to the level of detail they needed, when they needed it, how we could get that level of detail in a product that was usable to them. So, there was this huge learning process going on as we were trying to support these operations. That was one of the biggest turning points for us."

That was the intellectual part of DIA's evolution. The other part, physical, was the physics of the process. "The other thing, which goes along with that, was then figuring out how to get your national-level analysts here, out to the field from here to support those operations," Tyson said. "It is just critical to be actually tied to that operational unit. You just can't do it from DC, and that is one of the lessons we took away: You just can't do it from here."

Issue number one, he said, was getting traditionally desk-bound analysts into a mind-set that prepared them for going forward into these dangerous places. "We just hadn't been asked to do it, and it wasn't necessarily an expectation of someone coming into the agency at that time—like it is now," said Tyson, who has deployed to the combat zone as often as many military personnel. "So, there was a lot of learning on all our parts, absolutely." Issue number two was just exactly how do you do it? "How do you even equip an analyst to get out there? How do you get them out there? If they are on a military bird, do they need a visa for anyplace? All these little pieces that you had to get together," Tyson said. "When they get out there, what are you going to do, when are they going to contribute, what is their connectivity going to be? So, immediately after 9/11, that was sort of one piece that was swirling."

By the time of the Taji breakthrough in December 2006, those pieces were not swirling but were in place, and helped account for a big score.

What was pulled out of the Taji trove was so valuable that one military officer compared it to the Allies' success in breaking the Nazis' Enigma codes during World War II. In that conflict, the operation at Bletchley Park in England enabled British and American commanders to read the Nazis' operational orders for their land, sea, and air forces and to dispatch their own aircraft and ships to attack German troops and submarines. Intelligence helped win the day then, and was winning it again in Iraq. In advance of the Battle of Baghdad in 2007, the American commanders who were managing the successful deployment of the surge forces sent by President Bush would have the Taji cache to thank: They were given hand-drawn maps, one identified by intelligence officers as having been the work of Abu Musab al-Zarqawi, the leader of Al Qaeda in Iraq. Some showed exactly what the terrorists knew about the location of American checkpoints. There was Google

Earth imagery with Xs marking American forward operating bases and their perimeter defenses. And so much more.

"It gave us their whole game plan for Baghdad," said one intelligence officer who worked on the Taji trove. As tens of thousands of additional American forces were surging into Iraq in early 2007, Al Qaeda and its allies were planning their own offensive to take over the Iraqi capital. The intelligence seized at Taji contained the location of Al Qaeda safe houses and arms caches, detailed information on IED cells, and guides for planting roadside bombs. It showed the adversary's lines of attack as originating in the volatile belt of villages circling Baghdad along routes into the capital and the order for isolating the capital, neighborhood by neighborhood. The enemy military planners proved they had no lack of diabolical imagination for their tactical campaign of terror. There were orders for the mass murder of any sanitation workers spotted on the street, "so garbage would pile up and outrage the population against the central and local governments," recalled the intelligence officer. "When the trash piles up, it gets unbearable." There also were battle plans to kill all the bakers, since buying fresh bread daily is a sign of stable urban life and anger, frustration, and unease work in favor of the opposition. "This gave us the Al Qaeda order of battle, lines for their course of action, and operations for isolating neighborhoods and then the capital," said the officer.

The plan was sophisticated, too. "They had two or three different courses of action, branches, and sequels"—just like a concept of operations or mission plan drawn up by the American military, the officer said. The Taji material also told the military more than they had known about a shadowy terrorist group that claimed allegiance to Osama bin Laden. "There were names, faces, correspondence, notes between units; it's where we got to thinking that they did have some structure, did have some organization, did have an organization for battle, and chain of command," said the intelligence officer.

The influence of Saddam Hussein's loyalists was also seen in the battle plans for terrorists in Iraq who claimed allegiance to Al Qaeda. Military intelligence analysts realized that the terrorists' plan for squeezing Baghdad from the belts outside the capital used established communications, structures, housing, and lines of attack that Saddam Hussein's forces had planned to use to counter the American invasion.

"Once that stuff started coming back from exploitation and we grasped what we had, we set up countering operations to thwart what [Al Qaeda in Iraq] was trying to do at the time," recalled General Campbell of the 1st Cavalry. "We had not really understood how serious Al Qaeda was about Baghdad being their center of gravity, too," he said. "This gave us all of that and their routes into the city."

Using the hand-drawn maps and other battle campaign documents, the American military in central Iraq mounted raids northwest and west of Taji that uncovered huge arms caches and seized underground bunkers that were serving as terror cell headquarters. And illustrating the new and more cordial relations between the conventional and Special Operations forces, historic rivals within the American military, the intelligence was also passed to the elite counterterrorism force, which targeted high-value terror leaders whose locations were indicated by material in the Taji trove. As with any intelligence find, analysts and commanders had some disagreements over exactly how to interpret portions of the translated documents and how they should shape the deployment of American and allied combat forces. Some officers involved with the effort said some units were misdirected south of Baghdad as a result of the Taji haul, but General Campbell and others in command of the surge said they had no doubt about the value of the intelligence coup.

The American military, of course, did not make public the intelligence bonanza at the time, any more than the Allies bragged publicly about Enigma until many years after V-E Day. But the Iraq surge was a success, and General Odierno, who ran the day-to-day fight, was rewarded with a fourth star—and the job of turning security over to the Iraqis and trimming back the American force in Iraq that he had commanded as it grew again to invasion numbers.

Later, during one of his trips home to confer with President Obama and Defense Secretary Gates, General Odierno reflected on the secret elements that had made the surge a success: "What we found in those documents was the fact that they felt that if they could control very specific areas around Baghdad—north, west, and south of Baghdad—as long as they could control that, they would be able then to conduct operations," General Odierno said. "So we had to take away their sanctuaries. It's fundamental to see how a young lieutenant who stopped a vehicle and got this material gave us an extremely important piece of information that all of a sudden changed my thought processes on how to allocate my forces during the surge. I said, 'Hey. We've missed it here. We have to make sure we control these areas.' So I adjusted our plan."

First Lieutenant Garry Owen Flanders and the soldiers of 1st Platoon never got an official briefing on what they had found or on what it had meant to the war against Al Qaeda in Iraq. However, more than a year later, as their unit transitioned from combat to advising Iraqi security forces to take over the mission, they received a visitor. General Odierno helicoptered into their forward operating base and presented his official "coin"—a highly prized keepsake that carries a commander's official seal—to Flanders, his platoon sergeant, and two squad leaders, the soldiers who had landed one of the biggest intelligence catches in the war.

It was another September 11, this time in 2007, when members of an elite Special Operations team code-named Task Force 121 flew in darkness aboard helicopters, the pilots' eyes glowing green from the crystals of their night-vision scopes, as they dashed across the northwestern desert of Iraq toward Sinjar, a dusty village at the bottom of a low range of dry hills less than ten miles from the Syrian border that was a critical field station for the Islamic Republic of Iraq, the name for an Al Qaeda–affiliated group that chose an indigenous-sounding name to hide its foreign roots.

For weeks, a tent camp just outside Sinjar had been under constant watch. Unmanned Predator surveillance drones silently logged hundreds of hours overhead. Their pilots sat at a safe distance, many time zones away in the deserts of Nevada. In the "Pred" flight-control trailers, the consoles may look like video games with joysticks, but the weapons and targets are real. Those controlling the drones fly eight-hour shifts and then go home to their families in the suburbs of Las Vegas. The Predators captured full-motion video and infrared images of the Sinjar site around the clock, establishing what the military calls "a pattern of life": who comes, who goes, how often, how regularly.

At the same time, Rivet Joint aircraft manned by real pilots in planes the size of a Boeing passenger jet flew unseen overhead. These aircraft suck up cell phone and walkie-talkie signals from 30,000 feet. Joining the effort was the Joint Surveillance and Target Attack Radar System (JSTARS), carried aboard another converted Boeing passenger airframe, which can track personnel and vehicles traveling on the ground across a large swath of desert, from Sinjar to the Syrian border. This capability was critical to the surveillance mission, because operatives at Sinjar were believed to be responsible for smuggling jihadists on routes that ran like veins along the Syria-Iraq border all the way from Turkey to the town of Qaim in Iraq's western Anbar province, a hotbed of the Sunni insurgency.

Together, this massive effort at intelligence gathering had established beyond a doubt that Sinjar was the hub for a key Al Qaeda smuggling route, or "ratline," that brought fighters—especially suicide bombers—into Iraq. The Iraqis themselves, even the most virulently anti-American, did not volunteer in large numbers for suicide missions; that was the emotional commitment of foreigners who came into the country to make holy war. The network smuggling these would-be suicide bombers was operated by a terrorist commander named Muthanna, whose self-chosen title was Emir of the Iraq and Syrian Border. Military intelligence profiles identified him as a "close associate of key Syrian-based Al Qaeda in Iraq facilitators." He was king of a cross-border region of Iraq and Syria that stretched more than 450 miles, a length impossible to patrol, even if the checkpoints and official border crossings were not riddled with corruption. "If you don't lock your door, you can't complain about burglars," said one Marine officer stationed in the desolate desert of western Iraq along the border with Syria. By the time the Sinjar mission was mounted in the fall of 2007, an estimated 25,000 people had been killed in that year alone by suicide bombings in Iraq. The range of improvised explosives—dug into roads, carried aboard vehicles, or worn by jihadists—was becoming the gravest threat to American and allied forces, killing and maiming more personnel than did bullets and mortars. While technology and intelligence offered ways to discover and detonate at least some of the roadside and car bombs, "We were getting our asses kicked by suicide bombers," said one three-star American commander.

Muthanna was known to be an efficient and capable commander, but that was about all anybody knew. There were photographs of other terror leaders in Iraq: Abu Musab al-Zarqawi, the Jordanian who ran Al Qaeda in Mesopotamia; Abu Ayyub al-Masri, the Egyptian-born military strategist; Haythem Sabah Shaker Mahmud al-Badri, the emir of Greater Samarra; and Khalid al Mashadani, the senior Iraqi in the Al Qaeda network. Their mug shots were on wanted posters inside the coalition headquarters and on the baseball cards carried by troops in the field. But not Muthanna. His image was a black silhouette representing a terror leader for whom no photographs had been taken, bought, captured, or acquired. The military didn't know what he looked like, but it knew what he did. And so the order was issued to go after him. "It was the kind of thing done a thousand times before, and a thousand times after," said a senior operations officer. "It was a standard mission set."

Signals intelligence operators picked up a solid lead on exactly when Muthanna was crossing from Syria into Iraq on his way to a conference of senior terrorist leaders in Mosul, in north-central Iraq, which had effectively become Al Qaeda's capital in the country after having been pushed out of its safe haven in Anbar Province. The American military learned that Muthanna would stop at a tent camp outside Sinjar, just inside the border. Once the "go" order was given, dozens of Army Rangers, the elite light infantry of the American military, landed by helicopter at the four corners of what would be an imaginary square in the sand whose edges outlined what the military calls "a kill box" several hundred yards around the camp within which anybody moving is fair game. The commandos established this firm perimeter to keep innocents out and to capture or kill any "squirters" who might try and escape once the attack began.

Just before dawn, the Special Operations team hit, and hit hard, dropping from helicopters right onto the camp. In rapid spasms of violence, six terrorist fighters were killed by gunfire. Two other terrorist operatives died when they ran at the American commandos entering their tent and set off their suicide vests. Forensic identification identified one of them as Muthanna, who self-detonated inside his tent rather than be taken alive for interrogation. Muthanna's death was officially announced at a Baghdad news conference a month after the mission.

Even more important than having eliminated the mastermind of a significant smuggling route for foreign fighters and suicide bombers into Iraq, the Special Operations forces scooped up a treasure trove of documents and five terabytes of data on computer hard drives. Much of it had been erased in the minutes after the attack began, but computer wizards working for the National Security Agency were able to recover the zeros and ones. Word quickly spread throughout the American intelligence community and the military that the commandos had come up with what one senior spy boss in Washington called "an Al Qaeda Rolodex"—and not just for Iraq but for all of Southwest Asia and North Africa.

The identities of between six hundred and eight hundred foreigners who had entered Iraq at the behest of Al Qaeda were in the file. The documents and hard drives contained biographical material on one hundred others. Each file contained precious details of their personal lives: their misfortunes, their inspirations, their goals.

"These Al Qaeda were as—what's the right word?—as anal about taking notes and keeping records as the Nazis were in concentration camps," said one senior administration counterterrorism official who reviewed the Sinjar file. "They had the name of the guy. They had his alias, place of birth, phone number, facilitator when he got into Syria, what his profession was—all types of very magnificently helpful intelligence specifics. So this trove bought us a thousand names—or maybe eight hundred because of aliases." The terrorist network operating through Sinjar also had videotaped their training of bombers and their farewell tapes pledging a suicide in the name of jihad. "They videotape everything," said one young military analyst, "like Pamela and Tommy Lee."

The captured information also allowed the constellation of American intelligence agencies to dramatically refine its assessment of what animates a terrorist and who is susceptible to terrorist propaganda, inducements, manipulation, and indoctrination. According to a dossier completed by the military after the raid, the intelligence included "hand-written memos discussing personnel, weapons and ammunition procurement, the creation of passports and collection of money." The military gleaned details of how the would-be suicide bombers were crossing the border illegally and who was taking bribes. More gruesome was the task of matching the heads of suicide bombers—often recovered severed from their bodies after a self-detonation—with photographs found in the Sinjar computers.

According to senior American intelligence officers and military personnel who worked the mission, the captured files and computer information offered new clues for how to counter Al Qaeda's efforts in the marketplace of ideas. Experts learned how to mount super-secret counterattacks in the virtual world of online Al Qaeda Internet locations, since the hard drives included Web addresses of secret chat rooms, passwords to enter them, and coded "backdoors" for taking control of the sites. The hard drives from this raid, and from others across Iraq, Afghanistan, and in Pakistan, have become central to the "fight for intelligence."

"From Vietnam to 9/11, the military forgot that every operation has to be a fight for intelligence," said one veteran of the Special Operations community. "And this came right when the intelligence community was being downsized, too. It took us six to eight years after 9/11 to really relearn that the intelligence you exploit from a mission is just as important as who you might kill on the mission."

All this information scooped up on the battlefield is sent for translation, analysis, and exploitation to top-secret cybercenters at the CIA and the NSA, exploited by teams to create new strategies for using the information to deter, dissuade, and, it is hoped, defeat terrorists. "If you can learn something about whatever is on those hard drives, whatever that information might be, you could instill doubt on their part by just countermessaging whatever it is they said they wanted to do or planned to do," said Major General Mark Schissler, whose Pentagon duties have included serving as director of cyberoperations for the Air Force and as deputy director of the antiterrorism policy office for the Joint Chiefs of Staff. Terrorists tend to treat the Internet as a shield, not disclosing their whereabouts and using it to spread their ideology and influence. Schissler added, "You may be able to interfere with some of that, interrupt some of that. You can also post messages to the opposite of that." In this case, counterterrorism experts simply made the decision to release some of the Sinjar information that is true and that they knew would discredit terrorists with mainstream Muslims, like videotapes showing members of Al Qaeda in Iraq training children to kidnap and kill or a lengthy letter written by another terrorist leader that describes the organization as weak and plagued by poor morale.

At the same time, American diplomats abroad and counterterrorism experts at home were able to leverage the information in the documents by quietly working behind the scenes with moderate Middle Eastern governments—and some that had been openly hostile to American policy—to devise new ways to keep potential terrorists off balance, along with the networks that recruit, train, pay, and move them around the region. The attitude was that if these governments knew the truth, then the truth might prompt them to break up the smuggling rings and counsel, or lock up, potential suicide bombers before they even left the country.

The unit that carried out the Sinjar raid was named Task Force 121. The bland designation of the commando unit hid the fact that the American military's top-tier hunter-killer units had been reorganized for the mission of battling terrorists in Iraq and Afghanistan, a decision that in its own way was as significant a change of organization and focus as had been undertaken since the end of the Cold War. It was first disclosed in the *New York Times* in November 2003 that General John Abizaid and the senior leaders of the Special Operations community had created a covert force just for hunting Saddam Hussein and key terrorists across the region. In response to the story, Pentagon officials ordered the task force to change its name, and the unit's number has been redesignated on a regular basis ever since, just to throw off those trying to track its supersecret actions.

Its members are the most elite counterterrorist fighters in the American military, officially labeled "Tier 1" for readiness and with carte-blanche access to the nation's highest level of intelligence. The task force combines personnel from the Joint Special Operations Command (JSOC), the operational, war-fighting division of

the larger Special Operations Command that is charged with organizing, training, and equipping elite forces for all four armed services. The teams are drawn from members of the Army's Delta
Force, the Navy's SEAL Team 6, and Air Force and Army special
aviation units. There is a large talent pool of military intelligence
officers as well as officers and analysts from the CIA and the NSA.
As the war efforts in both Afghanistan and Iraq deteriorated, the
three-star commander of JSOC moved his headquarters forward to
Iraq from his base at Fort Bragg. His name was not well known
then, but it is now: Stanley A. McChrystal.

On the day in the summer of 2009 that a Senate vote confirmed General McChrystal and elevated him to his new command and he deployed to Afghanistan, he took two reporters from
the *New York Times* on a tour of his new "rear headquarters" in a
sealed corridor of the Pentagon basement, home for hundreds of
planners, operations officers, and intelligence analysts who would
be supporting his counterinsurgency and counterterrorism efforts
in Afghanistan, a place he called "downrange." The general—a tall,
lean, ascetic man who eats one meal every twenty-four hours and
listens to audiobooks on his daily long-distance runs to maximize
his time—said that the secret to his counterterrorism efforts had
been to break down walls that had divided the military and intelligence communities. "Every operation is a fight for intelligence," he
said. And every piece of information gathered on a raid—computers,
documents, photographs, videos, interrogations of prisoners, and
even the "pocket litter" taken from the militants' clothes—had to
be translated and analyzed quickly so that a follow-up raid could be
planned and executed in the few hours before the terrorist's cronies
knew one of their comrades had been taken out of action by the
JSOC task force.

The amount of material seized from terrorist and insurgent
targets soon grew to an incredible size. The DIA operates exploitation triage centers and massive warehouses for storing intelligence
product in the war zones as well as in Qatar and back in the

United States. One intelligence analyst said that walking into one of the warehouses for document and media exploitation reminded him of the final scene of *Raiders of the Lost Ark*, when the captured Ark of the Covenant is crated up and rolled into a cavernous storage area that contains all of the government's other, dangerous secrets. All told, more than two million individual documents and electronic files have been catalogued by media type: hard copy, phone number, thumb drive. Each is inspected by a linguist working with a communications analyst or a computer whiz. The DIA analysts are joined by experts from the FBI and the Drug Enforcement Administration. Given the volume, no more than 10 percent of the captured intelligence has ever been analyzed. Intelligence officers say they simply are overwhelmed, and untold quality leads may still be buried in the pile of computers, digital files, travel documents, and pocket litter. Technical and software improvements have made sorting and analyzing the material more efficient, but senior intelligence analysts still laugh at the chaotic early days when just about anything deemed of possible value was swept up and shipped back to exploitation centers. "I remember when we first started taking this stuff, it was coming back in Meals Ready to Eat rations boxes, discombobulated," said a bemused Defense Department intelligence analyst. "A live grenade came back in one of the boxes. It was shipped back here. This was in the early days when they were just grabbing everything and throwing it in boxes. Dirty underwear, half-eaten food—it was just amazing the crap that came back."

The specific hunter-killer-exploitation missions were planned, and the commandos themselves were based inside a giant military airfield north of Baghdad, which during the height of insurgent violence was hit so often by enemy fire that its nickname was "Mortar-itaville." The task force compound was walled off, a sign of the deep, dark, "black" units based there; it was off-limits to all non–task force military personnel, including even the Special Forces that operate on the "white" side to train Iraqi commandos and hunt the second tier of insurgent and terrorist targets.

Every night during the peak of the surge in Iraq in 2007, General McChrystal's troops carried out as many as a dozen raids on terrorist leaders, senior insurgent fighters, and top militia officers. The after-action reports of these raids were the first thing that General David H. Petraeus, the senior commander in Baghdad, read the next morning at dawn before he met with his advisers and wrote assessments for Washington. The vast majority—between 80 percent and 90 percent—of the missions were aimed at Al Qaeda–allied targets, while the rest attacked other extremist elements. Before major missions, a team of intelligence analysts would be on standby to exploit the material. If a big haul was expected, a "sensitive-site exploitation team" would be organized and would fly out with the Special Operations troops, setting up an ad hoc analytical cell in a tent or in an abandoned building near the attack site. The intelligence was not only used to find new targets and fresh missions but also employed in the high-level campaign to counter the terrorist message.

The focused missions of American commando teams were a combat solution to the threat that Michael Vickers, the Pentagon boss for Special Operations and low-intensity conflict, described as "more atomized—the individual guy who is bombing you every day." In Iraq, by 2007, "we had overwhelming force so that is how insurgents fought us. Faced with that kind of threat, that is where these counternetwork operations came in. It's the 'F3EA.' Find. Fix. Finish. Exploit. Analyze—and now! It's intelligence-driven operations and the use of technology, in particular persistent surveillance—an unblinking eye—that lets you conduct a sustained campaign. One mission leads to another. We didn't know how to do these kinds of operations before 9/11. A lot of intelligence investments we had made came together in 2007."

But amid the messy business of averting disaster in the war in

Iraq in 2007, the Sinjar raid was unheralded, though it is considered one of the task force's greatest successes and it validated the investments advocated by Vickers. Like all victories, it began on very different fields of combat. The Taji haul was a classic example of what can be accomplished by low-tech, boots-on-the-ground operations, which are and have always been a fundamental part of intelligence collection, though not many have proved to be so productive. But this is a two-front war in which the technical and human sides of intelligence gathering often intersect. In future wars involving the United States, there will be even greater interaction between local operations and high-tech intelligence gathering. One example of the latter is Sinjar, which was supported by a U.S. facility in a country that, apparently, dares not say its name.

Even from a great distance, the most distinctive landmark of the air base is not its military runways, some of the longest in the world, or the massive American air operations center there, but the large, double-tent structure that provides shade from the blazing desert sun over the outdoor recreation area that is the hub of social life for the American pilots, bombardiers, maintenance personnel, and intelligence officers based in this Persian Gulf state. A pair of giant, four-story-tall, beige cones explains why the unusual structure, visible from miles away, is referred to as The Bra by the airmen. Meeting at The Bra is what the Air Force crew members do most every night, gathering for camaraderie and karaoke after the blast-furnace Gulf sun has set. Best of all perks is the chit card issued on the first day of every month. While American ground combat forces throughout the Middle East operate under General Order No. 1, which forbids any consumption of alcohol in the combat zone, the American Air Force personnel assigned to this base can get two drinks a day, beer or wine, making the whole scene feel like a desert update of sailing the high seas with the Royal Navy as the grog ration was ladled out.

But serious business is done here, including command of all the airborne surveillance assets that nailed the Sinjar target set. American reporters who are granted access to the base must sign security agreements that forbid them from revealing its location. Odd, since a Google search for "Combined Air Operations Center" yields almost eighty thousand hits, many of them from official Defense Department sites and American military press releases identifying the location and describing the missions carried out there. (Although the official name of the headquarters overseeing American and allied aviation missions in the Middle East now is Combined Air and Space Operations Center, the old acronym, CAOC, pronounced KAY-ock, remains in standard use.)

The CAOC was quietly moved from its home in Saudi Arabia to its new location in the Persian Gulf in 2003, partly owing to restrictions on combat missions imposed by the Saudis but in no small measure to remove an irritant that had become a major propaganda cause for Muslim extremists: the presence of an American war-fighting headquarters in the same desert kingdom that was the protector of Islam's holiest sites, Mecca and Medina, the original grievance of Osama bin Laden and his Al Qaeda network.

The first CAOC looked like a gymnasium-sized garage occupied by hundreds of computer geeks who ate and slept at their terminals and simply uncoiled more electronic cable across the floor every time a new friend came over with yet another computer terminal to do homework. The giant electronic maps identifying and locating every single American and allied aircraft throughout the region were impressive, as were the six giant monitors showing real-time surveillance video feeds from Iraq and Afghanistan. But the place was so crummy looking that a member of a visiting congressional delegation actually asked a commander why he couldn't order someone to get a vacuum cleaner and give the headquarters a good dusting. The answer was that everyone feared the second-order effects of bringing in a cleaning crew with vacuums and brooms, because so much fine desert sand had entered the structure that kicking it up might bring the system down, halting air operations over Iraq and Afghanistan that were vital for protecting troops in contact with the enemy and gathering intelligence on adversary actions. The problem was solved when the headquarters moved into its new, multimillion-dollar structure; the replacement CAOC has a series of airlocks and blowers that were ostensibly installed to keep out poisons in a chemical or biological attack (the Pentagon has the same system, as official tour guides will tell you) but really put there simply to protect the sensitive computer systems from natural grit.

It is from this base that the Rivet Joint and JSTAR surveillance aircraft are launched, and it is home to the tanker jets that refuel them and the tactical fighters and long-range bombers sent over Iraq and Afghanistan for extended missions. It also is at the CAOC that a three-star Air Force general manages the precious number of Predator, Reaper, and Global Hawk surveillance drones available for orbits gathering vital intelligence in the skies over targets each day, such as those that found and figured out what the terrorist network was doing at Sinjar.

Lieutenant General Gary North, the CAOC commander from 2006 to 2009, during the run-up and execution of the Sinjar operation, said that the improvement in airborne surveillance in recent years, in particular the ability to capture and transmit full-motion video images in real time to help plan and guide combat missions, is like the transition "from the bow and arrow to the rifle."

"It changed the focus of battle," he said. "It is that entity which makes us, the coalition forces, able to have 'persistent stare.' And then tied to the platforms that now have full-motion video capability are weapons. We have deadly persistence."

As he spoke in his command suite overlooking the giant digital maps and video monitors of the sprawling CAOC floor, at least a half-dozen Predators were feeding live video surveillance on locations where insurgents were believed to be preparing to plant roadside bombs across Iraq and Afghanistan. Other images were boring, showing nothing but mud huts surrounded by parked trucks, a few male figures moving about. Yet, sometimes it is the least interesting sequence of images watched for days on end that tells the most about the way forward in the counterterrorism effort. And it was exactly such usually boring images that led the military to Sinjar and helped guide the Special Operations mission that scooped up the "Al Qaeda Rolodex."

The Sinjar records, according to analysts charged with creating a public summary of the captured material, "offer an unrivaled insight into foreign fighters entering Iraq." For the twelve months ending in August 2007, Saudi Arabia and Libya were the starting points for almost two-thirds of all foreigners who came to Iraq to take up arms against the Baghdad government and its American supporters, especially those who dreamed of serving as suicide bombers. Saudi Arabia, a vital partner in the post-9/11 global counterterrorism effort, was home to 41 percent of the would be terrorists, and Libya was home to 19 percent. Syria and Yemen were each the birthplace of about 8 percent of the Al Qaeda recruits, followed by Algeria with 7 percent, Morocco with 6 percent, and Jordan with just under 2 percent. The average age of all the jihadists was between twenty-two and twenty-three, with the oldest being fifty-four and the youngest having just turned fifteen. About 40 percent of those who listed occupations said they were students, and there were handfuls of teachers, doctors, and engineers. Intelligence officers snickered when the translation came through that one jihadist said he had previously worked as a massage therapist.

"The fighters' overall youth suggests that most of these individuals are first-time volunteers rather than veterans of previous Jihadi struggles," stated an analysis of the documents prepared by the Combating Terrorism Center at West Point, a research organization that draws on the U.S. Military Academy's scholarly and military resources. "The incitement of a new generation of Jihadis to join the fight in Iraq, or plan operations elsewhere, is one of the most worrisome aspects of the ongoing fight." And the analysis warned the American leadership not to confuse gains against the franchise Al Qaeda units inside Iraq "as fundamental blows against the organization outside of Iraq. So long as al Qaida is able to attract hundreds of young men to join its ranks, it will remain a serious threat to global security."

In a chilling list of career goals of the recruits, 56 percent said they had volunteered to be suicide bombers, far above the 42 percent who had expressed the goal of taking up combat arms as insurgent foot soldiers and had at least some prospects of living to fight another day. But countering this worrisome large percentage of those who chose martyrdom as their future was information in the documents that revealed holes in the terrorist recruiting network.

"The Sinjar records reinforce anecdotal accounts suggesting that Al Qaeda's Iraqi affiliates rely on smugglers and criminals—rather than their own personnel—to funnel recruits into Iraq," according to the West Point analysis. "Al Qaeda's reliance on criminal and smuggling networks exposes it to the greed of mercenaries. In many cases, the United States should target work to destroy these networks, but the U.S. must remain flexible enough to recognize opportunities to co-opt, rather than simply annihilate, such systems." It is a clear recognition that the corrosive effects of smuggling and organized crime are far less heinous than the effects of terrorism—and the trade-off to intelligence planners was obvious. The report suggests that "the U.S. may be able to use financial incentives and creative security guarantees to secure cooperation from some smugglers."

Another data point pounced on by the intelligence community was the demographics of the recruits: Most of the jihadists entering Iraq from the Middle East and North Africa crossed from Syria as part of a group from their hometown, suggesting that Al

Qaeda's recruiting efforts operated, at varying degrees of effective-ness, in only a few cities. "For example in Libya, about fifty of the names came from a city on the eastern border," said one counter-terrorism expert who worked on the Sinjar project, referring to Darnah, Libya. "And we said, 'What's the deal here?' And that's the first time the Libyan government had seen that, and they said, 'You know, I tell you what, we had problems there, too. We've brought troops in there twice before, for other reasons not neces-sarily tied to terrorism but it's not necessarily an area that's easy for us to control ourselves.' "

From the Libyan example, General McChrystal immediately realized the value of the documents, and he decided to break down a couple of walls. He believed that effective pressure could be mounted by sharing the information with the countries of ori-gin for the jihadists—even those countries with which the United States had little or no alliance in the struggle. And, even more, he thought pages of the highly classified intelligence findings should be thrust into the very public marketplace of ideas to shape the international debate on terrorism. Across the military and intelli-gence community, General McChrystal was credited with com-manding missions that captured and killed more of America's adversaries than any other living officer. But his legacy in shifting the culture of handling intelligence is just as important. "Whoever finds the intel, owns the intel," said one Special Operations com-mander who acknowledged that in past years there had been reluc-tance on the part of the military's elite units to share its most valuable finds with conventional military units, let alone the civilian intelligence community. General McChrystal put an end to that.

"McChrystal said this is not something that should stay in the intelligence world," said one senior official involved in the Sinjar effort. "This is too valuable. And if we wait for eight hundred leads to get run around the world, the full effect of this can't necessarily be felt. So McChrystal did something that was very audacious and not very well received on the intelligence side. He said, 'I'm going to declassify all of this, put it in "open source," and we're going to get this thing cooking.' Rather than wait for the law enforcement community or the intelligence community to exploit this stuff, McChrystal 'operationalized' it immediately: He just put it out there in a blanket release."

There was no precedent for declassifying such a large trove of classified intelligence materials seized by the most classified counter-terrorism unit in the American military. Not only no precedent but no unit, function, or team for doing it. The task fell to the military's Special Operations Command at MacDill Air Force Base, specifi-cally to one young and energetic noncommissioned officer and a naturalized Egyptian émigré—"a 9/11 patriot," his friends called him—who sat side by side in two cubicles inside the command's intelligence section. The project was officially referred to, by those with the requisite "need to know," as Red Beard. (The team has since grown to add another linguist and a civilian analyst.)

But the new unit's mission did not sit well at first with the troops in the field who had risked their lives to scoop up the intel-ligence in firefights and raids. "To do it, it involved dragging the shooters kicking and screaming," said the military member of the Red Beard team who believed that the quiet spread of information about terrorist networks was a necessary tool in the special opera-tor's arsenal. "We need to educate our planners."

The two men in those cubicles were given access to the DIA's database of two million captured documents, files, passports, pocket litter, hard drives, and electronic files. But they focused specifically on eight hundred files from the Sinjar raid; translating, cross-referencing, and collating them took about two weeks. Overwhelmed by the volume of the material, the Red Beard team came up with the unusual plan to enlist West Point's Combating Terrorism Center to analyze and publicize the find. "We did not have the bandwidth to do the study, so we used West Point for the academic side," said the Red Beard analyst. "Within thirty days of giving it to West Point, we had a rough draft. Academics read better, tell a better story, and this was apparent in the report. We have had a shift in how we do intel reports since then. Captured material resonates in their community."

As fate and the bureaucracy would have it, the government official given the task of leading the next phase of the larger Sinjar effort was a man who was fluent in the secret language of Special Operations and who had just moved on to lead the Bush administration's diplomatic efforts to marshal other nations to the cause of striking back at terrorists. They still call him general, although he traded his camouflage combat uniform for the pinstripes of diplomacy, laying his three stars and sidearm on the table for a Blackberry and leather binder. Not exactly in from the cold, retired Lieutenant General Dell L. Dailey had come in from the "black" world of the military's most top-secret Special Operations missions to be a key strategist in the growing effort to use American "soft power" of economic might, cultural influence, and democratic values to counter terrorism around the world. American movies, music, and lifestyle may remain popular throughout the Muslim world, the general knew from his decades of travel across the Middle East, but he also knew that American policies are decidedly not.

Born into a military family, General Dailey graduated from West Point in 1971 and served during the opening of the war in Afghanistan as the commander of the Joint Special Operations forces, including Delta and Navy SEAL Team Six, the nation's most secret counterterrorism units. After earning his third star, Dailey was given the choice job of directing day-to-day operations for the military's Special Operations Command before being named by the Bush administration as civilian point man for coordinating U.S. counterterrorism policies and programs with America's allies on behalf of Secretary of State Condoleezza Rice.

He brought military discipline to a State Department staff more comfortable with a work routine less structured than the armed forces, and a similar rigor to his diplomatic missions that routinely had him meeting senior counterterrorism officials around the globe at all hours of the night. Imposing in uniform and daunting in a suit—although you could miss him in civvies in a sports bar, since he looks like your favorite uncle—Dailey nonetheless could roll up his sleeves and lecture the Beltway leadership on the need to deal with complex terrorist threats using every instrument of national power—the economy, educational institutions, charitable organizations—not just the military. And he had learned through multiple deployments even before becoming a diplomat that it is important to pause and sip tea until dawn with Middle Eastern leaders. He may have preferred the company of defense ministry and intelligence types, but he also courted prime ministers and presidents.

General Dailey conducted exhaustive rounds of shuttle diplomacy as he circulated from December 2007 through the spring of 2008 among almost two dozen Middle Eastern and North African capitals to disclose—and exploit—the Sinjar findings. Many details of his marathon, closed-door negotiations remain secret, but members of the team that planned the effort and others who joined the delegation on the road described their work on condition that they never be identified publicly.

One member of the team recalled General Dailey's opening pep talk for the mission. "I can't walk into a country and say, 'Stop foreign fighters,'" the general said. "I've got to have intelligence. And it can be sophisticated, open-source intelligence, or it can be raw classified intelligence, but for these folks to listen to me I've got to lay something on the table." The Sinjar bonanza, which Dailey described to his aides as "super intelligence," was tailor-made for his diplomatic offensive, which initially focused on the countries that had supplied most of the foreign fighters and suicide bombers to Iraq: Saudi Arabia, Yemen, and, in a startling destination for a former Special Operations commander, Libya. (He had hoped to visit Syria, but diplomatic tensions made this impossible. Even so, the Syrian government was given details of the Sinjar file through other channels.)

At each stop along the way, Dailey was going to break china and not care about turf or traditional arrangements for country-to-country talks, ordering that appointments be made not just with the usual local foreign-ministry types in each country, which were the protocol destinations on State Department visits, but also with ministries of defense and of interior—the military and state police—and with the local spymaster as well. Members of the team credited embassy personnel in each stop on the itinerary for understanding the importance of the mission and identifying key leaders in the local government for meetings. The composition of Dailey's delegation was specifically designed to reflect the similar all-of-government nature of the American effort: His delegation included representatives from the State Department, the National Security Council, and the intelligence agencies as well as the Pentagon and the Department of Homeland Security. But it was the general-turned-ambassador who led the way. "This guy named Dailey would come in from the State Department bona fides in countries that recognize the horsepower of the State Department," said one official in the delegation. "And we'd come in under his military/special ops bona fides in countries that recognized the military side. It was an ideal relation. We walked both sides of the street. When one door was closed, you use the other one."

In each capital, the official recalled, "We gave them a briefing that showed where they were culpable, handed it to them—we had a customized 'hunter' briefing," of PowerPoint slides and graphic printouts created by the staff of the Office of the Director of National Intelligence in Washington. "It's good honest data. It was very evident that this stuff couldn't have been dreamt up, at least not by a bunch of gringos."

Some of the countries were offended. Some were so taken aback by the accuracy of the intelligence that they rounded up suspected recruits and facilitators of the terrorist transit network even before the Dailey delegation left town. "Now, a lot of these countries wanted to help not just for the effort in Iraq, but these guys come back to their country, and they're troublemakers," the official recalled. "Algeria had the same troublemakers from the mujahideen from Afghanistan, so a lot of these countries had already seen it historically so it wasn't hard to be convincing. But that was the thrust of our discussion. It was, 'You may have problems with the U.S. in other areas, but here's a spot where we're giving you information to help these folks decide to be helpful, so please take good heed there.' And they did."

American officials said that in scores of cases, the host government took the Sinjar data and sent its own security officials to speak with the family, community leaders, and local mullahs. "They would say, 'How could something like this happen?'" recalled one official who participated in the initiative. "There was a kind of finger pointing by the government to the family members. And then they'd say, 'Please contact us if he raises his head, let him know we're looking for him if he comes home, let us try to get inside his head to find out why he's doing this so we can try to fix problems like that for the future.' Most of these countries became pretty mature on their own internal security."

Sessions in Libya and Egypt were contentious. While the session in Saudi Arabia was calmer, it was in its own way just as complex. Since their country was the largest source of foreign fighters and suicide bombers flowing through Syria into Iraq, Saudi officials were eager to get the intelligence. But this had not always been the case. Saudi charities funded Al Qaeda, and weapons carried by terrorist fighters around the region originated there as well. Only after Al Qaeda turned on the Saudi leadership several years after the attacks of 9/11—breaking an unofficial cease-fire by launching attacks on local infrastructure and persons, including members of the royal family—did the Saudis embrace programs to combat their internal terrorist challenges with a vengeance. During a 4:00 a.m.

meeting over tea, one American official recalled, the Dailey delegation's hosts at the Saudi Interior Ministry described a delicate balancing act of cracking down on Islamic extremism while honoring Muslim religion and culture and sacred sites in ways that would not inflame radicalism.

In Algeria, the conversation took place over a lengthy dinner with internal security officials and senior representatives from the intelligence agencies. In Yemen, the hosts were the military and intelligence services. The problem there, however, was that the Yemeni government had not quite made it into the digital information era, so the list of more than one hundred names and addresses of potential jihadists and their recruiters and enablers had to be tabulated and sorted by hand. "They can't cross-check names on databases or anything," said one official who worked the Sinjar report for Yemen. "It was a bit of a challenge for them. They were conscientious. They were there for it all, but it took them a little bit longer, a little more work."

The Sinjar effort is being studied today at military academies and in closed-door, off-site intelligence seminars as a model of success in how to strike back at terrorists measured in two significant ways. From his suspected hideout in the tribal areas of Pakistan, Ayman al-Zawahri took to the terrorist communications channels to blast the Sinjar documents and the West Point Combating Terrorism Center report as American military lies. Obviously he reads the center's Web site.

The American military in Iraq learned from the Sinjar files and significantly changed its deployments along the Iraq-Syria border based on what was learned from the files captured in the raid. "Before Sinjar, we sort of 'soccer-Mom'ed' it with forces spread evenly all along the border," said a Marine officer who subsequently invested his forces more wisely by putting the intelligence into practice. "We realized there were huge swaths that were just not important, because the foreign fighters were using these smuggling ratlines. So we focused our forces more efficiently." General Petraeus

said the overall Sinjar effort did more to halt the terror networks
that flowed foreign fighters and suicide bombers into Iraq than
any other operation.

"You can see you have to work with other countries," he said.
"The State Department counterterrorist ambassador, of all people,
Lieutenant General (retired) Dell Dailey, former head of JSOC—
talk about getting one of those right—went out to all the different
countries from which foreign fighters had come into Iraq, talked
to them, tried to get them to reduce the opportunities for military-
age males to fly to Damascus, Syria, on a one-way ticket. And it
worked."

After the Sinjar raid and the exploitation of the intelligence
that animated the regional diplomatic effort, the flow of foreign
fighters and would-be suicide bombers into Iraq dropped from a
high of 120 a month to between 10 and 20 a month, according to
statistics compiled by the military's Central Command. The Sinjar
mission and the intelligence exploitation effort provided the platform for a crippling strike against the network funneling young
jihadists from across the Middle East for the grimly effective mission of becoming suicide bombers in Iraq. Even more, it proved
that there is no solely military solution to the threat of terrorism
and that every instrument of national power must be brought into
play. When commanders, diplomats, and intelligence officers are
asked to describe a success in the struggle against violent extremism since the attacks of 9/11, they cite Sinjar as a template for
melding intelligence collection and analysis, Special Operations
attacks, and global diplomacy to mitigate one of the most serious
terrorism problems of the war in Iraq, which was the flow of foreign fighters and would-be suicide bombers from North Africa,
the Persian Gulf, across the Middle East, and then through Syria
into the war zone.

4

THE PROBLEM OF PAKISTAN

On a searing summer day in July 2008, President Bush's senior foreign policy and national security advisers filed into the Yellow Oval Room on the second floor of the White House for a top-secret briefing. The subject was Al Qaeda's metastasizing presence in Pakistan's lawless tribal areas along the mountainous border with Afghanistan. The briefers were General Michael V. Hayden, the former head of the NSA who was now the CIA director, and his deputy, Stephen R. Kappes, just back from an exasperating visit with President Pervez Musharraf and other top civilian and military officials in Islamabad.

Bush settled into an overstuffed chair in front of a carved wooden table. Vice President Cheney, Secretary of State Rice, Defense Secretary Gates, National Security Adviser Hadley, and Admiral Mike Mullen, the chairman of the Joint Chiefs of Staff, took their seats along with the others. It was an unusual setting for such a momentous meeting. Bush typically held his war councils in the Oval Office or in the underground and windowless Situation Room. But this chandeliered room in the White House residence, with a view across the Truman Balcony of the South Lawn and the Ellipse, had a place in history: It was where, on

December 7, 1941, Franklin D. Roosevelt learned of the attack on Pearl Harbor—and where he vowed to strike back.

The high-level meeting represented the culmination of nearly two years of growing alarm within the administration about a resurgent Al Qaeda; its ally, the Pakistani Taliban; and an increasingly intertwined network of Islamic extremist groups working in a criminal-like syndicate in Pakistan's rugged borderlands. It also brought to a head months of frustration with an essential but often infuriating ally. After facing a with-us-or-against-us ultimatum from Bush immediately after the September 11 attacks, Pakistan had worked closely with American agents to capture such top Al Qaeda operators as Khalid Shaikh Mohammed, the mastermind of 9/11. The United States had given more than $10 billion in military aid to Pakistan since 2001, about half of which had gone to reimburse the counterinsurgency efforts by the Pakistani Army. However, Pakistan was also an ally whose main spy agency, the Inter-Services Intelligence (ISI) directorate, gave support and safe haven to militant groups in the tribal areas who killed American troops in Afghanistan and supported Al Qaeda, groups that also provided Pakistan with a strategic proxy force against its neighbor and longtime rival, India.

This paradox in the relationship underscores how America's "new deterrence" strategy requires an often exasperating reliance on difficult or undependable partners, like Pakistan, that need to be stroked, scolded, and supported—sometimes all at once. A parade of high-level American officials, including most of those gathered in the room that day, had flown to Islamabad over the past several months to coax, cajole, or confront Pakistani politicians, generals, and spies to take more aggressive action against the militants. The trips yielded little. Now, the threat emanating from Pakistan's tribal areas wasn't simply aimed against American and allied troops in neighboring Afghanistan; it had become a growing menace directed against the U.S. homeland. "This is the epicenter of terrorism in the world," said one senior military officer.

Pakistan's government had negotiated a series of peace agree-ments with the militants, cease-fires to pull Pakistani troops out of the tribal areas in exchange for a halt to attacks on army garrisons and other government targets. But those agreements had failed to keep the peace, and they had given Al Qaeda and the Pakistani Taliban time and space to rest, rearm, and recruit. Specifically, the CIA warned, Al Qaeda was now recruiting and training Western-ers in the deadly art of explosives and bomb making, and was sending them home to Europe and North America with orders to unleash attacks of their own.

"We kept building and building the case of the safe havens," Hayden would later recall. "They were coming at us. They were a threat to the homeland." Musharraf, distracted by political prob-lems of his own, held back his military and security forces and deflected the American offers of help and threats to do more. But even as tensions were rising, a debate within the administration had delayed this midsummer reckoning in the White House resi-dence. For months, the CIA and the Pentagon had wanted to launch commando raids into Pakistan and dramatically increase missile strikes from Predator drones against targets in the tribal areas to keep the militants off balance. But the State Department warned that any unilateral action could stoke the anti-American fires already blazing in Pakistan, further destabilize the weakened Mu-sharraf government, and perhaps even open the door for Islamic radicals to seize control of the country and its nuclear arsenal. The State Department position had prevailed, and for months the Americans worked with and through the Pakistani government, with few lasting results. "We were 0 for '07," Hayden said, using a baseball hitter's analogy to explain the lack of success against Al Qaeda and its confederates in the tribal areas.

But with fresh intelligence assessments that warned of a grow-ing threat to the United States itself now in hand, there was an unspoken understanding among the officials gathered in the Yel-low Oval Room, Hayden said, that "after the next attack, knowing

what we know now, there's no explaining it if we don't do something." Hayden and Kappes briefed the latest intelligence—by now
chillingly familiar to the group—and then presented a detailed plan
to address the threat. The plan called for ramping up the number
of armed CIA Predator and Reaper drones flying over the tribal
areas at any given time. It dropped the requirement that the agency
seek "concurrence" from Pakistan's government, instead authorizing unilateral Predator strikes with notification to the Pakistanis as
an attack was happening or shortly thereafter. This would shorten
to about forty-five minutes the time between when a target was
spotted and when a Predator could launch a Hellfire missile. It
would also reduce the chance that the ISI might tip off the target.

Equally important, the plan called for increasing an already burgeoning number of CIA case officers on the ground, vastly expanding the scope and depth of the American spy network inside the
tribal areas. A year earlier, in the summer of 2007, threats swirled
about Pakistan-based terrorist plots against Europe, and the CIA
had sharply increased the quality and quantity of intelligence collected along the Afghanistan-Pakistan border. Hayden's plan would
accelerate that trend. Finally, Special Operations forces would be
authorized to plan cross-border raids from Afghanistan into Pakistan to attack militant targets, demonstrating to Al Qaeda and to
the Pakistani military that Bush really meant business.

In short, one participant said, the thrust of the plan was to
increase all means to put pressure on Al Qaeda during George W.
Bush's last six months in office. The goal was to kill Osama bin
Laden before the president's term ended or at the very least leave
Al Qaeda in a much weakened state for his successor. Senator
Barack Obama's campaign pledge to ratchet up the pressure on Al
Qaeda—a bit of political one-upmanship—wasn't lost on Bush or
his national security team. "It wasn't just increase the Predator
campaign," said one senior official in the meeting. "It was to do
whatever was necessary to go after the network." After a limited
debate, Bush approved each measure. It was a decision that effec-

tively made the CIA director America's combatant commander in the hottest covert war in the global campaign against terror.

Later that night, more than seven thousand miles away, a Predator drone prowling over South Waziristan fired a Hellfire missile killing six men, including Abu Khabab al-Masri, one of Al Qaeda's most skilled chemical and biological weapons experts, and one of the top Al Qaeda operatives on the CIA's hit list. With less than six months left in the Bush presidency, the gloves were coming off.

The drumbeat of warnings from the tribal areas had been growing louder for two years by the time Bush signed off on the secret CIA campaign. On March 1, 2007, Lynne Tracy, an intrepid American diplomat in Peshawar, fired off an urgent diplomatic cable to her superiors at the State Department. Peshawar is the capital of Pakistan's North-West Frontier Province, since renamed Khyber Pakhtunkhwa, and a gateway to the tribal areas, home to most of Al Qaeda's leadership and their Pakistani Taliban hosts. If any American diplomat in Pakistan had a finger on the pulse of the militancy in western Pakistan, it was Tracy, a Dari-speaking career foreign service officer with experience in both Afghanistan and Pakistan. Two years later, gunmen would ambush her armored car as she left her residence for the consulate in Peshawar, firing shots at the vehicle. She would escape unhurt.

In her cable, Tracy warned not only of the rise of radicals in the tribal areas but also of "a creeping Talibanization" in the North-West Frontier Province itself. She warned that police officers in the Tank District had stopped wearing their uniforms after receiving threats against them and their families. Barbers in the region had been warned by Taliban gunmen to stop shaving the beards of young men—long beards being a sign of piety for Islamic extremists—or face grim consequences. Music shops were also being threatened and shut down. Extremists were enlisting new recruits by paying higher salaries than those offered by the government security and law enforcement agencies.

Other American and NATO officials as well as Afghan and Pakistani intelligence officials concluded that Islamic militants were openly flouting a peace deal with the government and were tightening their expanding grip in the north. The result was a Taliban ministate that was rapidly becoming a magnet for an influx of foreign fighters from throughout the Middle East as well as from Uzbekistan and Chechnya who were not only challenging government authority in the contested area but also seizing control from local tribes. More than one hundred local leaders, government sympathizers, or accused "American spies" had been slain in 2006, many of them in gruesome beheadings deliberately carried out to cow the region through a reign of terror. America's allies also voiced their growing concern. In November 2006, Dame Eliza Manningham-Buller, director general of the British Security Service, known as MI5, said in an unusual public statement that British authorities had some two hundred networks of Muslims of South Asian descent under surveillance. She linked many of these plots back to Al Qaeda in Pakistan's western borderlands, warning of the organization's guidance and tactical support of extremists.

In 2006 and early 2007, most of Bush's top national security aides were consumed with the floundering war in Iraq, which still had priority for troops, spies, military hardware, and the precious time on policy makers' schedules. But in corners of the government, a handful of aides trained their sights on the growing threat from Al Qaeda outside of Iraq. This made sense because the administration's "new deterrence" strategy relied increasingly on disrupting Al Qaeda's cyber operations or on interdicting flows of money into bank accounts rather than fighting solely with bullets.

The White House's day-to-day point man on counterterrorism issues was Juan Zarate, newly arrived from the Treasury Department, where, as a deputy assistant secretary and later assistant

secretary, he directed efforts to scour those flows of funds for terrorist financing, dissecting the sophisticated and shadowy networks
of donors, illicit activities, and other sources that filled terrorist
and insurgent coffers. Mapping the money trail offered the government new glimpses into Al Qaeda's organizational structure, scar-
ing analysts by how little they truly knew about the organization's
inner workings.

Like Jeffrey Schloesser and Art Cummings, Zarate was part
of the new breed of American counterterrorism experts who were
trained in other disciplines prior to 9/11 and then rose quickly
through the bureaucratic ranks and flourished as the government
hungrily sought specialists in what just a few years earlier had been
an underfunded and sparsely staffed backwater. In June 2005,
Zarate had moved to the White House to become deputy national
security adviser for combating terrorism. In his role to address
the transnational nature of terrorist threats, he reported to Ste-
.phen Hadley, the national security adviser, and to Frances Fragos
Townsend, another dynamic former federal prosecutor who headed
the White House's Homeland Security Council.

Zarate led the Counterterrorism Security Group, the government's frontline counterterrorism policy-making entity. Every
week, the group convened top experts from the Defense, State,
Justice, Homeland Security, and Treasury departments as well as
the intelligence agencies to focus on issues ranging from immediate terrorist threats in Pakistan and Afghanistan to longer-term
concerns like undercutting Al Qaeda's appeal in the Muslim world.
The group made day-to-day decisions on counterterrorism policies and directives and set up the discussion for top-level decisions
for the deputies and principals committees. "I saw my role as
coordinator, organizer, and gadfly to the interagency process,"
Zarate said, referring to the high-level coordination among federal
security agencies.

Soon after he arrived at the White House, Zarate also assembled
an ad hoc group of experts, including Henry A. Crumpton, a

career CIA officer who was the State Department's top counterter-rorism official, and Thomas W. O'Connell, the Pentagon's senior official for special-operations policy, to address the Pakistan prob-lem. The group produced a set of recommendations that became the framework in early 2007 for sensitive internal discussions within the administration. Among their recommendations were to train more Pakistani security forces, particularly the Pashtun-dominated Frontier Corps in the tribal areas, and to press for American intel-ligence agencies to increase their own intelligence gathering inside Pakistan, relying less on the ISI for information. Zarate told his colleagues that he had a mental checklist of the seven priorities he reviewed every day. Number one on the list was the safe haven in the Pakistani tribal areas and the threat it posed to the American homeland. "I kept a map of the FATA next to my desk," Zarate said.

Zarate was hardly alone in his worries about a resurgent Al Qaeda in Pakistan. By February 2007, concern was so intense that the White House dispatched the new secretary of defense, Robert Gates, on an unannounced trip to Pakistan to lay out the administration's growing concerns. After meeting with Musharraf in the garrison city of Rawalpindi, he told reporters, "If we weren't concerned about what was happening along the border, I wouldn't be here."

The visit had special resonance for the secretary. While with the CIA, Gates had first visited Pakistan twenty years earlier as part of the American effort to back the mujahideen in Afghanistan in their fight against the Soviet Union. The Soviets eventually were ousted, but the United States subsequently made a terrible mistake when it ceased to give any real attention to the region, Gates told reporters, allowing extremists to take over. The result was the Sep-tember 11 attacks, planned by Al Qaeda leaders under Taliban protection in Afghanistan. "We will not make that mistake again," Gates said. "We are here for the long haul."

Political turmoil in Pakistan was mounting, however, leaving Musharraf increasingly distracted from the militant threat in the tribal areas. In March 2007, Musharraf fired the chief justice of the Pakistani Supreme Court, Iftikhar Muhammad Chaudhry, after a standoff over the legitimacy of his presidency, setting off a months-long showdown that would further distract Musharraf from the escalating extremist threat. Then, in July, Pakistani security forces stormed the radical Red Mosque in Islamabad in a bloody end to an eight-day siege. The raid prompted a series of retaliatory attacks by Islamic militants against government forces.

In Washington, Bush and his national security team watched the unraveling political situation in Pakistan with growing alarm. A new syndicate of Pakistani Islamic extremist groups calling itself the Pakistani Taliban, or Tehrik-i-Taliban, was emerging in the tribal areas under the leadership of a firebrand named Baitullah Mehsud. The Pakistani Taliban was an organization distinct from the Taliban insurgency that the United States was fighting in Afghanistan, but it had links to that group and to Al Qaeda's senior leadership. The threat from Pakistan was growing.

A year earlier, in the summer of 2006, American and British authorities had broken up a London-based plot to bomb at least seven transatlantic airliners on a single day with liquid explosives smuggled aboard in soft-drink bottles and detonated by devices powered with AA batteries. In response, airline passengers were prohibited from bringing aboard their flights any containers of liquids larger than three fluid ounces.

The summer of 2007 was different. The threat, based largely on snippets of furtive conversations and the fear of a countdown ticking away, was more general and amorphous, with no specific time, date, or location, so the United States had no idea when it would trigger terror operations. As a result of communications intercepted by the NSA, American officials grew increasingly alarmed over reports that Westerners who had trained in Al Qaeda camps in Pakistan's tribal areas were beginning to filter back into Europe, possibly with plots already in the works. But there was nothing concrete for authorities to act on, as there had been the summer before. "There was just a lot of chatter," Stephen Hadley recalled. "The noise level was up very much like it was up before 9/11 so everybody's antennae came up."

These Western recruits were reputed to speak multiple languages. They were technologically savvy. They understood Western culture and knew how to blend in. Some of the recruits were of Pakistani descent and were part of the huge diaspora that now lived in Britain. But others were Caucasian. "Al Qaeda was bringing more and more people into the tribal region, people who wouldn't draw undue attention if they were next to you at the passport line at Dulles Airport," Hayden said.

At the Pentagon, Michael Vickers had just taken over as the Defense Department's top policy maker for special operations, succeeding Thomas O'Connell. Vickers, who had been the principal CIA strategist for arming anti-Soviet forces in Afghanistan in the mid-1980s, understandably thought he would need to spend most of that summer tracking the impact of the surge of additional American troops in Iraq. But after visiting Iraq, Afghanistan, and Pakistan, he quickly realized Iraq would take its own course. He needed to be on a plane to Islamabad every two to three months to keep tabs on the morphing enemy and Pakistan's response to it. "Pakistan was Job One from the beginning, I would say, for me and among the [counterterrorism] guys," Vickers said. "It dominated our attention more than anything else."

European allies with informants in Pakistan or in South Asian communities at home were enlisted to help look beyond their own borders. Fran Townsend, the White House Homeland Security adviser, quietly made the rounds in European capitals, including a trip to Rome on July 13, 2007, with FBI deputy director John Pistole to meet with senior Italian police and counterterrorism officials. "When you are looking for indications, technical intelligence becomes very important and the focus of our allies is very important because they are likely to pick up these plots first and may not realize that the intended target is in the U.S., which means they might not tell us," Townsend recalled later. "The Italian service, the British service are doing domestic counterterror investigations. They're not telling us about every one. They only tell us about the ones they think involve us or need our help on. So we're trying to make them sensitive to the fact that we need them to be very fulsome, take a very liberal view of sharing with us, because, by the way, we may have a piece that is relevant to your cell, we don't realize it and you don't know to ask us." Wary of past accusations that the White House had exaggerated terrorist threats to induce fear in the American public, the administration kept quiet about the latest threat warnings emanating from the tribal areas.

Two events changed that as the sixth anniversary of the 9/11 attacks approached in September 2007. On July 10, Homeland Security Secretary Michael Chertoff said in an interview with the *Chicago Tribune*'s editorial board that concerns about the Al Qaeda activity and public threats in Pakistan's tribal areas gave him a "gut feeling" that the United States faced an increased chance of a terrorist attack that summer. Some senior administration officials saw Chertoff's comments as part of the "new deterrence" strategy. By telling the militants their plot had been detected, officials said, Chertoff aimed to deter the terrorists from striking against defenses that would be better prepared. "There are data to support the idea that raising the level of difficulty does cause them to delay and sometimes divert what they are going to do," Chertoff said.

The comment made headlines and the evening news, and prompted Chertoff to expand his remarks. After reading highly classified intelligence reports for years, Chertoff said, he had a kind of sixth sense for gauging when the country might be vulnerable to attack, even if there were no specific evidence. "It is the same intuition people use in medicine when they make a diagnosis or in law when you try a case," he recalled later. The Al Qaeda safe havens in Pakistan posed just such a "gut instinct" problem. "Since you don't know exactly who is there necessarily or how long they've been there or exactly what their mission is, time is your enemy," Chertoff said. "If a year goes by and we haven't disrupted the activities over there, that's a year where you can do a lot of training and you can start to send people back. Because this pipeline had been open for a while and because the safe havens had been pretty unmolested for a while, we started to worry that we were going to start to see people coming out the other end."

Just as Juan Zarate sought to understand Al Qaeda's network and intentions by tracing its money trail while at the Treasury Department, Michael Chertoff had metrics, too, including an increasingly sophisticated system of monitoring the travel patterns of potential terrorists, using commercial airline passenger data and international travel records. "Where people come from, how they travel, what their travel activities might be in the United States and things of that sort," he said. "Is there some way we can tell if someone has spent six, seven, eight months in Waziristan?"

The second important public signal came a week later, on July 17, when the White House released a grim new intelligence assessment that openly acknowledged that the strategy of fighting Al Qaeda in Pakistan had failed. The intelligence report, the most formal assessment since the 9/11 attacks about the terrorist threat facing the United States, concluded that the United States was losing ground on a number of fronts in the fight against Al Qaeda. Indeed, the report concluded, the terrorist organization had significantly strengthened over the past two years. In identifying the main reasons for Al Qaeda's resurgence, intelligence officials and White House aides cited Musharraf's hands-off, peace-deal approach toward the tribal areas. "It hasn't worked for Pakistan," Townsend told reporters at the White House. "It hasn't worked for the United States."

In response to these developments, the federal government quietly went on heightened alert, and the National Security Council created a secret interagency task force to coordinate its response. The White House initially planned to have the FBI lead the task force, but Scott Redd and Michael E. Leiter, the two top officials of the National Counterterrorism Center, argued that their agency was uniquely suited to handle the challenge. Leiter appealed directly to Townsend, emphasizing that the center was prepared to show how far the government had come in addressing the failings on September 11 of sharing information and coordinating activities among federal agencies. Townsend agreed, and the NCTC was given the responsibility of leading the effort. It would also be a test run for some "new deterrence" principles.

It came as no surprise to those who knew Michael Leiter that his persuasion prevailed. Supremely self-confident and politically savvy, Leiter had managed complicated bureaucratic operations before. When the Office of the Director of National Intelligence was created in the wake of the 9/11 Commission Report in 2004, Leiter served as a deputy chief of staff coordinating the new agency's operations with the White House, the Pentagon, the CIA, and other agencies and departments. Now the challenge for Leiter was to harness the government's newly revamped counterterrorism structure to address the amorphous but potentially deadly threat. "In 2007, we're in a period where we were especially worried about Al Qaeda operatives ready for deployment to Europe or the United States," Leiter said. "That was our fear."

In response to this new challenge, Leiter oversaw a crash review of American vulnerabilities, heightening U.S. defenses, coordinating with European and Middle Eastern allies, and increasing clandestine intelligence operations along the Afghanistan-Pakistan border. In previous terrorism scares, experts from the Pentagon, the State Department, the FBI, and the intelligence agencies would meet to discuss the intelligence, return to their agencies to draft recommendations for possible actions, and then reconvene at the next interagency meeting to review the new set of options. This so-called stovepiping arrangement never fully integrated the government's resources and expertise. In addressing the 2007 summer threat emanating from Pakistan, a cadre of counterterrorism experts from across the government met repeatedly, tapping into the same information and drawing up potential action plans that complemented and coordinated with each other. It was a lesson drawn directly from the failures of 9/11. "What changed was that senior officials from every department and agency, overseas and domestic, were coming together with a common intelligence operating picture, saying, 'This is exactly what we're seeing, and this is what we're going to do about it,' " Leiter said. But Leiter and his colleagues still needed something tangible that would help everyone involved in the process, including the president in his daily briefings, quickly understand the threat, the responses available to government, and the cost, in terms of treasure, manpower, and economic impact of each option.

So was born the Horse Blanket.

It wasn't really a blanket at all. Rather, it was a large, multilayered briefing paper that unfolded, like a child's toy, to reveal a graduating series of contingencies that each federal agency could take in response to a potential or actual terrorist attack. It was a graphic device that distilled thousands of hours of analytical work and PowerPoint slides to a fold-up chart that policy makers could pull from their briefcases to handily compare and contrast options. The options were depicted on the document in green, yellow, or red, depending on how much it would cost (installing more screeners in airports), how much it would disrupt daily American lives (closing down portions of the border), or how it might impact foreign policy (increasing drone strikes).

"What it enabled you to do was say, 'If we have reason to believe we are facing an elevated threat picture, here is the menu of options we can look at on an interagency basis,' " Chertoff recalled. "Depending on the intelligence you could say, 'Well, we really ought to dial this up at the border or we ought to dial this up, we ought to do more internal investigation.' For example, this is purely hypothetical, but if we have an indication of an imminent nuclear weapon coming into the country, you would then say, 'Okay, that's just about as bad as it gets, we'll shut the border.' That'd be a red because you can't sustain shutting the border for a long time because it's a huge burden on us and it's a huge burden on the rest of the world. We never came near that, but I am trying to give you a feel for the burden of various levels of protection."

With no public fanfare, the CIA and other intelligence agencies intensified their spying and analysis along the Afghanistan-Pakistan border and coordinated even more closely with foreign intelligence services, culminating in the increased drone strikes a year later, in the summer of 2008. The FBI intensified its analyses of the threat to the United States itself. Homeland Security tightened border defenses, including some innovative reshuffling of Transportation Security Administration personnel at airports. Teams of bomb-sniffing dogs were more visibly deployed at train stations. "We were running and gunning," Townsend recalled. "We had an ability to surge the system in a very focused way and do it on a worldwide scale." As more information came in, officials could ramp efforts up or down accordingly, reflecting how the tools of the "new deterrence" could be employed and modulated according to the threat. Most of the steps taken and techniques employed remain classified because officials want to be able to use some variation of them in the future. "It was a full slate of things domestically and abroad," Zarate recalled. "You're trying to create a security blanket that tries to suss out what may be out there."

The threat eased after about a month, and Leiter's task force stood down. But the fears seemed justified when authorities in Germany and Denmark announced in early September that they had broken up two terrorist plots, each with connections to Pakistan's tribal areas. In Germany, the authorities said they had stopped a major terrorist attack against American and German targets in the country, possibly including the Ramstein Air Base, a crucial transportation hub for the American military, and Frankfurt

International Airport. Nearly three years later, a German court would sentence four Islamic militants to serve up to twelve years in prison for planning to create what a judge called a "monstrous blood bath." The group was known in Germany as "the Sauerland cell" after the region in North Rhine–Westphalia where three of the four men were arrested in possession of twenty-six military detonators and twelve drums of hydrogen peroxide, the main chemical in the explosives that had been used in the London transit bombings of July 2005. The court determined that three of the men were members of an Al Qaeda–linked terrorist group, the Islamic Jihad Union, which was a splinter organization of a Tajik terrorist group. The United States had helped the German authorities track the location of two of the suspects by eavesdropping on their cell phone conversations as they moved out of training camps in Pakistan.

A day before the German plot was disrupted, Danish authorities conducted predawn raids in nearly a dozen locations. American authorities helped Danish security officials locate the suspects through electronic intercepts from Pakistan, just as they did in the arrests in Germany. American intelligence officials said that one of the men in the Danish case had received instruction in explosives, surveillance, and other techniques at a terrorist training camp in Pakistan near the border with Afghanistan within the preceding twelve months. Just as American officials had feared, the extremists were seeping back into their European homes from the Al Qaeda training camps in Pakistan. It was only a matter of time, they believed, before these militants would make the hop across the Atlantic to American soil.

It was the most tantalizing of all tips, the Holy Grail of clues among the millions of pieces of information that intelligence analysts sifted through in the years after the 9/11 attack: the location of Osama bin Laden.

In the late summer of 2007, as tensions in Washington heated up over the reports of possible terrorist plots emanating from Pakistan, Afghan intelligence officers eavesdropping on Taliban conversations picked up strong indications that Taliban and Al Qaeda fighters were planning the largest gathering in Afghanistan since early in the war. The intelligence was so compelling that President Hamid Karzai summoned top American officers to his palace in Kabul to plead for a major American operation to crush the fighters. It wasn't just the Afghans who were worried. Independently, the secretive U.S. Special Operations teams assigned to hunt high-level Al Qaeda and Taliban targets in Afghanistan had also detected reports of the militant massing. "This looked to be bigger than Anaconda," said one senior American intelligence officer, referring to Operation Anaconda in March 2002, the final setpiece battle of the invasion of Afghanistan. Seven Americans died in that offensive in the Shahikot Valley.

This time, the intelligence indicated that more than one hundred Taliban and Al Qaeda fighters and commanders planned to enter Afghanistan through the Tora Bora mountains along the Pakistan border. The rugged, rocky region is honeycombed with caves, some of which had been used by the mujahideen in their standoff against the Soviet Army in the 1980s. The terrain was easy to defend and hard to attack and had been the site of bin Laden's last stand before he escaped into Pakistan in the winter of 2001–2002. What seized attention in Washington in 2007 were faint if tantalizing hints that bin Laden himself was going to join the new gathering. Even President Bush was briefed on the reports. "It was a big deal. We thought we had 'Number One' on this side of the border," said a senior American military officer involved in the operation. "It was the best intelligence we'd had on him in a long time."

Top military and intelligence officers who read the reports said the camps in Tora Bora were being used not merely as a staging area for attacks across Afghanistan, but, more worrisome, there were indications that the site was a planning and training area for a high-visibility, mass-casualty attack somewhere outside Afghanistan, in western Europe or perhaps even the United States. That larger threat is what led some to interpret the intelligence as indicating bin Laden himself might be in attendance to motivate suicide bombers and bless a mission that would attempt to replicate something big, perhaps even on the scale of another 9/11-style strike. "The threat stream was viable," said one senior officer. "The area was a hub for high-value leaders, mid-level commanders and foot soldiers. It was a command-and-control center. They went there as a launching pad to fight inside Afghanistan but also to plan and train for a spectacular attack outside the theater of combat."

Nobody disagreed that Tora Bora was a significant center of terrorists and militants. But there were deep divisions among the analysts over whether bin Laden would show up. "If UBL had been there, it would have been just luck," scoffed one military commander.

Those who read the intelligence tidbits as pointing to bin Laden's presence said it was one of the few areas of Afghanistan in which the Al Qaeda mastermind might feel safe moving and would have been the most recent confirmed presence of bin Laden. Other intelligence analysts rejected any suggestions that bin Laden would be foolish enough to move from hiding in Pakistan into a remote corner of Afghanistan, where the United States military could employ all its forces. As the analysts argued over the intelligence, the Special Operations planners were taking no chances. If this militancy council did happen and bin Laden was there, he would not escape again, they vowed.

Planners began building the largest combined air and Special Operations mission since the Vietnam War. The centerpiece of the operation, called Valiant Pursuit, would be carried out by as many as five B-2 bombers, the bat-wing stealth warplane initially designed to carry nuclear warheads into the Soviet Union. For this mission, each plane was to be loaded with about eighty satellite-guided conventional bombs. Dozens of attack planes would also be in place, ready to strike targets in the Tora Bora mountains. On the ground, the military would employ a new, long-range artillery system called HIMARS (High Mobility Artillery Rocket System). Helicopter gunships and Special Operations troops would stand ready to go in to kill or capture any insurgents who escaped the initial aerial bombardment. "It was going to be a piling on," said one senior American officer who was briefed on the mission, which is still highly classified.

The size of the operation, coupled with the ambiguity of the intelligence, alarmed some senior U.S. commanders, including Admiral William Fallon, the head of Central Command. "Fallon's view was you're swatting a fly with a sixteen-pound hammer," said the senior American officer. Other concerns surfaced. The B-2s would be utilizing a British air base in Diego Garcia, a tiny island in the Indian Ocean, and would likely need to fly through Pakistani air space to carry out the mission. While the B-2s' bombs were satellite guided, there was a risk that one could fall into Pakistani territory by mistake. "There was a lot of concern about how much ordnance we were going to put on target," said another senior American officer.

In late July, as the day of the militants' meeting approached, analysts pored over intelligence reports and communications intercepts to glean any clues. The picture was still murky. But commanders were given the green light several days later and ordered the B-2s to take off, to be in position if the meeting materialized. As the bombers approached the Indian Ocean, however, Admiral Fallon ordered the giant planes to return to base. President Bush was briefed on the decision, but he had left it in the hands of the military. "This was carpet bombing, pure and simple," said another top military officer who had openly voiced disagreement with the operation. "It was not precision-targeted. There was no way to separate the Al Qaeda leadership that might be on hand, and the fighters, from the local population and the camp followers." Even without the B-2s, however, a smaller, less ambitious operation later went forward with the HIMARS artillery, helicopter gunships, and Special Operations commandos pummeling the insurgent safe haven, and reclaiming control over the territory. Some senior White House officials said that the larger mission was cancelled because the meeting never happened, or at least not at the significant size that the intelligence officers had anticipated. Had the militants been tipped off? Was the original information wrong? To this day, government analysts still don't know.

At the White House, the disappointment was palpable. Senior officials had deliberately sought to maintain low expectations, but many had held out hope that this time they had bin Laden in their sights. It was not to be.

Nearly five months later, on December 27, 2007, the assassination of Benazir Bhutto, the Pakistani opposition leader and former prime minister, sent shock waves from Islamabad to Washington and marked an escalation of the militant threat. Al Qaeda and its Pakistani Taliban allies were increasingly bent on destabilizing the country. Distinguishing the various militant groups—sometimes working together, sometimes separately—had become an increasingly difficult task for American intelligence analysts. Among the groups they focused on most intently was one commanded by Sirajuddin Haqqani, son of the legendary militant leader Jalaluddin Haqqani and one of the many mujahideen commanders that Michael Vickers knew well from fighting the Soviets in Afghanistan in the 1980s. Another group, the Tehrik-i-Taliban, was a network led by the Islamic militant Baitullah Mehsud and was believed to be responsible for Bhutto's death. "It went from being a salad to a stew," Hayden told colleagues.

Just days after the assassination, President Bush's national security team met at the White House on January 4, 2008, to debate whether to expand the authority of the CIA and the military to conduct far more aggressive covert operations in the tribal areas. No decisions were made on the proposal, but five days later, the top two American intelligence officials traveled secretly to Pakistan to press Musharraf to allow the CIA greater latitude to operate in the tribal areas. The two officials, CIA director Mike Hayden and his boss, Mike McConnell, the director of national intelligence, jokingly called their fourteen-thousand-mile, round-trip, one-day visit the "trip from hell."

They had flown overnight from Washington and changed to a C-17 cargo plane in Turkey for the flight into Islamabad. There, the two men caught a few hours' sleep before heading to Musharraf's presidential suite for a late-morning appointment. Musharraf had resigned as Army chief of staff in late November 2007 but would remain president through mid-August 2008. He was joined by the powerful Pakistani Army chief, General Ashfaq Parvez Kayani, and the director of the ISI, Lieutenant General Nadeem Taj. For more than an hour, McConnell and Hayden reviewed their threat briefing with the Pakistanis. At one point, Hayden got down on one knee to spread out the maps and charts on a coffee table while explaining them.

"Mr. President, we've seen a merger," Hayden told Musharraf. "You've been slow in recognizing this merger between Al Qaeda and Pashtun extremists. Now they're coming out of the tribal areas, not just to kill us but to kill you. They're after you now."

At the end of the meeting, Musharraf rejected the American proposals to expand any U.S. combat presence in Pakistan through either unilateral covert CIA missions or joint operations with Pakistani security forces. Instead, Pakistan and the United States agreed to loosen restrictions on the CIA Predators flying secretly from a Pakistani air base at Shamsi in southwestern Pakistan. Rather than having to confirm the identity of a suspected militant leader before attacking, the shift allowed American operators to strike convoys of vehicles that bore the signature characteristics of

Al Qaeda or Taliban leaders on the run, for instance, as long as the risk of civilian casualties was judged to be low. The new procedures increased the CIA's freedom of action, but the drone program averaged only one strike a month for the first half of the year.

The election of a new coalition government in Pakistan in February 2008 presented new challenges for the Bush administration as it sought to weaken Al Qaeda in the tribal areas. American officials expressed alarm that the leaders of Pakistan's new coalition government, Asif Ali Zardari of the Pakistan Peoples Party (Benazir Bhutto's husband) and Nawaz Sharif of the Pakistan Muslim League, were negotiating with the same extremists believed to be responsible for an increasing number of suicide attacks against the security forces and political figures, including Bhutto.

The new government had signaled that it wanted to follow a more independent path with the United States than had been the case with Musharraf. But the new political face in Islamabad did little to curb the violence emanating from the tribal areas, where American officials and independent experts said between 150 and 500 hard-core Al Qaeda fighters were operating. Cross-border attacks into Afghanistan by militants based in Pakistan doubled during the month after the elections from the same period the year before, while Pakistani counterinsurgency operations in the tribal areas dropped sharply during the talks. Adding to the danger, American intelligence officials detected an increase in the number of foreign fighters infiltrating the tribal areas to join militants there. The flow of several dozen or more fighters reflected a change that made Pakistan, not Iraq, the preferred destination for many Sunni extremists from the Middle East, North Africa, and Central Asia who were seeking to take up arms against the West.

The classified diplomatic cables obtained by WikiLeaks, that were shared with the *New York Times* and other news organizations, document deep skepticism that Pakistan would ever cooperate fully in fighting the full array of extremist groups. This is partly because Pakistan sees some of the strongest militant groups as insurance against the inevitable day that the U.S. military withdraws from Afghanistan, and Pakistan wants to exert maximum influence inside Afghanistan and against Indian intervention. Indeed, the U.S. consul general in Peshawar, Lynne Tracy, wrote in July 2009 that she believed that some members of the Haqqani network—one of the most lethal groups attacking American and Afghan soldiers—had left North Waziristan to escape drone strikes. Some family members, she wrote, relocated south of Peshawar; others lived in Rawalpindi, where senior Pakistani military officials also live. In another cable, Ambassador Anne W. Patterson said that more money and military assistance would not be persuasive. "There is no chance that Pakistan will view enhanced assistance levels in any field as sufficient compensation for abandoning support for these groups, which it sees as an important part of its national security apparatus against India," she observed. In a rare dissent with Washington, she said that Pakistan would only dig in deeper if America continued to improve ties with India, which, she said, "feeds Pakistani establishment paranoia and pushes them closer to both Afghan and Kashmir focused terrorist groups." The groups to which she referred were almost certainly the Haqqani network, the Afghan Taliban, and Lashkar-e-Taiba, a group financed by Pakistan in the 1990s to fight India in Kashmir that has since been accused of being responsible for the November 2008 terrorist attacks in Mumbai, India.

The roller-coaster relations between the CIA and the ISI hit a new low on July 12, 2008, when Stephen Kappes, the deputy CIA director, traveled secretly to Islamabad with Admiral Mullen to confront officials there with evidence that the Pakistani spy service helped plan the bombing of India's embassy in Kabul, Afghanistan, five days earlier, which had killed fifty-four people, including an Indian defense attaché. The conclusion was based on intercepted communications between Pakistani intelligence officers and the militants who had carried out the attack, providing the clearest evidence to date that Pakistani intelligence officers were actively undermining American efforts to combat terrorism in the region. Kappes also presented new information showing that members of the Pakistani intelligence service were increasingly providing militants with details about the American campaign against them, in some cases enabling them to avoid American missile strikes in Pakistan's tribal areas.

Bush's decision to confront Pakistan over the embassy bombing and the ISI's ties to extremist groups was the bluntest American warning to Pakistan since the initial ultimatum immediately following the September 11 attacks. The tense meeting strained relations between the two countries, and by the time Mullen and Kappes had returned to Washington, the decision to ramp up unilateral American pressure on the tribal areas was gaining momentum. One participant in the late July 2008 meeting in the Yellow Oval Room said it seemed that the president had already made up his mind; he was just waiting for the command briefing.

Seven thousand miles away, Jeffrey Schloesser was looking at the Pakistani militancy from the Afghan side of the border. Schloesser had left Washington to take the prestigious command of the 101st Airborne Division in Fort Campbell, Kentucky, in November 2006. In April 2008, Schloesser, by now promoted to two-star general, deployed to Afghanistan for a fifteen-month tour to assume control over military operations in the rugged eastern portion of the country bordering Pakistan. It was a culmination of Schloesser's counterterrorism career, stretching from his days as a Special Operations helicopter pilot and liaison in Kuwait to his work after 9/11 in the Pentagon and at the National Counterterrorism Center. Deploying to one of the most dangerous areas in Afghanistan, Schloesser would be putting his policy experiences into ground-level practice. "I saw it in longer terms than I think others did," Schloesser said of the fight against the Al Qaeda–backed militancy in both Afghanistan and Pakistan. "I saw this thing as a continuum from what had been done in the area before, for better or worse."

For Schloesser, and for many of the best commanders in Afghanistan, the key was understanding the local culture, understanding that Afghanistan and the rugged Pakistani tribal areas would be won valley by valley against a tenacious enemy that sent out a global message but fought its battles, both tactical and ideological, at a very local level. "Whether you call it a syndicate in Afghanistan and Pakistan or a network globally, you find that these organizations are all very local," Schloesser said. "They have regional aspirations but they are localized because of where the people come from. If you don't pay attention to your enemy in a local way, you have no idea what they will do to you."

The consequences of not fully understanding that local culture and its complicated dynamics can often undermine the American-led mission in Afghanistan were amply demonstrated by an audacious American raid in the late summer of 2008, just a few weeks after the meeting in the Yellow Oval Room of the White House. On September 3, American Special Operations forces attacked Al Qaeda militants in a Pakistani village near the border with Afghanistan in the first publicly acknowledged instance of U.S. forces conducting a ground raid on Pakistani soil. With AC-130 aerial gunships overhead, more than two dozen Navy SEALs carried out running gun battles with insurgents for several hours, killing more than two dozen suspected Al Qaeda–related fighters and a small number of civilians before the commandos were whisked away by helicopters after completing the mission. Back in Washington, senior officials were stunned by what was supposed to have been a quick, stealthy raid. "The operation made a lot more noise on the ground than anticipated," a senior national security official said. "In retrospect the target was not as confined, the entering force was not as small as anticipated, and when they ran into trouble and firing started, lots of people came from around the neighboring areas which we were not fully aware were there."

The raid stirred such fierce protests from the Pakistani military that American commanders shelved plans for additional boots-on-the-ground attacks. But the CIA aggressively executed the rest of Bush's order. In the final six months of 2008, CIA drones launched twenty-eight attacks in the tribal areas, nearly double the total number carried out in the previous four and a half years. How ironic for an agency that in the late 1990s had fought hard against the armed Predator when the Air Force was developing it. In fact, it was one of John Tyson's DIA colleagues who was sent over to Langley to help manage the CIA's fledgling armed Predator program.

Within just over a year, American officials would assert that eleven of the twenty Al Qaeda or allied leaders most wanted by the United States in the Pakistani tribal areas had been killed or captured since the fateful July 2008 meeting at the White House. The officials would claim that the targeting had become so refined that few if any civilians were killed in the drone strikes, an assessment challenged by many human rights groups. But the strikes by the Predators and their bigger, more lethal cousins, the Reapers, were a tactic and not a strategy—a means to keep Al Qaeda and its confederates in the tribal areas off balance and buy time until the Pakistani military took more decisive action on the ground.

As President Obama took office in January 2009, the drone attacks would escalate sharply and drive senior Al Qaeda leaders further into hiding. But plots were being hatched in the tribal areas that the drones would not disrupt. The success or failure of those threatened attacks against the United States ultimately would hinge on a combination of luck and skill for both the terrorists and their pursuers.

5

TERROR 2.0

On a Monday morning just a year into the Obama administration, the Defense Department's top civilian and military leaders gathered for a war game built around a most urgent and emerging national security threat. This was the first time they had met in a large group at such a senior level to play out attack, defense, and counterattack in the new and worrisome environment of cyberspace. The assemblage was formally christened the Defense Senior Leadership Conference, but like all Pentagon terms, it was better known by its acronym, DSLC, or "D-Slick." Its membership included the secretary of defense, the deputy secretary, the top civilian policy and intelligence officials, the Joint Chiefs of Staff, and all the regional combatant commanders, who flew in from their headquarters around the globe.

Many of the items on the agenda for this particular morning session were the standard litany of strategic-level threats to the nation, including how the global recession and congressional concerns about the ballooning deficit would limit the Pentagon's ability to ask Congress for the money necessary to pay for national defense. But the agenda item on cyberwarfare was new. Sitting behind closed doors in a dining room on the outer ring of the

Pentagon's third floor of executive suites, the Defense Department's leaders, dressed in suits and in uniforms, played a war game to simulate how they would respond to a sophisticated cyberattack in which an adversary paralyzed America's power grids, communications systems, and financial networks.

The results were anything but encouraging. The mock enemy operating in the virtual battle space of the World Wide Web had anonymity, speed, and unpredictability—the hallmarks of a terrorist network. It was difficult to anticipate when the cyberadversary was about to move from aggressive probing of government and commercial networks (which occurs hundreds of thousands of times every day) to a crippling attack. It proved impossible to identify the country from which the attack originated—and even if that could be done, it would be impossible to say with certainty whether that government was actually an adversary itself, or if Internet servers on its territory had simply been hacked by outsiders to launch the attack. It was impossible even to say with certainty that the cyber-enemy had not simply set up shop over an espresso in a commercial cybercafé as a readily accessible but anonymous beachhead for the assault. Thus, there was no way to prevent further damage by threatening retaliation. What's more, the Pentagon officials and military commanders noted that they lacked the legal authority to respond, especially because it was never clear whether the attack was an act of terrorism, vandalism, commercial theft, or a state-sponsored effort to cripple the United States perhaps as a prelude to a conventional war.

While the implementation of the "new deterrence" against terrorism had been showing promise in some areas, in the emerging world of cyberwarfare, the military was starting from scratch, a situation somewhat analogous to the dawn of the nuclear age, when the United States and the Soviet Union had to develop new rules of behavior to deter each other from ever launching an attack. But unlike the 1950s, when theory kept somewhat closer pace with technology, America's cyberwarriors have come to realize that the capacity for computers to wreak havoc has far outpaced the unwritten rules and codified legal constraints that might govern combat operations across the Internet.

Pentagon officials said the cyberwar game in February 2010 marked the first time that all of the Defense Department's top leaders had sat together in one room for an exercise in virtual warfare. It was fitting, since the election of Barack Obama as president of the United States in November 2008 brought a number of notable firsts, including the first approval of a document laying out a national cyberpolicy with responsibilities assigned across the government, the appointment of a cyber "czar" to the National Security Council staff, and the finalization of plans to create for the military a new U.S. Cyber Command with responsibility for coordinating America's computer network defense as well as a capacity for attack.

For much of the decade since 9/11, terrorists operating in cyberspace have focused many of their efforts on communications, command, organization, fund-raising, and propaganda, but U.S. officials are preparing themselves for the day when violent religious militants adapt their tactics of hijacking and destructive attack to the digital world and strike at America's financial networks or critical computer infrastructure. The financial cost to the nation of crashing a regional power grid or taking the banking system off-line would make the dollar damage of 9/11 pale in comparison. Imagine the havoc if Wall Street could not trade, if power went off to hospitals in an entire time zone, if the safety system went down at a nuclear power plant. Just as the war on terror under George W. Bush repeatedly crashed against the wall of civil liberties and constitutional protections, so the Obama administration has wrestled with issues of privacy and domestic guarantees of individual rights while attempting to reshape cyberpolicy as a tool in combating global extremism.

Complicating matters is the fact that while 90 percent of the capability for cyberdefense and -offense resides in the military and intelligence community, about 90 percent of the vulnerable targets are in the private sector. Federal statutes and privacy concerns prevent the Defense Department's cybertools from being used to assist the Department of Homeland Security, the FBI, the Treasury Department, or the Department of Energy in defending American targets, short of a presidential directive in a time of crisis. With an attack traveling at network speed, there is simply no time to hit the pause button during a cyberbattle and ask the White House for a presidential order. The challenge is to design a linkage between the military's capabilities, designed for operations overseas, and domestic protections if an attack should hit the homeland. This has necessitated the drafting of new rules of engagement for military cyberoperations to defend the United States against digital attacks across the territory of neutral nations and allies. This effort provoked some of the Obama administration's most contentious debates.

In many ways, the debate over cyberwarfare mirrors the questions that were raised when the Bush administration first crafted its secret "Execute Orders" to deal with the Al Qaeda threat after the 9/11 attacks. "That AQ 'ExOrd' was the first designed against an enemy without defining an area of hostility," said one Bush administration official involved in those discussions. "That was a fundamental legal difference from past 'ExOrds' written to deal with a specific nation-state adversary. Al Qaeda could be anywhere—in an area of hostility, in a neutral nation, on the territory of an ally, not to mention operating in the homeland." Dealing with similar legal and logistical constraints that might dangerously limit the capacity for defense and counterattacks was a central consideration for the Obama administration as it wrote its new cyberwar plans. The United States needed a way to get past current barriers, foreign as well as domestic. Because of the speed of an attack, a response must be immediate, and only a presidential directive could brush aside the barriers that prevent the U.S. military from operating on American territory. Unless such limitations were overcome, the Pentagon's advanced cybercapabilities might be employed too late to do any good.

Operations abroad could be constrained as well. Recalling a political conflict that had complicated the deployment of troops to Iraq in 2003, one Bush administration official observed, "Just like if I want to go to Iraq with the Fourth Division, but the Turks say no, what happens if somebody says no to our desire to pass through their virtual territory to carry out cyber offense and defense? In cyber, we may be able to pass through and do no harm; or we may desire to do something active if bad things are propagating in networks on their territory. But another government can justifiably ask, 'What gave you the writ to go into a sovereign nation and do damage, even with zeros and ones?' We cannot keep arguing that we can go anyplace on the face of the earth and exercise our authorities. We have to build legal institutions to control it, the same way that we would if we want to drop a bomb."

The official in charge of the cybersimulation played out for the Pentagon leadership was William J. Lynn III, who had just taken office as deputy secretary of defense. He said that the most worrisome realization that emerged from the simulated combat was that the Internet had so blurred the line between military and civilian targets that an adversary could cripple a nation by crashing its credit markets or utilities infrastructure without even firing an electronic shot at a military or government installation. America's existing plans for protecting computer networks reminded him of one of defensive warfare's great failures, the Maginot Line of pre–World War II France. He argued that the billions of dollars spent on defensive firewalls and shields provided a similar illusory sense of security. "A fortress mentality will not work in cyber," he said. "If we stand still for a minute, our adversaries will overtake us."

In response, officials at the Pentagon and the White House are drawing on the same concepts that emerged for protecting the American homeland after the 9/11 attacks. Among the veteran military officers working on the problem is General Larry D. Welch, who served as Air Force chief of staff and the top officer overseeing America's nuclear arsenal at the former Strategic Air Command before retiring and becoming a defense policy analyst. He agrees that terrorists can be deterred in the physical world and in the digital world. "You don't just deter with costs, but also with benefits," he said. Layered defenses—blast walls, hardened buildings, metal detectors, chemical sniffers—are one step. So are obvious efforts toward "consequence management," the ability to respond to an attack with quick fixes and long-term recovery, all to convince a terrorist that even a successful attack will have limited effect. The goal, he said, is to "create resilience and thus diminish the prospects for benefits from terrorism." In the digital world, he continued, this means publicly announcing the overwhelming punishment the United States would inflict on any cyberattacker and building resiliency and redundancy into America's most critical and vulnerable computer networks. "We need to be able to fight through a cyber attack and sustain losses and damage," he said. "Some people say you can't deter terrorists. Nonsense. You can deter terrorists. Even if the suicide bomber cares nothing about the costs, and is willing to give up their life, they do care about the benefits."

Quietly, then, a strategy of cyberdeterrence has evolved to protect national security. "Deterrence has been a fundamental part of the administration's cybersecurity efforts from the start," said one Obama administration official. But that official would not say how the United States would respond after a major cyberattack, in keeping with a policy of deliberate ambiguity carried over from Cold War–era deterrence. As a precedent, the official cited how, in managing the standoff with the overwhelmingly superior conventional forces of the Soviet Union and its Warsaw Pact allies, the United States never declared that it would be bound to respond to an invasion of NATO territory with only conventional forces. The Kremlin's uncertainty about whether an invasion of Western Europe might go nuclear was viewed as crucial to Cold War deterrence and stability. Uncertainty about how the United States would respond to a cyberattack is intended to serve a similar purpose. "The United States reserves the right to respond to intrusions into government, military, and national infrastructure information systems and networks by nations, terrorist groups, or other adversaries in a manner it deems appropriate," said one high-level Pentagon official.

But many of the old principles of warfare do not really work in this new age. "We are looking beyond just the pure military might as the solution to every deterrence problem," said General Kevin P. Chilton, who retired in 2011 as the officer in charge of the military's Strategic Command, which defends military computer networks, in addition to overseeing America's nuclear arsenal. "There are other elements of national power that can be brought to bear. You could deter a country with some economic moves, for example." But terrorists on the Web have the same advantages as terrorists planting a bomb. Unless they are captured or leave behind a clear set of clues, the only attribution may be if they claim credit for the attack.

Secretary of State Hillary Rodham Clinton has also drawn on the language of the "new deterrence" to put potential adversaries on notice. "States, terrorists and those who would act as their proxies must know that the United States will protect our networks," she declared in January 2010. "Those who disrupt the free flow of information in our society, or any other, pose a threat to our economy, our government and our civil society." But Clinton did not say specifically how the United States would respond, except to hold responsible any country that knowingly allowed cyberattacks to be launched from its territory. Vague as they were, her comments were viewed as the first public articulation of an emerging government policy that, borrowing from Cold War deterrence, would issue a "declaratory policy" to officially warn potential cyber-aggressors of the immediate and very punitive response that could be expected.

The Pentagon's invigorated focus on the threat of computer-network warfare can be seen in the marching orders from Secretary of Defense Gates to the Defense Policy Board, his personal think tank, which draws its advisers from the ranks of retired military officers, the defense industry, and the academic community. In the transition from the Bush administration to the Obama administration, Gates gave the board three national security risks to ponder, analyze, and attempt to neutralize: One was China. One was Iran. And one was cyber.

It may seem surprising, but the cyberwar era began with America playing offense, not defense. In advance of the presidential order in March 2003 that sent American forces into Iraq to topple Saddam Hussein, American war planners proposed an opening salvo that would have given the invasion a true twenty-first-century capability. Before any bombs were dropped or artillery rounds fired, the military and its intelligence partners wanted to inject electronic poison pills into the Iraqi banking system. The plan was for massive computer network sabotage, a cyberattack to bring down Iraq's financial infrastructure, freezing billions of dollars in Saddam Hussein's official bank accounts and rendering him incapable of purchasing war supplies or paying his soldiers. "We knew we could pull it off," said one senior official serving in the Pentagon at the time. "We had the tools."

What would have been the most far-reaching cyberoffensive in history was questioned by Bush administration officials, who were unconvinced that the ripple effects—measured in economic collateral damage—could be contained inside Iraq. Given the linkages of the global economy, they feared that this cyberoffensive might spark worldwide financial havoc, starting in the Middle East and quickly spreading to Europe and even the United States. The plan was vetoed and never executed.

America's enemies are free from such discipline and self-restraint, and do not worry about a risk-versus-revenge calculus in waging their war of violent religious extremism on the Internet. Terrorists have proven far more agile and effective than the United States in turning the global computer network into a powerful tool, and it is their medium of choice for fund-raising, recruiting, propaganda, tactical planning, and mission execution. "The Internet forum is the connective tissue of the global Jihad," said one high-ranking intelligence officer. And American national security officials are poised for the day when terrorists use the Internet not just for communications, command, and control but for attack.

On Dolley Madison Boulevard in Langley, Virginia, a tree-lined throughway named for the First Lady who rescued presidential art, silver, and china along this evacuation route before the British burned the White House in 1814, the Central Intelligence Agency has surrendered its anonymity. A large sign points traffic toward the spy headquarters. A few miles farther up the road, in McLean, Virginia, sits the intelligence community's newest addition, the National Counterterrorism Center. It remains under cover, blending successfully with dozens of high-rise office parks hosting defense contractors, insurance conglomerates, and accounting firms surrounding the Tysons Corner shopping complex. When officials talk about the NCTC site, they refer cryptically to "LX1," in part for the letters and numeral shaped by the design of the office park when viewed via satellite image on Google Earth.

It was on September 30, 2005, a crisp autumn day, when General John Abizaid, the top officer of Central Command, showed up along with two other generals who ran Centcom's directorates for operations and for intelligence and special operations. They were there to meet with Vice Admiral Scott Redd, the NCTC director, to make their case for what became known as "counter-ing adversary use of the Internet," a phrase used so often that it got its own alien-sounding cyberacronym: CAUI.

For more than two hours, the generals made their presentation to the admiral. It went beyond the usual discussions about terror-ist fund-raising, recruiting, propaganda, and ideology over the Internet. The generals showed Admiral Redd that Al Qaeda's own and affiliated Web sites were using coded messages woven into apparently innocuous transmissions, messages that could instruct operatives what to do and when. Militants could learn how Amer-ican military convoys were organized and how they were vulner-able to IEDs. How to shoot a rocket-propelled grenade at just the right spot to take out a Humvee. How close you had to be, and at what angle, for a projectile to penetrate a soldier's bulletproof vest. And then there were the beheadings and other torture porn, some even showing gruesome executions of Americans. Some Web sites offered recipes for poison and guidelines for handling toxic chemicals. Others had explosives manuals on offer—a few of them stolen straight from the American military's training library. A quartet of Web sites had to be taken down, Abizaid argued, and immediately. These online offenders were known as "The Cent-com Four."

The problem was that the Internet service providers hosting the sites were not in Iraq or Afghanistan, war zones where the Americans had free rein to fight. The servers hosting some of the worst terrorist home pages were in Western Europe and Southeast Asia. Up to 80 percent of the militant sites had huge amounts of digital data and communications flowing through legitimate servers in the United States, many of which hosted millions of pages—too many for the operators of those servers to monitor. The question was how to deal with this problem. Military necessity had gotten out ahead of government policy. What authorities did the U.S. mili-tary have? What could be done?

"General Abizaid was the Centcom commander and he essentially felt like we were losing daily, not just the broader battle of ideas, but we were losing the information war in Iraq and Afghanistan because the way the terrorists dominate in either putting out beheadings or you just name it," said a counterterrorism official involved in the discussions. "He essentially wanted to shut down some of the Internet sites, and in a sense we did not have the proper authorities to do that. So we had to work a plan to establish the authorities, have them granted, and then to devise a means that would get them past the attorney general and the Department of Justice that people could live with as far as our own freedoms as citizens."

Looking back on his quandary, Abizaid observed in a 2010 interview that "this country, over its two-hundred-plus years of history, has been conditioned to fight wars against nation-states and to have a bureaucracy that's designed to attack it from a nation-state perspective. In the Napoleonic period, you had two realms of war and they were land and sea; in World War I and World War II it becomes land, sea, and air; in the Cold War it becomes land, sea, air, space—and in this war it becomes land, sea, air, space, and cyberspace. In this war there is a reluctance to admit, even within the services, that cyberspace is a domain of war where you have to conduct defensive and offensive operations. Yet when you looked at the enemy, the enemy was moving in the cyberspace world in a way that allowed them to recruit, train, organize, equip, proselytize, educate—you name it!—conduct intelligence operations. . . . We tried to get authority to operate in the Internet space aggressively, because we believed that the Internet space, the cyberworld, was an area that Al Qaeda was excelling in. It took years and very, very tough discussions—even at the presidential level."

Even to participants who struggled through the creation of the new counterterrorism cyberpolicy, the weeks following the NCTC conference were a blur of working-group meetings with participants ranging from the military and intelligence staff level all the way up to the deputies of the National Security Council. What emerged was an ad hoc, clumsy policy, with authority granted to a new panel, named the Strategic Operational Planning Interagency Group for Terrorist Use of the Internet. If that title was not sufficiently bureaucratic, the acronym was a howler: SOPIG-TUI. Meeting via secure video teleconference, the sessions sometimes drew three dozen participants from all across the government. "We invited everybody and their brother who has a lawyer to participate in these SOPIG-TUIs, almost to the point where we get new folks coming in over and over again," said one participant. Another official involved in the effort to counter adversary use of the Internet, reviewing his notes from those early meetings, noted a page with only one entry: PAINFUL, written in big block letters.

Even so, these meetings led to the creation of a powerful board of governors assigned to oversee counterstrikes on the Internet. Proposals to disrupt or take down terrorist Web sites were submitted to the SOPIG-TUI, which approved and forwarded them up the chain for a decision by the deputies at the National Security Council. But Abizaid and others were not completely satisfied. The process could take weeks, and it robbed the military of the essential capability to eliminate threats on the Web almost instantaneously. In response, SOPIG-TUI's advocates argued that it balanced the requirements of the intelligence and law enforcement communities with those of the armed forces. The rules of the SOPIG-TUI remain classified and have never been released, but it has since been superseded by a more formal process—a three-way agreement among the Pentagon, the intelligence community, and the Department of Justice—for considering timely attacks on terrorist Web sites, with the president making the final decision on whether to proceed.

Among the most closely guarded secrets of the military and the intelligence community are the tools that are used to defend against computer network attack and to carry out digital offensives on the

Internet. But just as Iraq became a proving ground for the nation's counterterrorism forces, it also served as a real-world laboratory for computer network warfare. In 2007 President Bush gave official but secret authorization that in effect declared Iraq an official battle space for America's cyberwarriors.

With the surge's success that year in knocking back Al Qaeda in Mesopotamia, the military command in Baghdad came to believe that one of the greatest long-term risks to stability in Iraq was a shadowy organization called Jaysh Rijal al-Tariqa al-Naqshbandia (JRTN)—the Men of the Army of al-Naqshbandia Order—based in the north-central part of the country. Its adherents were drawn from a large number of Iraqis who had not participated in the Sunni-led rebellion against the American invasion but who still opposed the government in Baghdad. "It is a Sufi sect—historically mystical, whirling-dervish kind of stuff," said one military intelligence officer. "It was not a mainstream movement of Islam, but it has organizational capacity far beyond most of the terror groups." It boasted that it had leadership and financial support from the Baathist elite hiding in their safe haven of Syria, among them Izzat Ibrahim al-Douri, a top aide to Saddam Hussein who was a member of the Iraqi leader's clan. JRTN established operational cells across Iraq, not just in its northern base, growing in its combat strength and becoming more sophisticated in waging information warfare. JRTN operated a pirate television station, bouncing images off an Egyptian-managed satellite from a primitive but effective broadcast studio inside a cargo truck that kept to the roads inside Syria to avoid detection and attack. Its programming specialty was video of snipers picking off American troops.

More ominous than the TV transmissions was JRTN's presence on the World Wide Web. Its Internet home page was a triptych—a map of the Arab world, the Iraqi flag, a rifle—with the name of the organization written along the bottom in Arabic. The site posted videos that were advertisements for the group itself, along with operational and how-to videos. JRTN members engaged in online training, demonstrating how to assemble bombs and prepare Katyusha rockets for use against American forces. The videos were accompanied by melodic recitations from the Koran. And then there were the videos of these attacks themselves. Like an MTV of hatred, these videos featured high-energy Arabic music with rhythmic beats and singing to celebrate successful attacks. One showed the downing of an American helicopter, the images captured by a video camera prepositioned beneath the anticipated flight path.

JRTN remained a strong presence on the Internet even as the United States drew down its troops and the Iraqi government prepared for national elections in March 2010. During this time, JRTN's inspirational and inciting propaganda videos were troubling enough, but in the run-up to the elections the JRTN Web site and other terror home pages took on a new operational edge. The government had kept secret the location of thousands of polling places, for obvious security reasons, but terror operatives began posting the information on these sites. It was a targeting list. And then a military raid turned up a trove of videos prepared by Al Qaeda in Mesopotamia, ready for posting on the Internet, meant to inspire preelection violence by showing successful attacks on American positions and the deaths of American troops. "When you're working against terrorists, you could win the battle but you could lose the war because you lost the information campaign," said one high-ranking military officer in Baghdad. "If you don't challenge that, you allow them to recruit and get money and keep growing. Cyber is their safe haven."

Deciding how to respond to this threat was not easy; it involved turf wars and competition within the different parts of the U.S. government. One agency's goals sometimes opposed another's. If the military made a strong case for taking a site down, it might still run up against equally powerful arguments from the intelligence agencies to keep the site alive in order to observe the terrorists' activities and plans. The debate was all about risk and benefits.

"Now, if there is a honey pot like that and you are Ray Odierno fighting Islamists in Iraq, your view is that anything that permits the Islamists to communicate with one another is killing my troops, shut it down," said a former senior official on the National Security Council. "And the counter argument is: Actually there are going to be Web sites around where they will communicate—you can't prevent them from communicating. The Internet is the Internet. If we get them communicating here, we can learn about them and we can give you intelligence that will allow you to go after these people and in the long run, it will keep the troops safer. These are difficult arguments to make.

"The other dilemma is, you think about shutting Web sites down. But of course servers are located in physical space and physical space falls within nation states and nation states have concerns about what happens on their territory. We don't have rules for any of this. You take down a Web site and, yes, it may be hosting Jihadis, but it also may be hosting things at home." The debate is paralleled by discussions over how the American national security bureaucracy should act against jihadist Web sites that are password encoded. While the software and passwords may allow militants to feel secure for meeting in these cyber back rooms, a decision to not attack the sites and let them operate allows America's cyberwarriors the opportunity to monitor and track who comes and goes. You can allow these sites to operate uninterrupted and follow those individuals who turn up on them in hopes of gathering intelligence and links to higher leaders.

It is an ironic but important footnote to history that these debates over taking down terror Web sites resulted in the largest interagency meetings held since the 9/11 attacks. Some of them were so large that the lawyers spilled over to a second conference room where they had to be tied in by video. At the end of debate, a weeks-long process described by participants as robust and passionate, two terrorist Internet sites, including the JRTN site, were knocked off the Web ahead of the election. They were posting specific operational information that was considered a clear and emerging threat to the security of the vote. At least one of the sites was hosted by an Internet service provider in the United States, and a visit from government lawyers presenting snapshots of virulent, extremist, and violent Web pages carried on their server prompted the company's executives to quietly pull the plug on that militant site. The ISP's managers later told government investigators that they could not be expected to monitor the content on each of the hundreds of thousands of pages hosted on their server.

Even so, both sites were soon able to reconstitute themselves on other servers, a new lesson for the emerging tactics of cyberwar. But the attacks and counterattacks continued. "We chased them all over the globe," said one senior Pentagon official. Yet even that silent war on the Web brought an unexpected but welcome second-order effect inside the jihadist leadership. "It took them a long time to figure out what happened, and that created infighting inside their own organizations," said another officer involved in the cyber-counterattack. The successful network strikes were not physical and left no digital fingerprints. "We can do the magic inside their systems, in a non-kinetic way," the officer said. "We have to be creative, very creative."

To achieve maximum results when launching counterstrikes like these, commanders made the case for extending their authorities to fight in the virtual battle space of terrorists hiding behind the anonymity of the Web and under the legal protections of other nations. The result was "a knock-down, drag-out interagency battle to grant NSA and CIA new authorities to shut down servers in the U.S. and allied countries," said one official involved in the high-level debate. The top officers of the Central Command, starting with General Abizaid and including General Petraeus, led the fight for the military's cause. But they ran headlong into objections from the Justice Department as well as resistance from the intelligence community. If the military perceived a threat to the force or the mission, it wanted the site taken down. The law enforcement community wanted to monitor the sites, to learn about terrorists and terrorist planning in order to identify suspects, deepen their defenses, and further their investigations. The intelligence agencies wanted to do likewise but also to exploit, provoke internal dissent, create confusion, and weaken the adversary.

"The community is split," said Arthur Cummings at the FBI. In the fierce interagency debates, those who advocated taking down Web sites that can pop back up in a matter of days were dismissed as adopting "whack-a-mole" tactics. They were warned about potential civil liberties lawsuits, since if the material passed through an American-based network there would be the implicit protection of freedom of speech and other rights of citizens. The debate was cast in terms of "collection capacity and knowledge that we gain from that collection versus the risk of allowing that entity to continue to do what it is doing," Cummings said, adding, "Is the radicalization on the Internet so bad now that it outweighs the gains of the collection?" It was capture-kill versus whole-of-government all over again but in the digital world: "We're back to the same equation, just using bits and bytes and electrons instead of flesh and bone," he said.

A half hour beyond the Washington Beltway, in the flat farmlands and gentle woods of Maryland, is a military post named for General George G. Meade, the commander of the Union forces who defeated Robert E. Lee's Confederates at Gettysburg. Small in area, Fort Meade looks more like a high-tech office park than an armed forces installation. But with the advent of the first power locks on automobiles, drivers passing by noticed something odd: Their doors would occasionally and mysteriously lock and unlock as they drove along the perimeter on a small state highway. What was deploying at Fort Meade was America's new army of electrons.

The outlines of operations at Fort Meade have since emerged from the shadows, and they no longer accidentally spoof electronic car door locks. The National Security Agency is the nation's premier signals intelligence organization, responsible for (among many other things) cracking codes and breaking into telephone conversations, computer networks, and e-mail traffic. As part of President Obama's cyberinitiatives, the director of the NSA, General Keith B. Alexander, was given a second job: pulling together the military's disparate components for computer network defense and computer network attack into one military command. In his position as head of the new Cyber Command, he is the global combatant commander for war on the Internet. His mission includes both securing the Defense Department's round-the-world computer networks and, if so ordered, taking the fight to adversaries by carrying out offensives in cyberspace.

For most of his career, Alexander had been reluctant to meet with the media. In part his reticence stemmed from the fact that his mission remained one of the most classified in the U.S. government, but there was doubtless another reason: the controversial role of the NSA in intercepting telephone calls to and from the United States, first approved by secret orders from President Bush and largely continued by President Obama. This mission generated intense contention within and scrutiny by Congress and the courts.

So it was a great surprise when Alexander agreed in September 2010 to be interviewed—his first after being confirmed by the Senate as the head of Cyber Command. Due to the rigorous secrecy surrounding everything inside Fort Meade's walls, the session was held in a conference room just outside the wire of the post, in the National Cryptologic Museum, which pays homage to code breakers throughout American history, with an actual Enigma machine, U-2 spy plane parts, and even a supercomputer on display. On a large field just beyond the museum, a variety of aircraft are mounted on static display: typical civilian and military types except for the Rube Goldberg contraptions of wires and antennae and dishes that mark them as retired reconnaissance, surveillance, and electronic signals-intercept platforms.

Soft-spoken and avuncular, Alexander began by describing the lay of the digital landscape. In 2010, he said, there were 1.9 billion Internet users worldwide, sending 247 billion e-mail messages daily. While 70 percent is spam, that presents an opaque thicket in which adversaries hide malicious messages and poisonous code. On top of that are the 4.6 billion cell phone subscribers around the world. That is a lot of digits to watch and listen to. And a cyber-threat travels fast at network speed. Divide one second on the clock into 1,000 parts. In just 70 of those, malicious code could strike a target in the United States from anywhere on the globe. "There's your decision space," Alexander said. "Wow. That's pretty quick. That's not a lot of time.

"There is a real probability that in the future, this country will get hit with a destructive attack, and we need to be ready for it," Alexander continued. "I believe this is one of the most critical problems our country faces. We need to get that right. I think we have to have a discussion about roles and responsibilities: What's the role of Cyber Command? What's the role of the 'intel' community? What's the role of the rest of the Defense Department? What's the role of DHS? And how do you make that team work? That's going to take time."

The lack of clearly defined legal authorities worried Alexander as well as civil libertarians. Some critics have questioned whether the Defense Department can enhance the protection of vital computer networks without threatening what many Americans see as their right to have unimpeded access to and use of the Internet without Big Brother watching and listening. "We can protect civil liberties and privacy and still do our mission," Alexander said. "We've got to do that." But Alexander expresses concern for the "what-if" in the event of an attack on civilian networks or infrastructure. "If one of those destructive attacks comes right now, I'm focused on the Defense Department," he said. "What are the responsibilities—and I think this is part of the discussion—for the power grid, for financial networks, for other critical infrastructure?

How do you protect the country when it comes to that kind of attack, and who is responsible for it?"

But even the Pentagon's advanced defenses, if ordered into play on American soil by emergency presidential order, would be static and not expected to prevent any more than 80 percent of potential attacks. And so Cyber Command is moving to a doctrine of active defense—"hunting on our network," Alexander called it. "You go look for stuff. Who could this be in our network, and why are they here? We have to up our game." While Cyber Command focuses mostly on potential computer network threats from nation-states, the risk of attack by a terrorist organization or lone-wolf militant remains a great concern as well. "Somebody who stumbles across something very bad in cyberspace and launches it—one person could cause a lot of damage," he warned. "Protecting yourself from nation-state and non-nation-state actors is going to be key."

Which brought Alexander to the emerging theories of deterrence and cyberspace. "We are cycling through deterrence strategy again," he said. Today, "the issue that you are going to quickly get to is who are you trying to deter in cyberspace? Who is a nation-state and who is a non-nation-state actor? You have both. So our deterrence strategy has to look at both of those. We may come up with a multilayered deterrence strategy."

Alexander pulled back the veil and acknowledged that policy directives and legal controls over digital combat had become outdated and outmoded and had failed to keep pace with the technical capabilities now under his command. The United States and the other nations of the world have not reached a consensus on what constitutes a cyberattack and have not been able to define what would be the appropriate response given the status of the laws of war based on traditional combat. Even if the U.S. government cannot instantly respond to an attack, it may still launch a counterattack, but it may do so too late to prevent the damage and serve only as an aid in the recovery or the forensics investigation into the adversary. Without defined legal authorities in place,

Alexander warned of a still-unresolved "mismatch between our technical capabilities to conduct operations and the governing laws and policies." One solution he advocated was to create a separate, secure computer network to protect civilian government agencies and critical industries like the nation's power grid against attacks mounted over the Internet. Alexander labeled the new network "a protected zone." Others have nicknamed it "dot-secure."

There is an old military saying that amateurs do strategy while the pros do logistics. Likewise, the lawyers often are in charge of developments in national security policy, and this was evident during the final years of the Bush administration and the first years of the Obama administration, as the government struggled to cope with the dramatic emergence of the terrorist threat on the Internet. The military, the intelligence community, and law enforcement agencies had battled to near exhaustion over whether threatening sites should be attacked or monitored. To end the interagency battles, what finally emerged, according to a four-star officer involved in the negotiations, was a legal document, the Trilateral Memorandum of Agreement, which set up a process to "deconflict" these disputes among the Pentagon, the Justice Department, and the intelligence community. This agreement put in place a formal, almost judicial system for arbitrating disputes. Under the classified arbitration system, if one of the military's regional combatant commanders proposed attacking an Internet site, the intelligence community and law enforcement agencies could then articulate their views, usually in opposition to taking down the sites. If disagreement remained, the case would be sent to General Alexander at Cyber Command, who would settle the dispute, although the loser could appeal to the National Security Council and even to the president. If it was a terrorist cyberissue, as opposed to a threat from a nation-state, then the National Counterterrorism Center could weigh in before the National Security Council reviewed the dispute. Alexander wrote to Congress in late 2010 to report that after years of vicious feuding about the rules of the road for attacking or monitoring a terror Web site, a formal accord for settling disputes had finally been reached.

One of the leading "unconstrained" Web sites sponsored by Al Qaeda is Al Falluja Forum, which maintains a robust presence on the Internet but also transmits its messages via social-networking sites and smart phones. Intelligence analysts believe that some of its individual sponsors, authors, and webmasters are not individuals at all but "ten guys in ten countries" who combine online into a specific "virtual persona" to avoid detection and arrest. The site and its affiliates operate from a main server, with multiple backups around the world. The forum has been attacked before—when, for example, the military believed it was about to post a particularly gruesome and provocative video of a captured American service member—but the effects of each successful intervention are short lived. "We can take them down for a brief time, if it's important to delay a release," said one military planner. But it pops up again within a few days. Even so, the tactical pause in the Web site's activities may provide a valuable effect for the military.

Another major player in the jihadist cyberscape is the Global Islamic Media Front, which intelligence and military officials call the Jihad Drudge. The site translates virulent speeches and extremist propaganda into fifteen languages for linking and reposting on sympathetic Web sites around the world. That makes it a "virtual company," more or less based everywhere and nowhere, but at times up to 80 percent of its content can be found hosted on servers in the United States. The organization uses a 128-byte advanced encryption software package with high-profile algorithms to keep out unwanted watchers, according to military and intelligence officers who have drilled into the site. It even includes tutorials on secure communications and is sophisticated in its IT support. The site offers aspiring jihadists a list of the nearest open servers from which to download the encoded software; the files are so big that time can be saved by finding the shortest distance to the encryption program.

The U.S. government, of course, fights back. One technique is called false band replacement, whereby the intelligence agencies infiltrate militants' networks and post their own material to counter extremist efforts onto those same jihadist Web sites. The trick is to copy the trademarks—"Web watermarks"—of Al Qaeda media sites. "All Al Qaeda products appear to go through a chain of preparation and approval," said one operations officer. "It's a complex system of validation. This makes messages posted on these sites official. They want to protect their message and brand—in particular from those who might go online in Al Qaeda's name and write or propose things that are counter-Koranic or non-Halal [not acceptable]." The ability of the intelligence community to persuasively forge Al Qaeda Web postings "does give an opportunity for confusion," the official said, "if we can post an almost-authentic message. We have learned to mimic their 'watermarks.' "

This Web spoofing can be used in support of more traditional combat missions. There is at least one case confirmed by American officials in which a jihadist Web site was hacked by American cyberwarriors to lure a high-value Al Qaeda leader to a surreptitious meeting with extremist counterparts only to find a U.S. military team in waiting. In another mission that now is a case study in the classified classrooms for cyberwarriors, the military and its partners in the intelligence community were able to undermine a senior-level Al Qaeda financier by secretly using computer code to take over the cell phones of members of the money network to sow confusion, distrust, and hatred. "We had the ability to hack into their phones and we would text message guys," said one senior officer familiar with the successful mission. "It was primarily telling them, 'Hey, brother, another guy is cheating you out of money.' The bad guys would get this text message and be like, 'Oh shit!' It was mainly to sow the distrust and that was at the higher levels of the network. We texted a few of his guys and basically some of his guys gave him up. It was really freaking cool."

Stories like this are useful for another reason. Many senior military and intelligence officers have pointed out that such broad descriptions of American capabilities are an important part of the "new deterrence." Terror leaders who know enough to fear America's technological advantages may come to distrust the electronic messages they receive, which in turn degrades their confidence and their ability to operate—all to America's benefit. To this day, the associates of the Al Qaeda money boss do not know that one of their key financial networks collapsed under an American cyberattack.

The military and the intelligence community also hire fluent speakers and writers of Arabic, Farsi, Urdu, Pashto, and other languages of the Muslim world to spend time in the jihadist online chat rooms. "They go into open forums where they can over time build up credibility and sow confusion," said one official who works on the program, which the military calls Digital Engagement Teams.

And then there are the efforts to take down the sites themselves. Some are pushed offline by what officials call "rods from the gods," a highly classified method of sending poisonous code into Web sites to knock them out. In Iraq, where the laws of war were preeminent over commercial regulations and freedom of speech, the military has been effective in attacking terror media centers with more traditional tools of combat. Four media emirs for Al Qaeda in Mesopotamia have been killed in Baghdad, and four others met a similar fate in Mosul. From a peak in 2006, when analysts counted more than one hundred fresh jihadist postings per day on sites operated by Iraqi terror cells, American military operations had forced those numbers down to barely a dozen per day by 2010. "With the decrease in online postings, the number of foreign fighters decreased as did donations," said one military officer. "If global jihadists cannot see the effectiveness of Al Qaeda in

Iraq, they don't want to give their lives or money." Iraqi detainees have also reported that a drop in postings led to demoralization within their ranks. By comparison, in Pakistan, where the American military did not have the freedom of action it enjoyed in Iraq, four of the six Al Qaeda media emirs running terror Web sites in 2001 were still on the job ten years later.

But if the offending Web site is hosted on a server in the United States or an allied or neutral nation, then the process is more a matter of solicitation than spycraft. If it's an American server, an office call is made to the Internet service provider by representatives from the Department of Justice, the Department of Commerce, or the Department of the Treasury. If overseas, then an American diplomat stops in. Fearing punitive reprisals for hosting a Web site fomenting lawless violence, most, like the Internet service provider cited earlier, quickly shut down the targeted terror home page. But these firms also want to know under what authority the U.S. government is asking them to break a contract, and they have requested legal protections.

Counterterrorism on the Web is a digital Darwinian process evolving at network speed. In the late 1970s, Ayatollah Khomeini successfully fomented revolution in Iran by using cassette tapes. But tape and video production is labor intensive and requires physical facilities that can be found and targeted. Today, less than 5 percent of violent extremist propaganda travels the globe via "old" media. It's Terror 2.0 that worries the U.S. government as Al Qaeda transforms itself from a top-heavy, hands-on terror organization capable of launching devastating 9/11-style attacks to one that has contracted out for smaller attacks and serves mostly as inspiration to like-minded groups around the world. The danger of online radicalization is visible in recent headlines: Five college students from suburban Washington, D.C., travel to Pakistan to train to wage jihad. Nidal Malik Hasan, a U.S. Army major, kills thirteen soldiers at Fort Hood. Umar Farouk Abdulmutallab, the Nigerian underwear bomber, almost brings down an airliner on

Christmas 2009. And Faisal Shahzad, a Pakistani American, parks an SUV filled with fireworks and propane gas primed to explode in Times Square. "They were substantially radicalized on the Internet," said Art Cummings of the FBI. The traditional model that required a potential terrorist to attend a religious school or indoctrination center in an isolated region of the Middle East is outmoded. "This was all done thousands of miles away," Cummings adds. But officials note one irony: The increase of online radicalization and training has in some significant ways dumbed down the sophistication of the attacks. Hands-on lessons at an isolated training camp in the tribal areas of Pakistan are far more effective in teaching recruits military and technological skills than instruction via the Web. But the Internet is available to any aspiring militant.

Law enforcement and intelligence officials describe a new, worrisome, and very dangerous trend. Aware that their Web sites are monitored, their cell phones tapped, and their cybercafés an easy target for surveillance, terror operatives are now increasingly communicating over the Internet via real-time video games. As X-Box and Wii and other online gaming systems offer opportunities for global pickup competition to gamers, extremists also have learned to log on at designated times to carry out their business during game programming and thereby use the chatter of countless other online users to mask themselves. Terrorist conference calls carried out over Internet gaming systems are nearly impossible to monitor. "There are tens of millions of people playing at one time," said one American counterterrorism official. "So hard to track." The NSA operates sophisticated electronic programs that listen for and locate suspect action via terror-related key words, but the language of online video war games exactly parallels, and covers, the language of violent, religious extremists. "They are talking about terrorist operations, but in play," the official said, making codeword tracking and tagging nearly impossible. Another trick terrorists are suspected of using is called steganography, whereby documents, operational orders, and planning guidance are minia-turized and hidden as an electronic dot embedded in an image on an otherwise innocuous Web site. It is the Internet version of a dead drop and nearly impossible to find in the global forest of Web pages.

It is a game of hide-and-seek with deadly consequences. Advo-cates for keeping quiet watch over the Web sites say the Internet is a honey pot attracting jihadists, with large amounts of informa-tion to be gathered by monitoring those who swarm. "You know, I could put up filters for every single one of those people, start banging them against current data, start using language filters to see which of them talk about violence and Jihad," said one senior counterterrorism officer. He ticked off the government's array of sensitive programs to monitor the adversaries' use of the Internet. "I could start using software network tools to see which of them are connected with each other based on phone records," he said. "I could do a million things with that stuff."

6

COUNTERING AL QAEDA'S MESSAGE

By the spring of 2009, the United States and its allies had made significant progress in disrupting Al Qaeda's ability to plan and carry out major operations from its safe havens in the tribal areas of Pakistan. Increasingly deadly CIA drone strikes and improved intelligence sharing between American and Pakistani spy agencies were squeezing Al Qaeda leaders in their mountain hideouts. But Al Qaeda and the other extremist groups still had the United States on the defensive in the ideological battlefield, whipping up anti-American sentiment and attracting a steady stream of new recruits and financial backing with a simple but venomously potent message to their followers: America is at war with Islam.

In June of that year, the new American president sought to counter that message and deter the spread of terrorist ideology with an even stronger narrative of his own: An African American named Barack Hussein Obama was standing on the podium in a Muslim capital as the leader of the United States. Obama came to Cairo on June 4, 2009, pledging "a new beginning." While America would continue to fight terrorism, he said, terrorism would no longer define America's approach to the Muslim world.

"We will, however, relentlessly confront violent extremists who pose a grave threat to our security—because we reject the same thing that people of all faiths reject: the killing of innocent men, women, and children," Obama said, speaking in forceful tones. "And it is my first duty as president to protect the American people." A few minutes later, Obama pivoted and took aim at Al Qaeda, signaling a shift in how the United States would confront it more directly and how America would frame a new narrative to chip away at Al Qaeda's legitimacy in the eyes of Muslims while appealing to their broader interests.

"They have killed in many countries," Obama said. "They have killed people of different faiths—but more than any other, they have killed Muslims. Their actions are irreconcilable with the rights of human beings, the progress of nations, and with Islam. The Holy Koran teaches that whoever kills an innocent, it is as if he has killed all mankind. And the Holy Koran also says whoever saves a person, it is as if he has saved all mankind. The enduring faith of over a billion people is so much bigger than the narrow hatred of a few. Islam is not part of the problem in combating violent extremism—it is an important part of promoting peace."

Obama's words were translated almost instantly into fourteen languages and posted on Web sites and blogs around the world. They were transmitted by text message to mobile phones in more than 170 countries. Staff members at more than 100 American embassies and consulates fanned out afterward to hold post-speech debates, conduct hundreds of media interviews, and pay visits to universities, mosques, and madrassas, with the goal to put a local American face on the president's promise of "a new beginning."

Obama sought to capitalize on his biography and the power of his own words to shift perceptions of the United States in the Muslim world and to deter a spreading terrorist ideology. The Bush administration, particularly in its waning months and with prodding from officials like Juan Zarate of the National Security Council, had embraced a broader counterterrorism strategy that included challenging Al Qaeda's messages and highlighting Al Qaeda's mis-steps whenever possible. But with the long-running war in Iraq, an expanding conflict in Afghanistan, and the damning images of Abu Ghraib and Guantánamo still fresh in people's minds, Bush's cred-ibility with Muslims was near zero.

After taking office, Obama quickly distanced himself from some of the harshest counterterrorism policies of the Bush administra-tion. He barred "enhanced" interrogation techniques and announced that the prison at Guantánamo Bay, Cuba, would finally close (a promise he has since had to put on hold). Even the rhetoric changed in the new administration with the phrase "countering (or combat-ing) violent extremism" replacing the "the war on terror" in official documents and pronouncements.

Rather than lecture the Muslim world, as members of the Bush administration often did, Obama sought to amplify credible Mus-lim voices to teach and condemn the evils of violent extremism. The challenge facing the United States, however, remains how to support these efforts without tainting them with a public embrace. A linchpin of the countermessaging strategy was to focus on Al Qaeda and its affiliates rather than on a wide range of terrorist organizations and hammer away at the group's hypocrisy and fail-ures while at the same time offering a positive alternative. This is a war of ideas where the goal is not so much to promote America but to destroy Al Qaeda's credibility. Some of this strategy is being carried out in secret war rooms created by the Pentagon, the State Department, and the intelligence agencies. Small cells of intelli-gence analysts prowl the Internet, hunting for examples of Al Qaeda excesses and mistakes: the bombing of a school in Jordan, the kill-ing of women and children by a suicide bomber in Algeria, the slaughter of dozens of civilians by a car bomb in an open-air mar-ket outside Baghdad. These upsetting events can be exploited in countermessaging that is transmitted not just by American offi-cials but also by radio broadcasts and speeches by more credible

Muslim voices, including respected clerics, throughout the Islamic world.

American officials know that if they damage the terrorists' reputations and credibility with their fellow Muslims, they are decreasing the "territory" that the extremists hold dear. British counterterrorism experts (schooled in the craft after decades of fighting the Irish Republican Army) and allies in the Muslim world are helping American officials devise a strategy to get in front of Al Qaeda's narrative. A Saudi militant captured in Iraq and nicknamed "Bernie" by the Americans (because he was badly burned in an attack) was sent home and conducted a series of television interviews in which he said that he had been lied to and manipulated by Al Qaeda's affiliate in Iraq. Worse, he said, there had been no long lines of Iraqi women willing to service him, as had been promised. Efforts like this are part of the war of persuasion and instantaneous countermessages, not unlike a modern political campaign.

Many of the American efforts center on drawing attention to civilian deaths caused not by allied forces in Iraq or Afghanistan but by Al Qaeda or the Taliban. A study by the West Point Center for Combating Terrorism in December 2009 found that only 15 percent of the people killed in Al Qaeda attacks between 2004 and 2008 were Westerners. The vast majority of the victims were Muslims. The report struck a nerve with Al Qaeda. Adam Gadahn, an American-born spokesman for Al Qaeda, responded within days with a poor-quality video in which he stuttered and tripped over words in denouncing the criticisms leveled in the report.

Obama's Cairo speech, in which he quoted repeatedly from the Koran and sprinkled his remarks with Arabic, began by identifying and confronting the tensions between the United States and the Muslim world: Al Qaeda, Afghanistan, Iraq, the Arab-Israeli conflict, Iran, nuclear weapons issues, democracy, women's rights. "Our view of the speech was pretty simple," said Ben Rhodes, the deputy national security adviser for strategic communications and the main speechwriter for the Cairo address. "It was acknowledge the tensions, name them and work through each of them." The second half of the address tackled what the president's aides said had been a glaring shortcoming in a comprehensive strategy to deter terrorist ideology. "We were countermessaging al Qaeda," said Rhodes, "but we weren't crafting a positive message that was relevant to people's lives in these countries."

To articulate that positive message, Rhodes studied public-opinion polling in several Muslim countries and American intelligence reports and also consulted a range of independent experts, businesspeople, and prominent Muslim Americans to determine what the people in the Muslim world cared about most. He was surprised by the results. "Terrorism usually wasn't on the list," Rhodes said. "Basically we were crafting messages in many cases based on what we cared about but not on what the audience cared about. Anyone who has run a political campaign or an ad campaign knows that if you want to communicate a message, you need to know your audience." What the people did care about in those Muslim countries was science, technology, education, and entrepreneurship. "The things they still admired about America and the areas they still wanted to partner with America were in areas that we weren't doing that much in," Rhodes said.

In response, and in the wake of the president's speech, the administration expanded business and education exchange programs. It dispatched science envoys. It started new health initiatives. President Obama hosted 250 entrepreneurs from around the Muslim world in April 2010 and created a fund to promote technological development. "We're basically trying to create deeper networks with Muslim majority publics," Rhodes said. "We don't expect Al Qaeda to surrender next year because we are having an entrepreneurship summit or expanding educational exchanges or sending a science envoy to Cairo. But we need a long game." A long game in political parlance is a long-term strategy. "The long game has to be just as it was in the Cold War, things that expand your networks into these places, things that expand not just government connections, but civil society connections—things that bring people here and give them a positive impression of America," Rhodes said.

In a sign of how important the president considers the legacy of the speech, Rhodes said that Obama keeps a checklist of its themes and goals, and demands regular memos updating him on the initiatives that were launched following the address. "We have an accountability loop on that," Rhodes said. "I can assure you that the interested groups on the outside also know we have a checklist."

However, more than a year after Obama's speech, there was a widespread feeling in the Muslim world that the president and his advisers had failed to follow through sufficiently on Cairo's lofty goals and that they had underestimated the difficulty in meeting the raised expectations. Rhodes's "long game" was in place, but the Muslim street wanted more dramatic short-term results. Despite the preparation and soaring rhetoric, Obama had failed to change the narrative he set out to destroy. A June 2010 report from the Pew Global Survey concluded, "Roughly one year since Obama's Cairo address, America's image shows few signs of improving in the Muslim world, where opposition to key elements of U.S. foreign policy remains pervasive and many continue to perceive the U.S. as a potential military threat to their countries." An Arab Public Opinion Poll (conducted by the University of Maryland and Zogby International) found that respondents in Egypt, Jordan, Lebanon, Morocco, Saudi Arabia, and the United Arab Emirates with a positive view of Obama had declined to 20 percent in 2010 from 45 percent a year earlier.

One senior State Department official said that Obama had boxed himself in by failing to deliver on a promise in the speech to take a hard line with Israel and to bridge the deep divisions between Israelis and Palestinians. "The Cairo speech, initially at least, was very important because he broke one of the major taboos of American foreign policy, which is to get tough with Israel and to bash heads with Netanyahu," said the official, referring to Israel's prime minister, Benjamin Netanyahu. "For a time period, he very clearly tackled a very critical issue in the Arab world. The Cairo speech was clearly a major dent into that image of steadfast American support for Israel. But he cornered himself by going really hard on Israel and not delivering." An American ambassador to a Muslim country also expressed disappointment at what he called a missed opportunity to build on the promises in the speech, citing the administration's failure to engage the Middle East peace process more aggressively or to seek closer ties to Yemen, Lebanon, and even Syria.

Rhodes acknowledged that the president may suffer in the short term but argued that the final judgment on the speech and what it achieved is still years away. He asserted that Obama's personal popularity in Muslim countries, which ranks higher than that of the United States overall, shows that the president's personal appeal remains a challenge to the terrorists' ideology. "What I think we got after that speech and what we didn't have at the end of the Bush administration is the benefit of the doubt," Rhodes said. "People want the president to do what he said he would do in the speech and he hasn't done that yet. That is good, they want him to continue, they want him to succeed." Nonetheless, Obama's checklist still has several empty boxes.

The turmoil in the Middle East and North Africa that erupted in January and February 2011 has complicated Obama's accounting. The White House faced strong criticism from human rights groups for not backing the pro-democracy movements in Tunisia, Egypt, and elsewhere sooner and more forcefully. Whether the populist uprisings help or hurt Al Qaeda's brand appeal is still playing out. Al Qaeda and its affiliates played no role in the initial rebellions and were caught flat-footed by the tumult. Osama bin Laden was silent, and his Egyptian deputy, Ayman al-Zawahri, issued only a handful of rambling statements. The largely nonviolent, secular revolts in Egypt and Tunisia amounted to a rejection of Al Qaeda's belief that murderous violence and religious fanaticism are necessary to topple the despots bin Laden denounced as puppets of the West and to replace them with an Islamic caliphate. "It's a discrediting of Al Qaeda's agenda," said John Brennan. By late March, however, Al Qaeda appeared to have regained its propagandist footing. Its leaders claimed that Islamist extremists delighted in the success of protest movements against regimes they abhorred, and they exhorted the protesters not to let up. Zawahri urged Egyptians who had toppled President Hosni Mubarak to disdain the United States, reject democracy, and embrace Islam as the answer to their grievances. Whether Al Qaeda successfully exploits the chaos in Libya to set up bases in the thinly populated southern desert or in Yemen to expand AQAP's influence is unclear. The long-term impact of these changes on Al Qaeda will depend partly on how leaders of the Middle East adapt. But if the underlying political and economic problems persist, Al Qaeda's siren song may once again sound attractive to a small but potentially lethal group of extremists.

The U.S. government has struggled mightily in the years since the September 11 attacks to develop an effective and credible campaign to counter the ideology and messaging of Al Qaeda and other extremist groups. In early 2002, the Pentagon quietly created the Office of Strategic Influence, a small but well-financed arm of the Defense Department's policy branch, in response to concerns that the United States was losing public support overseas for its war against terrorism, especially in Muslim countries. The program's supporters said they were filling a void left by traditional public diplomacy carried out by specialists at the State Department. The goal of the office was not only to broadcast messages into hostile countries but also to expand operations to friendly nations in the Middle East, Asia, and Western Europe. The proposals included aggressive campaigns that used foreign news media and the Internet as well as covert operations. But when the *New York Times* disclosed in February 2002 that the office planned to provide news items, possibly even false ones, to unwitting journalists to influence public sentiment abroad, Secretary Rumsfeld was forced to shut it down.

There were also efforts made to communicate with terrorist leaders directly, but these seemed like long shots at best. The Bush administration's secret program to send back-channel messages to bin Laden and his inner circle in 2001 was met with silence. It is unclear whether this highly classified program continued at all in President Obama's administration, which has carried out a significant review of all Bush-era covert intelligence programs as well as counterterrorism policies and initiatives. Under the Bush administration, which swore never to negotiate with terrorists, publicly defending such a program would have been extremely difficult.

American officials have searched for an ideological counterweight to Al Qaeda, whose protean and inspirational character has made it unlike any foe the military and the rest of the American government has ever dealt with. "You can destroy the people in Al Qaeda, but you can't destroy the idea of Al Qaeda," General Abizaid warned. "The idea of Al Qaeda needs to be attacked in a very, very whole-of-government, whole-of-international-agency way, and it has to be done in a way that's affordable."

The Bush administration struggled with how to organize the effort to counter Al Qaeda's message. The State and Defense departments fought any effort to subordinate their countermessaging efforts to the direction of a senior official at the National Security Council. And on a substantive level, many American officials admit that their most well-meaning efforts may fall short in combating Al Qaeda's narrative; it will require the efforts of Muslim leaders themselves to address the ideological threat. "You're putting your finger in the dike when you apply security measures against an ideological problem," said Philip Mudd, a former top counterterrorism official at the CIA and at the FBI. "The people who can beat this ideology are in the Islamic world, not here—we don't have the credibility in the ideological fight." In Saudi Arabia, for example, not only have security forces virtually eradicated the Al Qaeda cell there following a string of fatal bombings beginning in 2003, but religious leaders in the kingdom have been ordered to denounce suicide bombings and violence. The government has established and financed religion-based deradicalization centers for militants, which include education, job training and counseling, and a commitment by a militant's family to keep him from returning to violence. Counterterrorism experts say that these programs have had mixed success.

By 2007, these efforts and Al Qaeda's own excesses began to have an impact. Increasingly, there were signs of divisions within the once unified ideological ranks. Saudi Arabia's top cleric, Grand Mufti Sheik Abdul Aziz al-Asheik, gave a speech in October of that year warning Saudis not to join unauthorized jihadist activities, a statement directed mainly at those considering going to Iraq to fight the American led forces. Abdul-Aziz el-Sherif, a leader of the armed Egyptian movement Islamic Jihad and a longtime associate of Ayman al-Zawahri, the second-ranking Al Qaeda official, completed a book in 2007 that renounced violent jihad on legal and religious grounds. According to Western and Middle Eastern diplomats, such dissents have served to widen rifts between Al Qaeda leaders and some of their former loyal backers, depressing their recruiting success.

Dissent can also shift the initiative away from jihadist leaders. On December 16, 2007, Zawahri invited journalists and jihadists to ask him questions via the primary jihadist Web forums, but when his responses were released nearly four months later, he seemed to be on the defensive. "We haven't killed the innocents, not in Baghdad, nor in Morocco, nor in Algeria nor anywhere else," Zawahri said, according to a transcript posted on Web sites linked to Al Qaeda on April 2, 2008. In May 2010, Saudi Arabia's top religious leadership, known as the Council of Senior Ulema, issued a fatwa, or religious ruling, that denounced terrorism, including the financing of terrorist acts. Many other foreign governments, including those of the Netherlands and Pakistan, have employed counterrecruiting strategies, some aimed at the broad Muslim population, others tailored to reach disaffected young people who are easily radicalized.

And in Saudi Arabia, a government-supported program has enlisted hundreds of Islamic scholars-turned-bloggers to fight online radicalization by challenging the jihadist interpretations of the Koran on extremist social-networking forums. Many of these efforts to counter violent extremism on the Web are just getting off the ground, but there are signs that they may be having at least a temporary impact. Evan F. Kohlmann, who tracks militant Web sites at the security consulting firm Flashpoint Global Partners in New York, said a growing number of extremist forums are now using password-protected sites to thwart hackers and dissenters.

Striking back at the Al Qaeda message sometimes required American combat skills. One of the most successful efforts was undertaken on the ground in Iraq, in advance of the November 2004 offensive to retake Fallujah, effectively Al Qaeda's capital in western Anbar Province. The American military was fighting two wars, really, in Iraq: one to tamp down the roiling Sunni-Shia rivalry that risked civil war, the other a terrorist conflict inspired by Al Qaeda. "Fallujah was a festering cancer that was going to have to be dealt with," said Lieutenant General Thomas F. Metz, who spent fifteen months in Iraq in 2004 and 2005 as the commander in charge of the day-to-day fight across the country.

Metz is a mechanized infantry officer who rose to lead the Army's III Corps based at Fort Hood, Texas, where the multiple armored divisions under his command would have been the first sent to the Korean Peninsula in the event of a North Korean invasion. Hardly the most opportune training for the new kind of counterinsurgency and terror war under way in Iraq, but Metz had learned as a young man to be resourceful and agile when dealing with adversity. Metz tells a story about his having to find the cash for his first-year uniforms after his acceptance to West Point. (At the time, that was the only cost to entering cadets, since the Army did not want to be in the hole for outfitting those who wash out in the early months under academy pressure.) He won the money in a card game with other would-be cadets.

Metz never doubted that the American, Allied, and Iraqi forces could push Al Qaeda fighters from Fallujah and that civilian casualties could at least be minimized by an information campaign in advance to tell noncombatants to leave the city, which they did by the thousands. But the terrorist media cell run by the leader of Al Qaeda in Mesopotamia, Abu Musab al-Zarqawi, had routinely hammered out a successful narrative that American troops were killing and maiming civilians in Fallujah, in particular women and children. The terror media packages always had graphic images said to have been taken at the hospital in Fallujah. Metz had to silence that narrative before launching his offensive.

"There was an Al Qaeda guy who was always at the hospital showing these wounded children and females that were a result of the attack," Metz said. "We knew it wasn't the result of the attack because those kinds of attacks were launched with such precision—somebody has been constantly staring at these targets for a long time, and we knew the target enters that house alone or he is just with bad people. There are no family around, there are no children." You never get a second chance to tell your story first, Metz knew; no American military spokesman could push back. "You can prove all the facts wrong but it is over with: The perception is all that matters," he said. "If you are going to make the final assault on Fallujah, you want to ensure that they didn't have that platform."

So for the first tactical mission of the Fallujah operation, the Iraqi 36th Commando Battalion, supported by American Special

Operations forces, stealthily seized the hospital ahead of conventional troops advancing into Fallujah. And American and Iraqi media were embedded to show the mission in almost real time. "I don't think, at least in my experience, there are many military operations that you're doing for the purpose of affecting the information operations," Metz said. "But we wanted the 36th Commandos to take the hospital—Iraqis taking hospitals, on behalf of the Iraqi people who could be treated if harmed in the assault on Fallujah. They could come to their hospital and be treated at their hospital and it would not be an information operations platform for the enemy."

In the Bush administration's second term, Juan Zarate and other counterterrorism officials were increasingly seeking to capitalize on the intelligence collected in battlefield missions to fuel the high-level campaign to counter the terrorist message. It didn't always go well. In the spring of 2006, the National Security Council was running a weekly video teleconference among several federal agencies to coordinate what was called strategic messaging. Getting good propaganda to use against Zarqawi in Iraq was important; so senior administration officials who tuned into the American military briefing in Baghdad one day in early May were dismayed to see a senior Army spokesman, Major General Rick Lynch, briefing reporters about a captured videotape produced by Zarqawi and his fighters. The briefing focused on "outtakes" from a video that Zarqawi had aired earlier that were meant to show the leader of Al Qaeda in Mesopotamia as a fearsome warrior. But the outtakes seized by then–Lieutenant General Stanley McChrystal's Special Operations forces and aired that day were meant to embarrass and humiliate the Iraqi militant leader. They showed Zarqawi wearing white New Balance running shoes under his black jihadi garb and fumbling while trying to fire an automatic rifle. The video also made it clear that Zarqawi and his captains did not know much about weapons safety, and they burned their hands while passing the rifle, its searing hot muzzle first. The video even showed Zarqawi ignoring a call for prayer, something that would shock any pious Muslim. But the briefing itself was the first time that the senior officials in Washington had seen or heard about this video, and they were furious, feeling that the military had blown a golden chance. They believed that the video clips could have been exploited even more effectively if they had been made public by an Iraqi official or reporter. Anything with "Made in the USA" stamped on it could be viewed as tainted. "It was just a missed opportunity," said Michele Davis, a top communications strategist in the Bush White House.

Even if the release of the Zarqawi video was fumbled by headquarters personnel, the operators commanded by General McChrystal were able to neutralize Zarqawi permanently. Intelligence officials said that the public ridicule infuriated Zarqawi and prompted him to become increasingly irrational and reckless, issuing videotaped speeches on Islamic Web sites, vowing victory against the "crusaders" who had invaded Iraq. His outspoken rants helped the United States track and kill him a month later, on June 7, 2006, in an F-16 air strike at an isolated safe house north of Baghdad.

In Washington, Zarate and his boss, Steve Hadley, the national security adviser, struggled to wrap their arms around effective ways to counter Al Qaeda's narrative that the United States was at war with Islam. By early 2007, they were holding a series of brainstorming sessions in the Roosevelt Room in the White House, inviting outsiders to meet senior administration officials like Defense Secretary Robert Gates and Admiral Mike Mullen. In one meeting, the administration team met with social-network and Internet executives from Silicon Valley. Another convened philanthropists and nonprofit executives from organizations like the Smith Richardson Foundation and the German Marshall Fund. Another session invited marketing experts from Madison Avenue and Fortune

100 companies. Yet another gathered scholars like Peter Singer of the Brookings Institution and Walid Phares of the National Defense University. The sessions stirred provocative discussions but ultimately left many pivotal questions unanswered. Why can't the United States combat the narrative effectively? Why is the Iraqi enemy using the Internet more effectively than the American military? The government was being whipsawed between two objectives. On the one hand, the administration clearly had to be engaged in countering Al Qaeda's potent message. But Zarate and his colleagues in the White House also recognized that the U.S. government was not the most credible messenger for this task. "We were struggling with, what does a messaging and ideological battle look like in this new technical and ideological landscape," Zarate recalled. "The U.S. government just wasn't prepared and organized to deal with this."

And the efforts the government did make were tightly managed from Washington, too tightly for some commanders' liking. General McChrystal complained that the countermessaging campaign was too centralized. "I had the authority to drop a bomb," he said to his aides, "but I didn't have authority to send someone an e-mail. I couldn't send a targeted person, an enemy person, an e-mail. If you centralize too much, you tie everyone's hands and it doesn't work."

By 2008, the National Security Council, working closely with the Pentagon, the military commands in Iraq and Afghanistan, intelligence analysts, and embassy officials, developed a plan to use examples of civilian killings and other atrocities by Al Qaeda or the Taliban to undermine the terrorist groups' credibility. Strategic-communications specialists seized on terrorist attacks reported in the Western and Arabic-language media, and sent summaries to some two thousand domestic and international reporters, congressional staff members from both parties, think-tank scholars, columnists, bloggers, and government officials in the United States, Iraq, and Afghanistan.

Officials picked stories with arresting headlines:

TALIBAN KILL TWO UN DOCTORS, CHILDREN AND A SCHOOLTEACHER

TWO SCHOOLGIRLS BLINDED IN ACID ATTACK

TALIBAN SEIZES BUS, EXECUTES 2 DOZEN PASSENGERS, BEHEADING ONE

TERRORIST ATTACK KILLS 14 CHILDREN ON LAST DAY OF SCHOOL

"The main goal was to create a constant drumbeat of anti–Al Qaeda information that was factual, directly quoted, and heavily sourced with credible, direct links to verify," said Mark Pfeifle, the deputy national security adviser for strategic communications and global outreach. "We put a priority on using photos and video to tell the story with the theme throughout being Al Qaeda and its supporters are killing, maiming innocent Muslims, including women and children."

Officials in Washington also coordinated with military commanders to exploit operations for their propaganda value. In December 2007, American and Iraqi special operations forces raided a safe house that had been used by Al Qaeda in Iraq to torture their enemies. Within hours of the operation, commanders and diplomats on the ground invited Western and Arabic-language media to tour the safe house, to view the site and talk to victims, to take their photographs, and to hear their personal stories firsthand. The photos and video worked their way into the Iraqi and larger Arabic-language media over time, Pfeifle said.

These campaigns were more effective than earlier efforts. But persuading non-Americans to step forward, often in a war zone, proved challenging. "Sometimes that was difficult as the Afghan or Pakistani or Iraqi public officials and everyday people, for obvious security reasons, many times didn't want to comment out of fear," Pfeifle said.

In other locations, the messaging was integrated more seamlessly into existing aid programs. In 2008, the U.S. Agency for
International Development spent about $9 million on counterter-
rorism measures in Mali, an impoverished desert country in West
Africa where an offshoot of Al Qaeda was operating. Some of the
money went to expand an existing job-training program for women
and another one to provide young Malian men in the north with
the basic skills to set up businesses like tiny flour mills or cattle
enterprises. Some aid trained teachers in Muslim parochial schools
in an effort to prevent them from becoming incubators of anti-
American vitriol. But the agency also built twelve FM radio stations in the north of the country to link far-flung villages to an
early-warning network that sends bulletins on bandits and other
threats. Financing from the Pentagon would produce, in four
national languages, radio soap operas promoting peace and tolerance. "Young men in the north are looking for jobs or something
to do with their lives," said Alexander D. Newton, the director of
USAID's mission in Mali. "These are the same people who could be
susceptible to other messages of economic security."

In June of that year, the Bush administration's efforts to counter Al Qaeda's narrative got a major boost when James K. Glassman
was appointed as the undersecretary of state for public diplomacy
and public affairs. Glassman, a Harvard graduate and a journalist
by training, had been the publisher of the *New Republic* magazine
and an economics columnist for the *Washington Post* before serving as chairman of the Broadcasting Board of Governors, which
oversees Voice of America. Glassman was the fourth appointee to
head an office with a troubled past. The first, Charlotte Beers, a
Madison Avenue executive, produced a promotional video about
Muslims in America that was rejected by some Arab nations and
was criticized by many of her State Department colleagues. Her
successor, Margaret D. Tutwiler, a former State Department spokes-
woman, lasted barely five months. Just before Tutwiler assumed
the job, a report issued in October 2003 by a bipartisan panel led

by Edward P. Djerejian, an Arab specialist and former U.S. ambassador to Syria and Israel, painted a grim picture of American public diplomacy in the Arab and Muslim world.

Tutweiler was succeeded by Karen Hughes, a longtime Bush aide and confidante who led an aggressive effort to repair America's poor image in Muslim countries. She set up "rapid-response" teams of communications specialists in the Middle East and elsewhere to counter bad news and defend administration policies around the globe. But Hughes's emphasis on polishing America's image and increasing the number of visiting Fulbright scholars failed to make a meaningful dent in Al Qaeda's growing anti-American narrative.

In contrast, Glassman moved quickly to attack the extremists' ideological message and divert young people from the path that led them to become terrorists, areas Hughes studiously avoided. The biggest obstacle facing Glassman, besides Al Qaeda itself, was time. He had just over six months in the waning days of a lame-duck presidency to make an impact, but he took on the challenge, arguing that the rise of the Internet, long considered an ally of extremists, could be turned against them. Glassman explained that Al Qaeda was more in control of what he called Web 1.0, where terrorists broadcast messages and followers receive them. In Web 2.0, where social networks are ascendant and followers can challenge their leaders, Al Qaeda could lose its strict control of the narrative, as Zawahri did when he was forced to respond to the online questions. He recognized that terrorists were moving away from old media like CDs, DVDs, and cassette tapes, which were cumbersome and expensive. New media was cheaper and mostly online. "What terrorists want to do with young people is indoctrinate them, isolate them, bombard them with messages and exhortations, like a cult does," Glassman said. "But once you open that up, they [Al Qaeda] are at a major disadvantage.

"The one thing we saw over and over again being a major obstacle was the narrative that the United States and the West are out to destroy Islam and replace it with Christianity," he continued. "If that becomes the prism through which you see everything, it's a big problem."

When Glassman arrived at his offices at the State Department, he had not only scant time to make headway but little money to work with. Glassman said that of Public Diplomacy's $800-million budget, two thirds was designated for student exchange programs. Little was left for what Glassman called "diversion" programs, initiatives to steer young people into various activities and away from terrorist ideology. But he worked with what he had. He gave $300,000 to an organization called the International Center for Religion and Diplomacy, which aims to reform radical madrassas in Pakistan. He and Zarate championed support for a range of emerging grassroots organizations that opposed violent extremism, including the Alliance of Youth Movements, Sisters Against Violent Extremism, Global Survivors Network, and the Quilliam Foundation, an anti-extremist think tank. But even Glassman acknowledged that in such a short time, it was difficult to gauge the impact of his new approach. "How do you measure whether you are effective or not?" he said. "Nobody really knows the answer."

Fledgling efforts at strategically important U.S. embassies in the Muslim world also faced an uphill fight to change the financing priorities for public diplomacy that in many ways still seem locked in the Cold War. When Gonzalo Gallegos, a longtime State Department spokesman, arrived at the U.S. Embassy in Islamabad in 2008, his budget for public diplomacy was a paltry $1.4 million, only about twice the amount allotted to the U.S. Embassy in Costa Rica, a peaceful tourist mecca, for the same purposes. Traditionally, that budget paid for educational and cultural exchanges and for travel expenses to bring teachers, musicians, and Pakistani American professors or imams from the United States to give voice to a positive American experience. These programs, while well-meaning, had little effect on the anti-American sentiment building in the country. "We were losing the battle," Gallegos said. "We needed a way to get ground back." Armed with funds from Glassman, the embassy teamed with a group of Pakistanis in Islamabad to run a print advertising campaign and a polling project. The ad campaign targeted the culprits responsible for exploding a truck bomb at the entrance to the Marriott Hotel in Islamabad on September 20, 2008, that killed more than 50 people and wounded more than 250 in one of the worst acts of terrorism in Pakistan's history. The blast had gone off just a few hundred yards from the prime minister's house, where all the leaders of government were dining after the president's address to Parliament. The campaign bought half-page and full-page ads in the Urdu and English-language press that showed photographs of the mangled hotel front and these messages: "This is horrible." "What kind of people do this?" To measure the impact of the campaign, a poll was taken. The results were discouraging, as few people remembered seeing the ads. Due to limited funds, the campaign ran only for a week, and it was limited by the fact that it ran at the end of the Ramadan holiday, when newspapers shut down.

Gallegos figured that to make another campaign work, the embassy would have to coordinate more closely with the Pakistani government and with the powerful media arm of the Pakistani Army. Any further effort would also need a lot more money. As the clock ran out on the Bush administration, the embassy went hat in hand to the State Department as well as to the military's Central Command and Special Operations Command for financing to combat the extremist narrative in Pakistan. In the end, the military commands and the civilian departments could find only about $10 million to give to the embassy to address one of the country's top counterterrorism priorities.

In June 2009, Glassman's successor, Judith A. McHale, vowed that the United States would combat Al Qaeda with both "new and old media." "This is not a propaganda contest—it is a relationship race," she said. "And we have got to get back in the game." But unity of effort was lacking, and painfully so, across the government. Despite the Obama administration's best intentions to capitalize on America's media expertise—in styles ranging from Madison Avenue to YouTube, Facebook, and Twitter—the bureaucracy confounded those efforts at many turns. In meeting after meeting, Pentagon and military officers showed up and applied their standard rule to planning new missions, whether on the battlefield or on the airwaves: First, figure out the desired end state— exactly what was to be accomplished—then figure out what to do. Diplomats spoke a different language and shaped their mission more in terms of themes and outreach and audiences. "The Defense Department would identify the gaps, really the vacuum, in our communications to the Islamic world," said one top administration official directly involved in the negotiations. "The State Department would show up basically talking mostly about the need to respond faster."

Meetings also were marked by a tug-of-war over whether the messages would focus on specific themes of countering terrorism or address the broader range of underlying causes across a specific region of the Islamic world. And the coordination of those messages with military action, if required, continued to create abrasive relationships between soldiers and diplomats. "It's both microphones and drones," said one Pentagon official. "Communications is a tool. It can take you a certain distance down the road. But if the road gets dangerous, you need guns."

And even as the administration committed to building up the capabilities of partner nations to fight violent extremism on their own, Pentagon officials continued to express deep frustration that the State Department, with only a tiny fraction of the military's manpower, did not have the capacity to run the countermessaging campaign. The discussions ranged from low-level negotiations about sending military personnel on temporary duty to assist the State

Department to a cabinet-level dialogue where Secretary of Defense Gates turned to Secretary of State Clinton and in essence offered to write a check for whatever she needed to get the crisis communications effort off the ground. That check wasn't accepted, and others couldn't be cashed. In fact, Pentagon officials kept a record of the number of official budget transfers from Defense to State for countermessaging efforts that were returned. One, in particular, was galling. The Pentagon offered to pay the bill for one State Department communications project but then called for the funds to be returned when the State Department, short of personnel, let out a bid for contracts to outsource the mission.

The State Department's efforts to counter violent extremism picked up pace following President Obama's Cairo speech in June 2009. However, the department struggled to align the personnel, authority, and resources needed to follow up on the president's message. In July 2010, more than a year after the speech, President Obama grew frustrated by the lack of progress in institutionalizing the countermessaging capabilities of the U.S. government. When Daniel Benjamin, the State Department's top counterterrorism official, briefed Obama that month on upcoming initiatives to counter violent extremism in the Muslim world, he included in his briefing the concept of a Center for Strategic Counterterrorism Communications, an interagency cell within the State Department that would be designed to counter the effects of terrorist messaging around the world. The new communication center would double the size of the department's existing digital outreach teams to about twenty native Arabic, Farsi, and Urdu speakers who would operate in online chat rooms, Web forums, and other social media to try to break up the "echo chamber" effect of jihadist movements. The teams would monitor more Web sites than before and be more aggressive in confronting the extremist narrative rather than just parroting American policy. The center's staff would also include military officers specializing in information operations; intelligence specialists from the CIA, the National Counterterrorism

Center, and other agencies; as well as State Department public diplomacy experts. Obama immediately embraced the idea but also vented his anger and irritation at the delay in getting it up and running. "I thought I asked for this a year ago," he complained. "What do I have to do to get this done around here?"

White House officials winced at the president's scolding. "I got my butt chewed in that meeting pretty hard," said Denis McDonough, the deputy national security adviser. "It won't happen again, I can tell you that." Following the meeting, there was a rush within the State Department to start the new communications center to comply with the president's order. Further complicating the project was the need to find suitable space for the new center, adequate funding, and a trained staff. (The center was designed to draw on specialists from the State Department, the military, and the intelligence agencies. It would build upon the digital outreach team that had been established years before.) After initial delays, the center received $6 million to cover start-up costs. Despite the president's clear directives to the State Department and other government agencies stating that this was one of his top priorities, the communications center was still at a very nascent and understaffed stage five months later, and the U.S. government's message against terrorism and other expressions of violent extremism still was not making the desired headway.

By early 2011 the center finally seemed poised to turn a corner. Its coordinator, Richard LeBaron, a respected career diplomat and former U.S. ambassador to Kuwait, acknowledged the initial difficulties as well as the long-term challenges facing his effort. "If this were easy, people would have done it a long time ago," he said. The center's focus is as much about understanding its target audience—eighteen-to-thirty-year-old men, mostly in the Middle East—as it is about devising messages that steer them away from violent extremism. "The words are important, but they only get you so far," said LeBaron. "It's about translating those messages so they resonate with the right people and people around them who have influence." In one online video mash-up posted to You-Tube in February 2011, the digital outreach teams spliced together scenes of jubilant protesters celebrating the resignation of Egyptian president Hosni Mubarak with a videotaped statement in 2008 from Ayman al-Zawahri insisting that "there is no hope to remove the corrupt regimes in Muslim countries except by force." When Zawahri asked, "Let anyone who disagrees give me a single example," the video clip shifted to the jubiliant throng in Cairo's Tahrir Square. Forty-eight hours after the video was posted, it had garnered 42,000 hits.

Within Benjamin's office, another small team oversees global efforts to combat extremist voices. The effort seeks to identify and support grassroots campaigns intent on organizing civil society against violent extremism. These groups must operate independently of the U.S. government in order to have credibility in challenging extremist ideologues. One such organization is Sisters Against Violent Extremism, part of the global Women Without Borders campaign. This organization links women in countries like India, Pakistan, Yemen, Northern Ireland, and Israel into a global network. SAVE organizes country-specific training programs for women interested in participating, programs that cover topics such as computer literacy, English-language education, and small-business skills. The State Department helps to support this organization with a small grant every year to supplement its own fund-raising efforts. According to an official involved in the program, the State Department does not participate in any of the program's planning or advocacy programs.

Even as Obama aimed his rhetorical missiles at Al Qaeda, the Pentagon and State Department were drawing on state-of-the-art technology to thwart the militants' message from literally reaching its intended target. American officials in Kabul devised a sophisticated jamming campaign, and the technology and techniques used by the U.S. military in Afghanistan are something they want to share with the Pakistanis to employ on their side of the border. It is a specific type of jamming called overbroadcast, whereby favorable programming is sent with a stronger signal over the precise frequency used by insurgent "pirate" radio stations. That's the first step. The second step is to have counterprogramming also broadcast to either side of the dial from the pirate station that is the target of the overbroadcast. What happens then is that the insurgents' audience spins the dial left or right in search of the insurgent programming but lands instead on the favorable programming on the adjacent channel. This system not only blots out the insurgent transmissions but also drives listeners to channels filled with programming that counters the extremist message. The trick is that this has to happen in real time, since some of the pirate stations are in the backs of trucks or even towed in trailers behind motorcycles. But the United States has technology to track the pirate signals, determine the broadcast frequency, and set in motion a system of overbroadcast and adjacent counterprogramming. "The goal is fuzzing out the militants' radio broadcasts so everybody has to turn to another station—and that station is yours," said one official involved in the effort. "The capability to track, direction-find, locate and overbroadcast a signal is commercial, off-the-shelf stuff for about $10,000," the official said. "Put it on a truck with a little power, say fifty watts, and you're in business. Most of the bad pirate radio is just two or three watts—village-level stuff."

But in the most contested battle spaces, the extremists have proved more nimble and adaptive in fighting the strategic narrative. In two audio recordings from Osama bin Laden released in early October 2010, the Al Qaeda founder showed a softer side by urging help for victims of the recent massive floods in Pakistan. Despite a considerable effort by the United States to get food, medical, and other supplies to the hard-hit areas, bin Laden's call for disaster relief appeared to show that his concerns range beyond plotting murderous violence. In Afghanistan, allied officials acknowledge that the sophisticated multimillion-dollar propa-

ganda campaign that the Taliban runs out of Pakistan has become
adept at exploiting rifts between the Obama administration and
the Afghan government, portraying the West as at the edge of failure in its campaign to defeat the insurgents and disparaging the
Karzai government as a corrupt stooge of the West. Moreover, the
Taliban appears nimble enough to respond to external criticisms.
In September 2010, Mullah Muhammad Omar, the leader of the
Afghan Taliban, issued a statement saying that his group would
respect the rights of all Afghans, a reference to criticism of the Taliban's treatment of women. Omar also said that the Taliban had a
specific plan for leading the country again. While the Taliban posts
messages on Facebook and Twitter that are easy to disseminate
online, the American-led coalition is struggling to keep up by translating some of its own news releases into Dari and Pashto, the main
languages spoken in Afghanistan.

With the Obama administration's focus on "combating violent
extremism," government agencies are also revamping strategic
messages at home and abroad. Daniel Benjamin at the State Department has launched a new program in coordination with embassies worldwide, designed to tailor counternarratives for specific
communities, even neighborhoods, rather than a one-size-fits-all
approach. In town hall–style talks and media interviews, tackling
violent extremism is a major theme for top Obama advisers,
including Secretary of State Clinton, Homeland Security Secretary
Janet Napolitano, and counterterrorism czar John Brennan. Denis
McDonough underscored it in a speech to a mosque in Sterling,
Virginia, in March 2011: "We can either play into Al Qaeda's narrative and messaging or we can challenge it and thereby undermine it. We're determined to undermine it." The theme is often
embedded in the memos Ben Rhodes regularly sends to Obama,
updating him on the progress of initiatives launched after the
speech in Cairo. And American officials are becoming more aware
of their strengths and their limits in countering the violent extremist message. "We have come to a realization of what is in the art of

the possible and what is not and what's our role, and more importantly, what is not our role," said John Tyson, the DIA analyst.
"Now it is learning how to better execute those parts that we think
we actually have a role in."

In Washington, the officials from the Pentagon, the State
Department, the FBI, Homeland Security, and the National Counterterrorism Center are dividing up responsibilities for countering the extremist narrative, assigning people to new jobs and
allotting them budgets, and then making necessary adjustments.
The first step, officials say, is to prevent extremism from spreading, before dismantling and defeating terrorist networks. That
means engaging with groups who may not admire the United
States but oppose Al Qaeda even more. "This is not about getting
them to love us," said one Defense Department official who is
deeply involved in the discussions. "It is about getting them not to
challenge our interests."

Second, the Obama administration is confronting the same
obstacles as the Bush administration before it. Is there a coordinated plan among all the federal agencies to combat violent
extremism? "Every night, I get on my knees and pray for this kind
of coordination," the Defense Department official said, warning
that terrorist networks are much more agile and fast-moving than
large government bureaucracies. "We're a half step behind or
more," the official added. "That gap ebbs and flows. Sometimes,
we're way behind." Al Qaeda's narrative can draw sustenance from
the most unexpected quarters: a little known Florida pastor who
set off a deadly rampage in Afghanistan when he burned a copy of
the Koran in the spring of 2011, or an American-born radical
cleric named Anwar al-Awlaki, now hiding in a remote corner of
Yemen, whose English-language diatribes against the United States
have motivated a new generation of Western jihadists.

The third major challenge is to tackle the growing threat from
American citizens and residents who have been radicalized at
home or abroad. A report published in September 2010 by the

Bipartisan Policy Center's National Security Preparedness Group, which is headed by 9/11 Commission Chairman Thomas Kean and Vice Chairman Lee Hamilton, found that no agency in the U.S. government is charged with monitoring and stopping the radicalization and recruitment of Americans. Michael Leiter of the National Counterterrorism Center argues that no single agency in the government should have that responsibility because no single organization has all the tools to counter radicalization effectively. Leiter's strategy to counter the extremist narrative is multipronged, focusing on highlighting Al Qaeda's failures but in a relatively quiet way: to deny the terrorists the publicity and stature they seek. "It is not always best for us to hammer the counterterrorism drum over and over again, because by doing so we can in fact glorify Al Qaeda," he said in a speech in December 2010.

The United States, Leiter maintained, must also empower local governments and local organizations that have credibility in working with Muslim communities to solve local grievances. That will help counter Al Qaeda's effort to wrap those local grievances into a global jihad with the toxic message that the West is at war with Islam. "The U.S. government clearly has a challenge in terms of messaging," he said in an earlier speech in June 2010. "The single biggest change from the Bush administration to the Obama administration is the greater focus, though still not a perfect one, on counterradicalization and messaging rather than the hard elements of national power."

Though Leiter warned that "we are farther behind than I would like" in reversing the trend toward the radicalization of American extremists, he remained confident. "We help make our own luck," he said, referring to all the steps that have been taken since 9/11 to prevent another attack. However, the day is coming for the United States when that luck runs out.

7

THE NEW NETWORK WARFARE

The community of professional national-security strategists in Washington travels on what some dismiss as a merry-go-round but really is an industrial-strength conveyor belt. By late 2010 both Barry Pavel and Matt Kroenig were back at the Pentagon; Pavel after a senior-level tour of duty on the National Security Council and Kroenig on a break from academic duties at Georgetown University. Pavel was there only briefly before moving out of public service and into the policy-analyst community. Kroenig remained into 2011, still working on deterrence issues, but this time applying lessons of Cold War deterrence to another twenty-first-century threat: how the United States should respond to the potential of Iran acquiring nuclear weapons. A half decade after their proposal had been handed to President Bush at his Texas ranch by Donald Rumsfeld, their initiatives had been disseminated throughout the national-security apparatus and embraced by like-minded thinkers across the military, intelligence, diplomatic, and law enforcement communities. Their language had expanded to become part of the daily operational vernacular. Perhaps General Stanley McChrystal gave this broad analysis its most succinct expression: "It takes a network to defeat a network."

Vickers said. "But if we can deter the support network—recruiters, financial supporters, local security providers, and states who provide sanctuary—then we can start achieving a deterrent effect on the whole terrorist network and constrain terrorists' ability to operate. We have not deterred terrorists from their intention to do us great harm, but by constraining their means and taking away various tools, we approach the overall deterrent effect we want."

"It doesn't take a lot of money to be a terrorist. But it takes a lot of money to be a terrorist organization." That is the mantra of the financial tracking teams operating out of Central Command's headquarters at MacDill Air Force Base in Tampa. "If it's not job number one, then it's number one-A," said a senior officer. The challenges in cracking the financial support of terrorism are daunting. Significant funds are raised over the Internet, a virtual safe haven for terror organizations. "There are these terror web sites where, in essence, it says: 'You know it's your Koranic duty to make Jihad. If you can't, click here to send money . . .'" said another Central Command money specialist. The Web relationship does more than fund militancy; it's a scouting service. Any donation could be a first step to greater commitment by a potential future jihadist.

The other challenge to cutting off the movement of money by terror networks is the historic system of Hawalas, the money transfer houses operating throughout the Muslim world, an incredibly efficient and effective method based on honor, trust, and confidentiality. Walk into a Hawala office in one city. Hand over funds with a name and destination city. That Hawala operator phones or e-mails his contacts in that second city with instructions and, just as easily, a code phrase to identify the recipient. No paperwork. No wire transaction record. No signed receipts of deposit or transfer. Just a promise to settle the debt later, minus a small commission.

One successful military campaign was mounted in late 2009

and early 2010 against the Hawala network in Nangarhar, Afghanistan, which was funding vicious Taliban attacks in villages along
the border with Pakistan. "Many Hawala buildings have three-
hundred-plus separate family businesses doing the same work, so
the Taliban and other insurgents have options if we take out one,"
said a Central Command officer involved in the campaign. "So we
took out six. We mounted an information-operations campaign
that said to the others, 'If you pick up the Taliban business, you will
lose the quality of life and your families will suffer a drop in well-
being.' This requires patience and maturity."

Mature terror networks that want to move larger sums interna-
tionally do have to accept the visibility of the modern financial system, which makes them susceptible to notice, tracking, and penalty
by governments, including the U.S. Department of the Treasury.
Juan Zarate had been particularly successful in this kind of financial
detective work. "At Treasury, we used financial information and
tracks to lead to terrorist cells and networks, worked to disrupt and
dismantle funding networks and aggressively freeze assets," he said.
As government analysts crack the relationships in the money-
transfer arm of a militant organization, "The question is, which key
person to affect?" said one American official. "There are more lawyers involved in this effort than shooters." The goal is to identify
and sanction any individual who has influence on a financial network at multiple levels or is involved with several militant money
networks. That's simple financial theory: economies of scale.

"The important person in this chain is the one with the relationships, whose skill set is required to find and hide the money,
who knows the laws and customs necessary to move it around,"
said one intelligence community money tracker. "He might not be
so willing to so quickly enter the hereafter as a hard-core Jihadi,
and so is susceptible to pressure and probably easier to find and
arrest." The death of Mustafa Abu al-Yazid, Al Qaeda's chief
financial officer, in May 2010 from an American missile strike in
northwest Pakistan underscored how removing a vital link in the

terrorist chain can seriously disrupt the entire network. Yazid was one of Al Qaeda's founders and was considered by American intelligence officials to be the organization's number-three leader, behind bin Laden and Zawahri.

Even before Yazid's death, American intelligence officials said that Al Qaeda was in such tight financial straits that it was requiring its operatives to pay for their own room and board, training, and weapons. Yazid's demise put a serious dent in Al Qaeda's ability to tap its donor Rolodex and forced the group to turn to more junior financial facilitators who lacked Yazid's contacts and his understanding of the most effective ways to move money. "More than anyone else, Yazid possessed links to the deep-pocketed donors in the Arabian Peninsula and beyond who have historically formed the backbone of al Qaeda's financial support network," said Stuart A. Levey, the undersecretary of the treasury for terrorism and financial intelligence, soon after Yazid was killed. "Wealthy donors gave their money and, more important, placed their trust in Yazid, which makes him exceedingly difficult to replace."

By 2010, however, many millions of dollars were still flowing largely unimpeded to extremist groups worldwide, and the Obama administration was exasperated by frequent resistance from allies in the Middle East to combating the problem. As revealed in the secret State Department cables originally obtained by WikiLeaks, terrorist financiers use a cunning array of strategies to fill their coffers, including kidnappings for ransom in North Africa, the harvesting of drug proceeds in Afghanistan, and fund-raising at religious pilgrimages to Mecca, where large amounts of currency change hands. One episode that ignited particular concern occurred in August 2009 in Yemen, when armed robbers stormed a bank truck on a busy downtown street in Aden during daylight hours and stole 100 million Yemeni *riyals*, or about $500,000. American diplomats said the sophistication of the robbery and other indicators bore the hallmarks of an Al Qaeda mission. A February 2010 cable to Richard C. Holbrooke, the administration's special representative for Afghanistan and Pakistan, said that "sensitive reporting indicates that al Qaeda's ability to raise funds has deteriorated substantially, and that it is now in its weakest state since 9/11." But many other cables noted the terrorist group's knack for generating money almost at will from wealthy individuals and sympathetic groups, including charities, throughout the Middle East while often outfoxing counterterrorism officials with a bewildering spectrum of money-shifting schemes. "Emerging trends include mobile banking, pre-paid cards, and Internet banking," the cable observed.

In recent years, officials in the Bush and Obama administrations have sounded upbeat about their advances in disrupting terrorist financing. But internal State Department cables offer a more pessimistic view, with blunt assessments of the threats to the United States from money flowing to militants affiliated with Al Qaeda, the Taliban, Hamas, Lashkar-e-Taiba, and other groups. A classified memo sent by Secretary of State Clinton in December 2009 singled out residents of Saudi Arabia and its neighbors, all allies of the United States, as the chief financial supporters of many extremist activities. "It has been an ongoing challenge to persuade Saudi officials to treat terrorist financing emanating from Saudi Arabia as a strategic priority," the cable said, concluding that "donors in Saudi Arabia constitute the most significant source of funding to Sunni terrorist groups worldwide."

Of course, this was the same Saudi Arabia that is a staunch military and diplomatic ally of Washington. Saudi spies have funneled information about suspected terrorist plots involving militants in neighboring Yemen to the United States and its European allies. They provided the tip that helped uncover the October 2010 plot to blow up American-bound cargo planes with computer printer cartridges packed with explosives. By that time, American officials said that Saudi Arabia was taking actions that they had long hesitated to take or had resisted, including holding financiers accountable through prosecutions and making terrorist financing a higher priority. A leading group of Saudi religious scholars issued a fatwa against terrorist financing in May 2010, and the Saudis created a new financial intelligence unit.

But even with this progress, "terrorist funding emanating from Saudi Arabia remains a serious concern," according to a cable in February 2010 written by diplomats at the U.S. Embassy in Riyadh. The diplomats expressed frustration that the Saudis remained "almost completely dependent on the Central Intelligence Agency for names, addresses and other direction on terrorist financing." They said in an earlier cable that while the Saudis appeared earnest in wanting to stanch the flow of terrorist money, they often lacked the training and expertise to do it. "Their capabilities often fall short of their aspirations," read this cable from November 2009. The cables reveal that Saudi leaders appear equally resigned to the situation. "We are trying to do our best," one cable quoted Prince Mohammed bin Nayef, who led the Saudis' antiterrorism activities, as telling Holbrooke in a May 2009 meeting. But, the Saudi prince said, "If money wants to go" to terrorist causes, "it will go."

The diplomatic cables offered similarly grim views about the United Arab Emirates ("a strategic gap" that terrorists can exploit), Qatar ("the worst in the region" on counterterrorism), and Kuwait ("a key transit point"). Secretary Clinton stressed the need to "generate the political will necessary" to block money to terrorist networks—groups that she said were "threatening stability in Pakistan and Afghanistan and targeting coalition soldiers."

While President George W. Bush often vowed to cut off financing for militants and pledged to make financiers as culpable as the terrorists who carried out plots, President Obama has struck a more muted public position on the issue as he has tried to adopt a more conciliatory tone with Arab nations. The Obama administration has used many of the same covert diplomatic, intelligence, and law enforcement tools as its predecessor and set up a special task force in the summer of 2009 to deal with the growing problem.

While federal officials can point to some successes—prosecutions, seizures of money, and tightened money-laundering regulations in foreign countries—the results have often been frustrating, the cables show. Even as the United States urged its Persian Gulf allies to crack down on suspected supporters of terrorism, these countries' leaders have pushed back. In private meetings, they accused American officials of heavy-handedness and of presenting thin evidence of wrongdoing by Arab charities or individuals, according to numerous cables. Kuwaiti officials, for example, resisted what they called "draconian" measures sought by the United States against a prominent charity and dismissed allegations against it as "unconvincing."

The same goal of neutralizing financiers held true for the gun runners, explosives procurers, and weapons handlers. "The guys who are doing the weapons transfers? This became a blinding flash of the obvious to us," said one commander with multiple tours tracking terror networks in the Middle East. "These guys aren't part of a terrorist network; they are just running guns. They are just trying to make money. So you could take apart another strand of that network—the gun runners and the guys who would provide the ammunition and stuff like that. It's easy to put the squeeze on them. They were just in it for making cash."

Another linchpin of a terror network is the religious leader who blesses an attack. Heavenly reward will not await a suicide bomber unless his death and those of his victims is deemed halal, in keeping with Islam's sacred Sharia law. Each militant network has a Sharia emir, usually at the level of a sheik or mullah. According to one military officer with command experience in Iraq, the cleric is the essential piece of the puzzle: "Take him out, and suicide bombings from that network are frozen until he is replaced. Suicide bombers won't go ahead with a mission without the blessing."

Targeting experts at Central Command also made a specialty of toying with the egos of terror commanders, upgrading and downgrading the hefty federal bounties offered for Al Qaeda, Taliban, and other insurgent captains. "They are very proud," said one action officer. "Hubris is a sin. We can play to their psychology." To be sure, senior leaders like bin Laden or Zawahri were viewed as too sophisticated to fall for the ploy. "But with a midlevel commander, it has great tactical effect," the officer said. Here's how it works: Military and intelligence analysts draw up a list of high-value targets. There is a public announcement that the bounty on a particular terrorist leader's head has been slashed. Word is whispered in the local markets that the commander isn't worth a higher reward because he has been injured or has been deemed incompetent. "This smokes him out," said the Central Command officer. "If we think they are wounded, we can pull the money, as if to say he's dead. He'll try and do something that brings him up on the net. He wants to say I'm alive. He wants to prove he is still important and worthy of the higher bounty." Even senior members of Al Qaeda's global network have been suckered by the ruse and have been picked up after they made themselves more visible not long after the bounty on their heads was reduced. General McChrystal was fond of telling his subordinates in Special Operations units, "When a person moves, that's when we can get them. If they sit in a hole and are not taking any chances, we can't get them."

There is another tactic to reduce enemy effectiveness. "You have to take the people with specialized expertise off the battlefield," Michael Leiter said. "You can have strategic effect. What appear to be tactical wins can have strategic effect." He cited the death of Abu Khabab al-Masri, one of the lead planners in Pakistan for Al Qaeda's program to develop or obtain chemical, biological, radiological, or nuclear weapons (CBRN). "That had, we believe, a strategic effect on Al Qaeda's ability to come up with complicated CBRN," Leiter said. "So, there are times where what seems like just a guy can really change the whole outlook."

■ ■ ■

The military will go to the ends of the earth to get those militants and their networks. They go to the tiny desert nation of Djibouti on the Horn of Africa. It may not be the end of the world,
but you can see it from there. Which is why the American military
scraped the hard rock and sandy soil; rebuilt a former French Foreign Legion base, Camp Lemonier; and quietly installed a couple
of thousand troops on a mission that is a model for how the Pentagon tries to get ahead of the terrorists before they have a chance
to plant their colors and set up networks in inhospitable, barely
governed places.

The emphasis is on a near-invisible military presence that is not
a political burden on host governments. In this place where American forces never were based before, they now operate from a
Spartan forward position within easy reach of the wild, ungoverned swaths across the Horn of Africa that prove attractive to
terrorists seeking a safe haven. To an unusual degree, the mission
has lashed together the government's entire national security structure. Officers there describe a high level of cooperation among conventional military forces, the more secretive Special Operations
teams, and the American intelligence community. Representatives
from other government agencies, including customs and agricul-
ture, routinely pass through.

Despite fractures between the United States and some of its
closest allies over the war in Iraq, the Djibouti mission is cited as
an example of smooth coalition cooperation. The American-led
ground force closely coordinates with the international naval
armada plying waters just offshore to deter and, if required, to
interdict terrorists who may try to sneak past. That naval mission
swaps command among allies, giving them a stake and a share of
the effort. With small forces keeping the pressure on terrorists who
may try to operate across a huge corner of the world, the mission at

Camp Lemonier has attracted the attention, and the praise, of the nation's most senior military commanders.

High-level military and intelligence officers, pressed by the accountants back in Washington to explain the cost of a base in the middle of nowhere that rarely fires a shot, argue that it represents part of the "new deterrence," one carried out by troops and civilian analysts and a healthy dose of public works engineers. If America didn't have such a focused effort in that particular piece of geography, it could lead to new terrorist safe havens and certainly would invite the movement of terrorists and perhaps even new training camps, the officers maintain. The mission has settled into a quiet rhythm since Combined Joint Task Force–Horn of Africa was established in late 2002 at a base so primitive that the most serious security threat comes from attacks by hyenas and jackals that do not heed the barbed wire and guard towers that rise from the hardscrabble desert floor around the base.

The task force was initially designed to trap terrorists that Pentagon leaders believed would flee Afghanistan along traditional smugglers' routes down the Persian Gulf, into the Arabian Sea, and past the Horn of Africa. But the overlapping ground, maritime, and air patrols across the region appear to have deterred the use of that route, prompting Al Qaeda senior leaders to hunker down in the tribal areas of Pakistan and some, perhaps, to travel instead to Iraq to fight American and coalition forces there.

"We by ourselves don't really pursue the threat of terrorism in the Horn of Africa," said Major General Samuel T. Helland of the Marine Corps, one of the task force commanders. "Our job is to prevent it, deter it, and to support the host nations as they develop the capability that they require to fight the terrorist threat that is germane to their countries." The headquarters began the mission aboard a ship off the Horn of Africa in 2002 and moved ashore in 2003. But many within the Pentagon did not see the virtue of this mission and argued for reassigning the personnel back to a combat zone. One of those who fought to secure the mission was Lieutenant General Douglas E. Lute, the director of operations for Central Command from 2004 to 2006. He has since moved on to the National Security Council, where he served Presidents Bush and Obama as a director for policy on Iraq and Afghanistan. The Horn of Africa task force, he said, "is a model of how we can deter terrorists by interacting with local nationals in an effort to help them help themselves without the burden of a large American military presence. The model includes the ability to lace together not only all of the agencies and components of the American government, but also to reach out and bring in the strength of coalition partners."

American intelligence and military officers are certain that members of Al Qaeda and other terrorist groups continue to move through the region, with some small numbers setting up and operating in ungoverned corners of Somalia, Sudan, and Yemen. Camp Lemonier is just a dozen miles from the Somali border. And as if to emphasize the danger of not keeping an eye on the region, pictures hanging on headquarters walls at the base serve as reminders of the simultaneous Al Qaeda attacks in 1998 on the American embassies in Kenya and Tanzania. Those were the powerful images of Al Qaeda terror before bin Laden's organization attacked the *Cole*, brought down the twin towers, and destroyed a wedge of the Pentagon.

Those reminders help offset the burden of serving in a very uncomfortable climate. Djibouti is the hottest place on the planet that sustains non-nomadic habitation, so it's easy to see, and feel, how it and neighboring countries remain ripe to becoming a habitat for terrorists, too. Large youth population. Few jobs. Hot time waiting for a flight out can be spent counting the number of government cargo planes off-loading the country's only cash crop: khat, the light narcotic, in chewable form, that for decades has been a revenue-generating crop for the government.

The task force was organized with responsibilities for the coun-

terterrorism mission not only in Djibouti but also in Eritrea, Ethio-
pia, Kenya, Somalia, Sudan, and Yemen, an area almost 70 percent
of the size of the continental United States. The location provides
a unique platform for intelligence officers to watch for terrorists'
movements, and the military forces on the ground, along with
those at other bases in the region always on call, keep the pressure
on. The Special Operations and intelligence communities, under
presidential "execute orders," maintain smaller presences in some
of those countries, missions they have tried to keep invisible.

Should military action be required, commanders say they have
not forgotten the lesson of the CIA's mission in November 2002,
when a Predator surveillance aircraft blasted a car in Yemen, killing an Al Qaeda operative and five others, including an American
citizen. The strike was characterized as a success, but it only added
to the outrage of many leaders across the Horn of Africa that their
sovereignty would not be respected. Djibouti continues to be a base
for Predator reconnaissance missions across the region, but as a
concession to local political sensitivities, and in an acknowledgment
of the need to preserve relations with Ali Abdullah Saleh, the
Yemeni president, for at least the next eight years there were no
more armed Predator strikes against terror targets in Yemen flown
from Djibouti. In the years since that strike, the United States has
invested hundreds of millions of dollars in Yemen's security forces,
hoping to give that vulnerable nation the ability to carry out the
fight on its own.

The commanders at Camp Lemonier and senior officers at the
Pentagon say that American forces in the Horn of Africa would
act only in support of and at the request of the host government, a
legal formulation that also characterizes past missions in such
places as Pakistan, where unilateral American action always carries a heavy political price. The mission also focuses on border
security and teaching counterterrorism skills to local forces, so
they can better deter and disrupt terror networks on their territory
by themselves. Those efforts, Pentagon officials say, represent an

important focus of the policy of deterrence. In this region, that means preventing the creation of another Taliban-run Afghanistan, which served as a safe haven for Al Qaeda to plan the September 11 attacks. "It is a deterrent mission," said one senior Pentagon policy planner involved in standing up the Horn of Africa task force. "Just the fact that it is not a problem does not mean it is a mistake to pay attention. We have prevented a problem. It is a place we keep an eye on lest it become a problem."

Perhaps none of the military's far-flung efforts at establishing counterterrorist networks to fight terror networks better illustrates the cost-benefit analysis than the small force committed to the Philippines. The decision on whether to maintain an elite six-hundred-troop unit there went all the way to Defense Secretary Gates, who ordered the military to sustain the effort despite the military's difficulty in finding enough of these highly trained units for assignments to two wars as well as for the wider effort to combat insurgencies and militancy in other parts of the world deemed to be threats to American interests. The mission of the Combined Joint Special Operations Task Force–Philippines continues to be training local security units and providing logistical and intelligence support to Filipino forces to better understand and fight a local insurgency that has played host to terrorists with global ambitions. Nobody at the Pentagon or CIA has to be reminded that Khalid Shaikh Mohammed and Ramzi Yousef met in the Philippines for an operational planning session in advance of the September 11 attacks.

Senior officials say the American unit has been instrumental in successes by the Filipino armed forces in the years since 2001 in killing and capturing leaders of the militant group Abu Sayyaf and the Moro Island Liberation front, antigovernment organizations operating in the south. In a simultaneous counterinsurgency effort in the Philippines, members of the American force have completed hundreds of infrastructure projects, including roads, schools, clinics, and firehouses, and have conducted medical examinations and administered vaccines.

Admiral Timothy J. Keating, who oversaw the mission when he was commander of American forces in the Pacific, said that the task force's work, with its tiny footprint, might never be completed. "The successes we enjoy, and the gains, can tend to anesthetize us a little bit," he said. In making his case, he had the support of Leon E. Panetta, the CIA director at the time, who made quiet—and unannounced—visits to personally inspect the unit's operations. The task force even gets high marks from the often skeptical international development and human rights community. "In general, the Joint Special Operations Task Force–Philippines has been regarded as a success story, especially in terms of winning hearts and minds through civic action and medical assistance projects," said Mark L. Schneider, the senior vice president of the International Crisis Group.

Colonel Bill Coultrup, a veteran Special Operations officer picked to serve as Philippines task force commander, said that his goal was simple: "Help the Philippines security forces. It's their fight. We don't want to take over." Coultrup, a veteran of General McChrystal's Special Operations units, understands how it takes a network to fight one. His service includes deployments with Special Operations units in Iraq, Afghanistan, Somalia, and Bosnia, where the mission focused on capturing or killing adversaries. But in the Philippines, Coultrup's work has been only 20 percent combat related. That portion of the military mission is designed to "help the armed forces of the Philippines neutralize high-value targets—individuals who will never change their minds," he said. Eighty percent of the effort, though, has been "civil-military operations to change the conditions that allow those high-value targets to have a safe haven," Coultrup added. "We do that through helping give a better life to the citizens: good governance, better health care, a higher standard of living. That's our network. If ours is stronger, and is there first—that's how we prevent the bad guys from getting a grip on the local population."

But none of those regional missions can compare to the delicate, sensitive, and critically important American support of Pakistan as it battles terror networks operating from safe havens on its territory. It is a mission that American officials do not like to talk about.

At an observation post in the bare brown foothills of the soaring mountains of South Waziristan, Major Shazad Saleem of the Pakistani Army's 57th Punjab Regiment pointed across the Makeen valley to the craggy nine-thousand-foot peaks and warned two visiting reporters to pull their armored vests tight. "There are still snipers out there," he said, with only a faint smile. It was June 2010, and nine months earlier thousands of Pakistani soldiers, including Major Saleem's 326th Brigade, had fought through ambushes and roadside bombings to take back this strategically vital passageway between North and South Waziristan from militants sheltered in scrub and riverbank hideouts. Makeen, a small village fifteen miles east of the Afghan border, had been the home base for the Pakistani Taliban leader Baitullah Mehsud before he was killed by a CIA drone attack in August 2009. At that time, the region teemed with Uzbek, Arab, Afghan, and Pakistani fighters. Makeen was also the village where the *New York Times* correspondent David Rohde and his two Afghan companions were held hostage during part of their seven months in captivity with the Taliban. A walled school compound that had been Mehsud's headquarters lay in ruins, its metal corrugated roofing twisted like taffy from American drone strikes and Pakistani artillery fire. Makeen and several other small villages in the valley were quiet now except for Pakistani Army patrols motoring up and down the two-lane road. The army had ordered all civilians to leave Makeen before launching its offensive, an edict that extended throughout South Waziristan.

The tactic enabled the army to turn the region into a free-fire zone, figuring anyone who stayed was a militant. But it also forced hundreds of thousands of men, women, and children into make-shift tent camps set up on the edge of the combat zone.

Major Saleem, a sixteen-year veteran whose grandfather served in the British Army when Pakistan was still a part of British India, said that his troops were the vanguard of a new program to train Pakistani soldiers for up to a year in "low-intensity conflict" before deploying. The Pakistanis do not use the term *counterinsurgency*, favored by the Americans, because they say it suggests the militants have some popular support among local residents. The soldiers have also borrowed tactics from the militants, employing surprise and deception to thwart ambushes and roadside bombings. With only a handful of night-vision goggles to share among them, Major Saleem's soldiers have become more adept at operating by moon-light, often hugging the edges of steep riverbanks while on patrols to avoid detection. "We are determined to stay until we finish this menace," he said.

In a larger regional offensive that had been under way for two years, the Pakistani Army was finding counterinsurgency warfare tougher and more costly than anticipated. On this day automatic rifle fire could be heard from deep in the valley. At a makeshift trauma center at the army's base in Razmak, North Waziristan, a young Pakistani soldier lay anesthetized on the operating table, blood-soaked bandages applied in the field a testament to a near-fatal wound. The bullet through his neck from a Taliban fighter had narrowly missed an artery, and after some minor surgery, the army medics declared the patient out of danger.

Much like the challenge facing American and NATO forces in Afghanistan, a lack of Pakistani civilian authority has made it nearly impossible to consolidate military gains in contested areas like South Waziristan. While the long campaign has eliminated some Pakistani Taliban insurgents, it has also dispersed many other fighters, forcing the Pakistani Army in effect to chase them from one part of the tribal areas to another. The country's devastating floods in 2010 have forced the military to shelve new attacks against safe havens in North Waziristan and settle for trying to hold areas already cleared of militants.

Part of America's evolving "new deterrence" strategy is to train and assist national armies and security forces to fight their own insurgencies so American troops do not have to. From the Philippines to Mali to Pakistan, American forces are imparting their skills in marksmanship, tactics, and strategy, while trading on their partners' knowledge of language, culture, and terrain to counter their local enemies.

A graduation ceremony in June 2010 for Pakistani troops trained by Americans to fight the Taliban and Al Qaeda was the scene of festivities at the Warsak Center, north of Peshawar, which were intended as a show of fresh cooperation between the Pakistani and American militaries. But it said just as much about the limitations of such cooperation. Nearly 250 Pakistani paramilitary troops in khaki uniforms and green berets snapped to attention, with the top students accepting a certificate from a U.S. Army colonel after completing the specialized training for snipers and for platoon and company leaders. But the new center, twenty miles from the Afghanistan border, was built to train as many as two thousand soldiers at a time. The largest component of the American-financed instruction—a ten-week basic-training course—was months behind schedule, largely because Pakistani commanders said they could not afford to send troops for new training as fighting intensified in the border areas.

Pakistan restricts the number of American trainers throughout the country to no more than about 120 Special Operations personnel, fearful of being identified too closely with the unpopular United States, even though the Americans reimburse Pakistan more than $1 billion a year for its military operations in the border areas. "We want to keep a low signature," a senior Pakistani officer said. The deep suspicion with which every American move in

Pakistan is regarded has become a fact of life that American officers must work through as they try to reverse the effects of the
many years when the United States had cut Pakistan off from military aid because of its nuclear weapons program. That period of
estrangement through the 1990s left the Pakistanis feeling scorned
and abandoned by the United States, and its military disenchanted
with America and seeded with officers and soldiers sympathetic to
conservative Islam—and even at times to the very militants they
vow to fight today. The training program at Warsak is one of the
first steps the American military has taken to help soothe the
rising anti-American sentiment, even among the Pakistani officer
corps. "This is the most complex operating environment I've
ever dealt with," said Colonel Kurt Sonntag, the West Point graduate and Special Forces officer who handed out the graduation
certificates.

The personnel training is just one part of what is now a multi-
faceted security relationship aimed at improving Pakistan's security forces so they can combat a militancy that is spreading beyond
the remote tribal areas to the more populated "settled" areas of
Punjab and Sindh. To combat Al Qaeda and the Taliban, the United
States provides Pakistan with a wide array of weapons from body
armor to F-16 fighter jets, shares intelligence about the militants,
and has given the country more than $10 billion toward the cost
of deploying nearly 150,000 Pakistani troops in and around the
border areas since 2001—with the promise of much more to
come.

About a dozen American trainers were assigned in 2010 to
yearlong duty at the training center in Warsak, for which the United
States spent $23 million on construction, plus another $30 million
on training and equipment. Much of the training at Warsak is
aimed at building the confidence of the Frontier Corps scouts, some
of whom have relatives in the Taliban and who speak the same language, Pashto, as many militants. One of the challenges is that the
militants are often better armed and more handsomely paid than

the scouts. Three basic skills were built into the course: how to shoot straight, how to administer battlefield first aid, and how to provide covering fire for advancing troops. Until a few years ago, the Frontier Corps was widely ridiculed as corrupt and incompetent, but under the leadership of Lieutenant General Tariq Khan, salaries quadrupled to about $200 a month, and new equipment is flowing in. The scouts are winning praise in combat and attracting young men who might otherwise fall prey to jihadist entreaties and ideology.

General Khan, a portly former tank commander who battled Baitullah Mehsud in South Waziristan, offered an early and qualified judgment on the effort. He said that the training was still "settling down and maturing."

One of the most violent terror networks that bloodied the people of Iraq, and the American and allied forces fighting to secure the country, was the diabolical genius of Al Qaeda in organizing attacks by female suicide bombers in markets, polling places, police stations, and theaters. It is all but impossible to detect an explosive vest hidden under a woman's loose-fitting *abaya*; in a traditional Muslim society, women cannot be searched by men, and the all-male Iraqi Army is bound by tradition. There were never enough women in the Iraqi Interior Ministry's police force for the task. This makes deterrence even more crucial.

Over the years, there had been specific, if tactical, successes against the female suicide bombing cells. Ahead of any elections in Iraq, for example, the military issued warnings that insurgents would try to slip bomb-laden suicide vests into polling places beneath the long gowns of Iraqi women or of men in women's clothing. But a snap program first organized by Lieutenant General Thomas Metz in Iraq helped address the problem. He set up a system in which one of the first women to arrive at a large polling place for any vote would be searched and cleared. That woman would in turn be asked to search ten others. Each of those ten would then search ten others before voting and so on in a daisy chain throughout election day. The solution was a success but can hardly be replicated every day at every public gathering spot across Iraq.

Commanders were cognizant that there had to be a more permanent effort to take down the female suicide bombing network. Lieutenant General Mark P. Hertling, on his second tour in Iraq—this time in command of the 1st Armored Division—took up the challenge. Hertling, one of the Army's new breed of "pentathlete commanders" to come out of the wars since 9/11, understands not only the role of physical combat in counterinsurgency but also that of economic and political development, programs to train local forces, and efforts to manage the information war inside the war. Hertling and his wife, Sue, also typify the military family that is sustaining the all-volunteer force, proof that while politicians may talk of America as a nation at war, it's really just a tiny percentage of military families at war: The Hertlings have two sons and a daughter-in-law in uniform, all having completed multiple combat tours.

Hertling and his troops based in northern Iraq, who saw the rising chaos from Al Qaeda bombings, sought innovative ways to disrupt the larger female suicide network and, even more, to deter women from signing up. Part of their campaign was to find ways to counter the idea that the bombings were justified under religious tenets. The Americans wanted to get the word out that at least some of the women who carried out the attacks had been coerced, although some were widows of terrorists and some appeared driven by outrage over the deaths of brothers and fathers. Hertling sought the counsel of prominent Iraqi women, including politicians and cultural leaders. What he learned, he said, was that "the bombers often had been child brides of terrorists, and their husbands had been killed. The culture is such that there were a lot of young girls—even as young as twelve or thirteen years old—who were forced to marry these Al Qaeda in Mesopotamia guys that came into the country that were all strangers. [They] just came in and went around town grabbing women to satisfy their fighters. If you are forced to marry in a society like that, that's one thing. But when your husband dies, and he was a terrorist, the related shame the women would then feel makes the shaving of collaborating French girls' heads in World War II tame in comparison. Not only do they then become an outcast in society because they've been with these terrorists, but because of the religious-cultural norms, no one else is going marry them, or even take care of them. So they have no food or money, they are extremely poor, they are living in the outskirts of town because that is where they were hiding, and they can't remarry or get any kind of job. So what else is there left other than to revert to the belief in religious propaganda: Blow yourself up, kill an infidel, and go to heaven? I went back to the staff and said, How do we get after this kind of thinking while going after these networks?"

Hertling ordered his division headquarters to organize a first-of-its-kind women's conference, which they held in Erbil, a major city. The general and a senior colonel were the only American men present, and he recruited most of the female soldiers from within the division and the various brigades he commanded to help run the forum. Hertling's wife spoke to the group via satellite TV link-up from the 1st Armored Division's rear headquarters in Germany, sharing her thoughts with the "sisterhood" in Iraq. Hertling then challenged the participants to break with old ways and assist with security. A group of female political leaders from Diyala Province, where most of the female suicide-vest activity had taken place, drew Hertling into a closed discussion about how they could help. Their suggestion: Put Iraqi women into the police academies and make them a part of the security force. Hertling seized the opportunity. "If you can give me a list of two hundred women who will be good police officers," he said, "I'll see if I can work this." By the next day, he had four hundred names. With this roster of volunteers in hand, he went to the police commander in Diyala Province. With great reluctance, the commander eventually agreed that women could enter training as an experiment. A first class of twenty-seven policewomen graduated within weeks, growing within a year to more than sixty women across Diyala, all assigned to markets and other public locations to search for female suicide bombers. This effort then expanded to Kirkuk Province and later Salah Ad Din Province, all hotbeds of female suicide activity.

An unexpected breakthrough in Hertling's effort came when Rania, a fifteen-year-old girl, was captured in Diyala before her explosive vest could be detonated. She told interrogators that she had been given juice that made her queasy and dizzy and that she was wrapped in the vest before being pushed toward a checkpoint. Rania said that her mother was an Al Qaeda sympathizer. The debriefing enabled the Americans and the Iraqis to gain a better understanding of how at least some of these women were recruited, and her information led to the further capture of six other women in the same cell, all widows of Al Qaeda fighters who were primed as suicide bombers. American commanders wanted to spread the word that Rania and others appeared not to have been willing bombers and that the killing of innocent Iraqis could not be defended as an approved religious act. But that had to be done without American fingerprints, which would undermine the message. American officers convened sessions with Iraqi politicians, human rights activists, and journalists, and provided information about the suicide bombers, including specific and significant details of Rania's debriefing. They wanted this information to promote a public debate, but unlike in the early years of the war—when the American military wrote and produced information campaigns and even paid off local reporters—the content of this discussion was left to the Iraqis.

The Iraqi news media leapt on the story. A young female radio host initiated a call-in show outside Baqubah, where Rania was captured, and called the program "Doves of Peace." The discussions of Rania's case became the most popular talk show on regional radio, and the host became an Iraqi wartime Oprah. By the time the 1st Armored Division turned over command of northern Iraq to Iraqi forces as part of the reduction of American troops across the country, instances of female suicide bombers in the region had dropped significantly, although the threat has not disappeared.

"We will never win the hearts and minds of those from Arab cultures, and that's even a bad expression to use as we work with other cultures," Hertling concluded. "Many in the Arab world don't want to be like us. They have no desire to have their hearts and minds won. They have their own cultures, their own values, and they want to keep it that way." If American policy wants Muslim populations to join the effort to counter militant networks, then the United States should strive for winning something different from hearts and minds. The most important goal, Hertling said, "is to win trust and confidence."

There is a grim aphorism cited in counterterrorism circles that describes America's technological advantages but warns of a more compelling national deficit of patience required in tackling militant networks around the globe: America has all the watches, but the terrorists have all the time. Making the case for public commitment to a sustained national security agenda is the job for elected officials. The military and intelligence communities are atop the technology.

No tool has revolutionized the nation's ability to take apart terror networks, or received less acclaim, than the computer or, more specifically, the vast array of supercomputers devoted to the mission. Driven by the NSA, the system can collect, analyze, sort, and store data from a range of communications, in particular cell phone conversations, e-mails, and Web sites, billions of times faster than humans can. It's the same case with data from documents seized on raids or forensic analysis of bombs.

"It's a brute-force effort, but done electronically, and quite elegant," said a longtime member of America's cyberwarfare community now working under General Alexander at the NSA and Cyber Command. This official described how their superclassified computer system can do in seconds the work that otherwise would require tens of thousands of human beings working hundreds of thousands of hours. Just as important, a secure communications system operated by the military and intelligence community offers immediate access to precise data on an entire militant network under review, from high-value terrorists to the lowliest courier, all available via data link to interrogators at remote detainee units in Iraq or Afghanistan and up to senior policy makers preparing for meetings in the corridors of Washington.

Tens of thousands of detainees have passed through American-run camps in Iraq and Afghanistan. Most were seized carrying cell phones, each of which had a dialing history. That raw information is entered into the American database. When recruits voluntarily walk in off the street to apply for a position with the Afghan or Iraqi security forces or a more mundane government job, they check their cell phones at the door. Same with local nationals entering an American compound in the war zones. Each of these cell phones can be copied or cloned in seconds, with the supercomputers scanning the calling history for matches to known terror network members. If there is a match, a team of "strategic debriefers" is called in to question the person about why his phone has been in contact with a targeted terror cell. "We can unravel that," said one military officer who has worked in the program. "It opens the door to a whole command-and-control network. Now we know who we are dealing with." Especially in Iraq, officials said, the cross-referencing of cell phones has led American and Iraqi investigators to government employees, even some serving senior Iraqi leaders, who were hiding direct ties to terror and insurgent networks. The other benefit of the huge archive of cell phone numbers is that the military can track the specific users. "Another major breakthrough: finding and fixing 'bad actors' through technology, in particular cell phones and geo-location," said one official.

The process of "massing intelligence" on an individual has proven to be a more valuable tool than harsh interrogation techniques when a detainee needs to be questioned. "We can go into an interrogation knowing more about a guy than he does—and this is a guy we didn't even care about two hours before," said one military officer. Pictures captured on his cell phone or ones that linked to his. Family names, even of his kids; family history. People with whom he had spoken and knowledge of where he had traveled. "This is the technique: 'We know all,' " the officer said. "We wouldn't just make the detainee think we already knew everything about him, but we actually do know everything about him. It gives us great leverage in forcing a detainee to give up others. There are no secrets left. It is futile to lie." No detail is too small to be left off the counterterror database. "Knowing about a missing toe can help us ID a guy," said one analyst. Forensic review of the kinds of copper wire or rubber washer favored by an explosives network is just as important. Bits of debris remaining after an explosion can be identified and tracked back to the original manufacturer. Not that a chemical company in Florida or a machine-parts plant in Michigan or a wire-bending shop in Italy would be aware that its multiuse parts ended up inside a bomb after purchases by many middlemen. But bomb makers are creatures of habit. They like the same parts. Working the purchase chain can often lead directly to the heart of the network.

Despite these advances in the brute-force power of supercomputer technology, human beings must remain in the decision loop, even though they also remain a weak link. The reason is straightforward: There is no software perceptive enough to look at a video image and separate a Taliban fighter carrying an AK-47 from an Afghan villager carrying a shovel. But the challenge to human analysts has been magnified as the military continues to accelerate its efforts to find, fix, and finish off Al Qaeda and its franchises.

Major General James O. Poss sits atop the Air Force effort as his service's assistant deputy chief of staff for intelligence, surveillance, and reconnaissance, and from a Pentagon office decorated with models of the newest and coolest spy planes, he revels in the accelerating advancements in his technology even as he worries about the ability of human beings to keep up. He confessed that the Air Force has reached out to at least two unusual allies for advice on how to manage its intelligence overload: first, to the National Football League, to see how the organization categorizes and stores years of game film and video, and manages still to quickly access the files; and second, to YouTube, to explore better ways to gather, analyze, and store voluminous video files. "The bad news is, we don't know how to manage all of the information yet," Poss said.

The challenge is obvious at Langley Air Force Base, inside what looks like a redbrick schoolhouse where a warehouse-sized room with dim lighting is home to hundreds of flat-screen TVs that hang from industrial metal skeletons. Air-conditioning guarantees gooseflesh. The occupants are strikingly young. They consume a lot of caffeine and sugar. They speak their own language. The building is called Distributed Common Ground System-1, one of the Air Force's most sensitive installations for processing, exploiting, and disseminating information from the global battlefield. And it is costly: The Air Force piece of this global intelligence, surveillance, and reconnaissance mission alone is priced at $5 billion. Using this network, and for the Air Force alone, each day brings the task of processing one thousand hours of full-motion video, one thousand still images, and hundreds of hours of "signals intelligence," usually cell phone calls, in thirty-eight different languages. That flood of data has fundamentally changed how the military thinks about the fog of war. No longer is it too little information. Today, the problem is too much, and the challenge is seeking new ways to analyze it, prioritize it, and distribute it.

Deep concerns over how to manage all of this information have risen to the very top of the military. General James E. Cartwright, the former head of Strategic Command who became vice chairman of the Joint Chiefs of Staff in 2007 and is an expert on new technology and warfare, worries about how the military will manage with its introduction of the next generation of sensors, which are vastly more capable than even those on the battlefield today. "Today, an analyst sits there and stares at 'Death TV' for hours on end trying to find a single target or see something move or see something do something that makes it a valid target," Cartwright said. "It is just a waste of manpower. It is inefficient."

And it's only going to get worse, as the next generation of sensors can watch multiple targets over a larger area. This so-called Gorgon Stare technology could require two thousand analysts to fully process the data feeds from a single flying platform, compared to the nineteen analysts required per drone today, he said. "We just can't do that," Cartwright warned. "I now have run into a problem of generating analysts that I can't solve." That's why, he said, the military is searching for new algorithms and new digital technology to help analyze, sort, and store at speeds impossible for a human to manage in this new world of battling shadowy terrorist and insurgent networks.

John Tyson, the DIA's top Al Qaeda expert, has watched as the government's force of professional counterterrorism analysts has grown from a group small enough to know each other's phone numbers to a vast army linked by supercomputers processing hundreds of thousands of bits of data in nanoseconds. Al Qaeda and its associated terror networks may have been degraded, but they are adapting. "If you look at it from a network standpoint, perhaps they are less capable," Tyson said. "However, I think it is more distributed now, but I think you have more people looking at the problem set. It is sort of a crapshoot. Put your bet down on red or black."

8

THE RISE OF
HOME-GROWN EXTREMISM

On the cold, soggy morning of December 1, 2010, Juan Zarate and Michael Leiter met in a conference room just a few blocks from the White House, where together they had managed one terrorism crisis after another. The two old friends and longtime colleagues in the Bush administration had taken different paths after President Obama was sworn in. Zarate had left government and was now a senior adviser at the Center for Strategic and International Studies (CSIS), an influential Washington think tank, as well as a national security analyst for CBS News. The White House had asked Leiter to stay on as head of the National Counterterrorism Center, a nod to the former Navy pilot's professionalism as well as to the new team's desire to maintain continuity among the country's top terror fighters during the transition.

Zarate had invited Leiter to CSIS to speak on the shifting terrorist threat facing the country and how Leiter's center was responding to the new challenges. The two men traded compliments during the introductions. "He's not Jack Bauer," Zarate said of Leiter, referring to the star of the television drama *24*, "but he's probably the closest thing we have in Washington in a suit to Jack Bauer." "Minus the torture," Leiter quipped to the audience of policy analysts, journalists, and government experts. He then joked that he was still trying to catch up on the flood of e-mails the indefatigable Zarate had sent to him at two a.m.—nearly three years earlier.

But the message Leiter delivered that morning was anything but light-hearted: The American homeland is not immune to the ideological poison of Al Qaeda and its affiliates and followers, as there are American citizens and permanent legal residents infected by the virus of violent religious extremism, often spread by the Internet.

The Obama administration is grappling with the fact that the nation is hurtling down a bloody and familiar road already traveled by Britain, Spain, Germany, and Israel. Despite a spate of recent thwarted bomb plots, Leiter warned, the country was facing an increasing threat from homegrown terrorists. "We have to be honest that some things will get through," he said. "In this era of these more complicated threats and a more diverse threat and lower-scale attacks, to include individuals who have been radicalized here in the homeland, stopping all of the attacks has become that much harder."

Leiter's sobering comments were sandwiched between two cases that vividly illustrated his concern about the growing number of Americans who are choosing to self-radicalize and carry out terror attacks on their own.

Five days earlier, on November 26, the FBI arrested Mohamed Osman Mohamud, a nineteen-year-old Somali-born U.S. citizen who tried to detonate what he thought was a car bomb at a Christmas tree lighting ceremony in Portland, Oregon, where some ten thousand people had gathered. While he was planning the bombing, Mohamud was spotted by the FBI and put under surveillance. He told undercover agents that in 2009 he published three articles on the Web site Jihad Recollections, which was edited by Samir Khan, a Saudi-born American, from his home in North Carolina. (Khan had since moved to Yemen, where he ran *Inspire*, an English-language magazine and Web site, on behalf of Al Qaeda in the Arabian Peninsula.) Mohamud also told the agents that for four years he had been dreaming of carrying out a terrorist attack. "Since I was fifteen," he said. "I thought about all these things before."

A week after Leiter's address in Washington, federal prosecutors charged a Baltimore construction worker with plotting to blow up a military recruiting station in Maryland. The FBI had been tipped off to his radical statements on Facebook, joined his plot, and gave him a phony car bomb that he tried to explode. The worker, Antonio Martínez, a twenty-one-year-old American citizen who had recently converted to Islam and changed his name to Muhammad Hussain, had declared on his Facebook page that he hated "Any who opposes Allah." The indictment charged that Martínez was focused on killing American military personnel in the United States because they were killing Muslims overseas. In this case, as in the Mohamud case, the FBI used undercover agents to monitor the suspects for months, befriend them, and ultimately supply them with fake explosives. In both cases, federal agents said they offered the men several chances to back out, proposing nonviolent options to help the cause of Islam. But the men wanted to attack.

They were not alone. In September 2009, a nineteen-year-old Jordanian national was arrested after placing a fake bomb in a sixty-story Dallas skyscraper. The same month, a twenty-nine-year-old Muslim convert was charged with placing a bomb in the federal building in Springfield, Illinois. And in October 2010, a thirty-four-year-old naturalized American citizen born in Pakistan was arrested and charged with plotting to bomb the Washington Metro after meeting with undercover agents and discussing his plans and surveillance activities. All these plots were thwarted. (In October 2010, the Jordanian was sentenced to twenty-four years in prison. The other cases were all pending, as of the spring of 2011.) But Leiter's message was clear: Eventually, one of these homegrown terrorists would succeed.

■ ■ ■

As the years passed after September 11 with no major attacks in the homeland, terrorism analysts cautiously embraced the notion that Muslims in the United States were less vulnerable to radicalization than Muslims in Europe or the Middle East. American Muslims were better assimilated culturally and economically, the experts said, and they were well positioned to climb the ladder of prosperity in this country. They were said to exhibit little of the alienation that often gripped their counterparts in Europe, much less an attraction to extremist violence. But that began to change noticeably, starting in 2009. In all, there have been more than forty plots involving American citizens or permanent residents in the ten years since the 9/11 attacks, and roughly half of these were launched in 2009 or 2010. The jihadist plots or attacks inside the United States have baffled terrorism experts because the would-be bombers have no evident links to one another and little in common beyond their apparent ideological motive.

Even more disturbing to counterterrorism officials are three cases with ties to Pakistan's tribal region, where the American perpetrators received training in bomb making and terrorist tactics from Al Qaeda or Lashkar-e-Taiba operatives. These plots involved Najibullah Zazi, a former Manhattan coffee vendor who pleaded guilty to traveling to Pakistan for explosives training and plotting a deadly assault on New York City subway trains in September 2009; David C. Headley of Chicago, who pleaded guilty to aiding the 2008 terrorist assault on Mumbai and plotting attacks in Denmark; and Faisal Shahzad, a Pakistani American who loaded his Nissan Pathfinder with fertilizer, propane, and gasoline in a failed attempt to detonate a car bomb in Times Square in May 2010. "The past thirteen months have been as intense, if not more intense, because of the variety of threats than any time since 2001," Leiter told the CSIS audience.

Why was this happening now?

The New York Police Department, after more than two years of reviewing cases of homegrown terrorism in the United States and around the world, offered one of the earliest explanations in a wide-ranging report issued in August 2007 that described a four-phase process that transforms what it called "unremarkable" people into terrorists. In the first phase, or "preradicalization," most home-grown terrorists are strikingly unexceptional; they have ordinary jobs, live ordinary lives and, for the most part, have had little if any criminal history. The second phase, "self-identification," occurs when individuals are influenced by external or internal events, often through the Internet, and begin to explore the jihadist brand of Islam on their own. This phase could result from losing a job, experiencing a death in the family, or feeling anger about the treatment of Muslims in international conflicts, such as in Afghanistan and Iraq. The third phase, "indoctrination," happens when an individual wholly accepts the extremist ideology and is willing to commit violence to achieve its goals. This stage is often facilitated by someone with spiritual influence, such as an imam or other respected figure with religious training or credentials, who sanctions the violent act as a religious duty. The final stage, "jihadization," is reached when individuals or members of a small group accept their duty to commit violence in the name of Islam and begin preparing and executing a plot.

"The transformation of a Western-based individual to a terrorist is not triggered by oppression, suffering, revenge or desperation," the study concluded. "Rather, it is a phenomenon that occurs because the individual is looking for an identity and a cause and unfortunately, often finds them in extremist Islam. There is no useful profile to assist law enforcement or intelligence to predict who will follow this trajectory of radicalization. The radicalization process is accelerating in terms of how long it takes and the individuals are continuing to get younger."

Leiter expressed a similar frustration, confiding to guests at a dinner in Washington several months earlier: "I have a better understanding of radicals in London than anywhere in the U.S., except New York City." Entering the radicalization process does not necessarily mean that a terrorist will pop out the other end of "the funnel" every time; the NYPD report concluded that individuals who stop short of carrying out attacks are still dangerous, serving as "mentors and agents of influence to those who might become the terrorists of tomorrow."

What concerns Leiter and other senior officials is not just the number of Americans becoming radicalized but the worrisome number of those who are becoming "mobilized for action." Homeland Security Secretary Janet Napolitano put it this way: "It is difficult to understand why someone goes from a nice upper-middle-class household in the United States to a training camp in Yemen or the FATA and then comes back and wants to kill people." The tougher defenses the United States has erected since 9/11 to prevent foreign-based terrorists from entering the country have put a premium on terrorist groups recruiting or at least inspiring those living in America, who can operate freely and under the radar. "We have a good capability to detect and disrupt these sort of multipurpose teams that take months to plan, rehearse, fund, provide the logistics support for an attack," said Dennis Blair, the director of national intelligence, in testimony to the Senate Homeland Security Committee on January 20, 2010, less than a month after the Christmas Day plot that nearly brought down an airliner landing in Detroit. "But we are not as capable as we should be of carrying out the much more difficult task of detecting these self-radicalized citizens of the United States, Europe, other countries like Nigeria, who are given a very simple mission—with an advanced bomb to carry it out—or who plan their own attacks, inspired by Al Qaeda's message but not directed by Al Qaeda." Thus it becomes imperative for the government to get smarter on tracking what Philip Mudd, a former top CIA and FBI official, calls "the digital exhaust that a human being leaves around the world," including e-mail messages, cell phone calls, and travel information. "Counterterrorism in newspapers is about plots," Mudd said. "Counterterrorism in practice is about people," with a premium placed on "how we understand the distinction of tracking that person over-seas and tracking that person domestically."

The homegrown terrorist threat within America's borders defies easy description. A growing number of individuals have been self-radicalized through the Internet. Others have traveled to Paki-stan's tribal areas, seeking to join the militants who are fighting American troops in Afghanistan, only to be recruited by Al Qaeda for suicide missions back home. Three cases illustrate the range of threats facing counterterrorism officials.

Najibullah Zazi

On Monday afternoon, September 7, 2009, Jim Davis, the head of the FBI's office in Denver, was enjoying the Labor Day holiday grilling hamburgers and drinking beer on his patio when the phone rang. It was Steve Olson, Davis's top deputy for national security issues, relaying an urgent message from FBI headquarters in Wash-ington. A sharp-eyed CIA analyst monitoring intercepts from the e-mail account of an Al Qaeda facilitator in Peshawar, Pakistan, had spotted a chilling message sent from the United States: "The marriage is ready"—terrorist code that a major attack is set to go. "Everyone knows what that means," said Davis, who served with the FBI in Afghanistan and Iraq, where he was one of the first fed-eral investigators to interview Saddam Hussein after he was cap-tured in December 2003. "There was no doubt in my mind that at that moment we were talking about an Al Qaeda operative." And that Al Qaeda operative, it turned out, was living quietly in Aurora, Colorado, a Denver suburb. His name was Najibullah Zazi. And he was seeking advice from an Al Qaeda facilitator in three increasingly frantic e-mails about how to mix the proper ingredients for a flour-based explosive.

Zazi was a twenty-four-year-old former Manhattan coffee-cart vendor who was now working as a shuttle bus driver at the Denver international airport. As Davis ordered round-the-clock surveillance on the suspect, FBI analysts scoured law enforcement and intelligence databases but found little to go on. Two days later, early in the morning of Wednesday, September 9, Davis got another jolting phone call: Zazi had left town in a Hertz rental car, heading east on Interstate 70 at speeds exceeding one hundred miles an hour. "At that point we don't know if he's running to something or if he's running from something," said Davis. "We don't have any idea what his intent is at that point." A Colorado state patrolman pulled Zazi over as he approached the Kansas border and asked where he was going. New York City, Zazi told the officer, who let him go with a warning.

The timing was ominous. The eighth anniversary of 9/11 was two days away. The end of Ramadan and the opening of the UN General Assembly, with scores of world leaders arriving in New York, was near. Hundreds of agents scrambled in what became known as Operation High Rise, as Zazi sped toward New York. As Zazi arrived in New York on Thursday, September 10, he was stopped on the George Washington Bridge as part of what was meant to look like a routine random check of cars entering the city. But the law enforcement officials at the bridge failed to find two pounds of high explosives hidden in his trunk. Spooked by the traffic stop, Zazi gave the explosives to a high school friend and accomplice, who flushed them down the toilet. Zazi also learned that New York City detectives had visited an imam he knew, asking questions about him.

The next day, Friday, September 11, the police towed Zazi's illegally parked car and searched the laptop computer they found inside. Among the files was a nine-page bomb-making guide. That night, the FBI raided the homes of suspected sympathizers, bringing the plot to an end. But federal prosecutors still did not have enough evidence to charge Zazi with a crime, and he was allowed to fly home to Denver on Saturday, September 12. Reporters, tipped off by the raid in New York, hounded Zazi, who gave impromptu interviews to deny any wrongdoing. After spending two days in a furious media frenzy with television crews camped outside his apartment, Zazi paid a surprise visit to the FBI office in Denver on Monday, September 14, accompanied by his lawyer. "He thought he could talk his way out of this," Steve Olson said. Instead, after twenty-eight hours of interviews spread over three days, Zazi was arrested and charged on Saturday, September 19, and the full outlines of a harrowing plot that had been unfolding for months came into focus. Zazi and two accomplices had planned to carry homemade backpack bombs into the middle of packed rush-hour subway cars running between Grand Central Terminal and the financial district, and blow themselves up. Zazi characterized the plot as a "martyrdom operation" that he was just days away from executing when he realized he was under government surveillance.

The plot had been hatched soon after Zazi and his two accomplices, high school friends from Flushing, Queens, flew to Peshawar the previous year, on August 28, 2008, eager to join the fight in Afghanistan and avenge what Zazi believed were the senseless deaths of women and children at the hands of American soldiers. In Pakistan, however, they met three senior Al Qaeda leaders who persuaded them that they could help the jihadist cause more by returning to New York and carrying out an attack there. The Al Qaeda leaders were the brain trust for the group's operations against the United States and other Western countries: Saleh al-Somali, Rashid Rauf, and Adnan G. el-Shukrijumah, a Saudi-born naturalized American who is still considered one of the most dangerous Al Qaeda figures at large. (Rauf and al-Somali have since been killed by CIA drone strikes in Pakistan.) Zazi's plot was one of three, including thwarted attacks in Britain and Norway, that the three Al Qaeda planners orchestrated.

Zazi remained in Pakistan, taking terrorist training courses in how to handle AK-47s and other weapons, how to make suicide vests, and how to fire rocket-propelled grenades. He returned to New York on January 15, 2009, and soon moved to Colorado, where his aunt and uncle lived. Zazi got a job driving an airport shuttle van and started buying bomb ingredients in beauty-supply stores, telling one clerk who commented on the volumes of materials he was buying, "I have a lot of girlfriends." Zazi experimented with bomb materials in a hotel suite he rented in Aurora. It was from that hotel that Zazi sent his fateful e-mails to Pakistan over Labor Day weekend after he failed to cook up the correct lethal concoction. Had Zazi mixed the chemicals correctly the first time, Olson said, "there would have been no need for the follow-on emails that started this whole case. That's how close this was. He was going for mass casualties."

Zazi pleaded guilty to terrorism charges on February 22, 2010, and has been cooperating with the FBI. Investigators point to Zazi as the archetype of the most difficult challenge facing authorities today: a homegrown operative who travels freely, is skilled in interpersonal relations, and who understands the intricacies of American life so well that he gave several interviews to journalists after the FBI had identified him as a terrorism suspect following the raids in New York. And yet beneath that confident surface lay deep-seated anxieties that apparently pressed him to plot against his country. "He felt somewhat of a misfit, an outcast," said Eric Jergenson, the agent who led the FBI team that interviewed Zazi in Denver. "He wanted to make a statement and accomplish something."

Nidal Hasan

Major Nidal Hasan, an Army psychiatrist of Palestinian ancestry, looked like any one of the hundreds of troops on November 5, 2009, when he walked into a processing center at Fort Hood, Texas, where troops receive medical attention before being deployed or after returning from overseas. At first, he sat silently at an empty table. Then he bowed his head for several seconds, as if praying, rose, and pulled a high-powered pistol from beneath his coat. "*Allahu akbar*," he cried—"God is great." And then he sprayed gunfire across the room, killing thirteen people within minutes. In retrospect the warning signs were blinking red. Beginning in late 2008, Hasan wrote about twenty e-mail messages to the radical Yemeni American cleric Anwar al-Awlaki, asking whether his religious obligations would justify a Muslim American soldier to kill fellow soldiers. Some of the e-mail messages were intercepted and forwarded for investigation to a Joint Terrorism Task Force led by the FBI. But a Pentagon analyst who scrutinized the e-mails decided they were in line with Hasan's clinical research and warranted no further inquiry.

Hasan's relatives, however, recall that five years before the fatal shootings, he had grown disgruntled with the Army, complaining about anti-Muslim harassment. They said that he looked into getting a discharge from the service, but because of a shortage of mental-health specialists and Arab Americans in the military, he feared his chances of getting out were slim. In the meantime, Hasan alarmed some colleagues by voicing increasing opposition to the wars in Afghanistan and Iraq, whose traumatized and injured veterans he was counseling. He anguished over reconciling his religion with his military duties, but his supervisors paid little heed. In a 2007 PowerPoint demonstration to explain why some Muslim American soldiers might feel divided loyalties, he quoted incendiary passages from the Koran, including "And whoever kills a believer intentionally, his punishment is hell." In his presentation, Hasan wrote, "If Muslim groups can convince Muslims that they are fighting for God against injustices of the 'infidels,' then Muslims can become a potent adversary; i.e., suicide bombing."

The Defense Department's review of the incident, released in January 2011, recommended that the Pentagon spend as much time and effort protecting its personnel from internal threats as it does safeguarding them from external dangers. It also urged the Pentagon to work more closely with the FBI, and to develop awareness programs to train commanders to identify risky behavior within the ranks. Secretary Gates has said that he is especially concerned that the military does not seem to be alert to signs of radicalization in its own ranks, to be able to detect its symptoms, or to understand its causes.

Faisal Shahzad

Faisal Shahzad seemed to be an ideal example of the American immigrant success story. In 2006, at the age of twenty-six, he was working as a financial analyst at Elizabeth Arden, the global cosmetics firm; he had married a Pakistani American from Colorado; he had purchased a new home in Shelton, Connecticut; and he was on the path to becoming an American citizen and a father. But even as the Pakistani-born young man was enjoying America's financial promise and expansive culture, however, he was growing increasingly bitter toward his adopted country's foreign policy, particularly the wars in Iraq and Afghanistan. His anger fueled a religiously infused alienation that caused deep concern among his friends. "Can you tell me a way to save the oppressed? And a way to fight back when rockets are fired at us and Muslim blood flows?" he wrote in a lengthy e-mail to friends. "Everyone knows how the Muslim country bows down to pressure from west. Everyone knows the kind of humiliation we are faced with around the globe."

A pivotal moment came on July 10, 2007, when Pakistani commandos stormed the Red Mosque in Islamabad, ending a lengthy standoff with armed militants in a firefight that left more than one hundred people dead. While policy makers in Washington praised the Pakistani government's decision to confront the Islamist militants, Shahzad was outraged by the assault at the mosque he had frequented during his periodic visits home. During one of those trips a year later, Shahzad's pathway to militancy seemed clearer than ever. He asked his father for permission to fight in Afghanistan, a request his father turned down. Shahzad's resentment continued to build, and by April 2009, when he got his American citizenship, he sent an e-mail message to friends saying that his "sheikhs are in the field." By June, he had left for Pakistan. His wife packed up their children and moved to Dhahran, Saudi Arabia, where her parents were living. Six months later, Shahzad had linked up with Pakistani associates and had found his way to Waziristan and the Pakistani Taliban through a connection at the Red Mosque.

Over the next five weeks, the young man went through the Taliban's boot camp and learned how to make bombs. The Pakistani Taliban leaders saw a special prize in Shahzad, who carried an American passport, and, like Al Qaeda with Zazi, asked him to return to the United States to carry out an attack. Ultimately, the Pakistan Taliban wired Shahzad $12,000 to bankroll his failed plot to plant a car bomb in Times Square on Saturday night, May 1, 2010. After his arrest, Shahzad cooperated with investigators, but he sounded a defiant note at his sentencing in federal court in Manhattan on June 21, declaring himself "a Muslim soldier." "Brace yourselves, because the war with Muslims has just begun," Shahzad said. "Consider me only a first droplet of the flood that will follow me."

All three men—Zazi, Hasan, and Shahzad—used their understanding of American lifestyles, their American citizenship or residency, and their American freedoms to fly under the radar of authorities. Hasan's deadly attack succeeded. Zazi came within days of carrying out his plan. And Shahzad actually parked his explosives-packed SUV in Times Square, only to be foiled by faulty workmanship and an alert street vendor nearby who reported the smoking vehicle. But as Michael Leiter would warn seven months later, one day in the future, a homegrown terrorist will prevail.

In the Obama administration, efforts to combat domestic radicalization remain largely without a central coordinator. FBI field offices have stepped up their outreach programs to Muslim communities, seeking to build trust even as they defend undercover sting operations designed to weed out the aspiring homegrown terrorist seeking the means to go operational. Using rules revised at the end of the Bush administration, the FBI also has freer rein to begin investigating a person or group as a potential security threat, even without evidence of wrongdoing. Agents are allowed to use religion or ethnicity as a factor—as long as it is not the only factor—when selecting subjects for scrutiny. The Homeland Security Department is seeking to strengthen ties to local, state, and tribal law enforcement and emergency services departments through support to regional intelligence fusion centers. And the Department of Education is working to share information on counterradicalization programs with several school districts from around the country that have significant Somali American populations. More than thirty young men from Somalia who are now U.S. citizens or have permanent resident status have left the United States to fight in Somalia, and American counterterrorism officials fear that one day some may return to attack the United States. "As the pace of mobilization increases, we have also increased the capacity of domestic programs," Leiter said, noting that President Obama has ordered regular briefings on national and global counterradicalization programs.

But the government is struggling to settle on a common strategy for identifying and defeating a homegrown threat that is becoming increasingly diverse and difficult to track. Counterterrorism experts at the National Counterterrorism Center, at the FBI, and at Homeland Security are analyzing patterns of behavior, Internet communications, and travel patterns. In the battle of measures and countermeasures, Al Qaeda and other extremist groups are looking to speed up the time between radicalizing an individual and mobilizing that person for action. "What we have seen is that the distance between radicalization and putting a bomb on is sometimes days and weeks," said Michael Chertoff, the former secretary of Homeland Security.

This narrowing of the "radicalization gap" is putting more

pressure on state and local authorities as well as on the general public to be more keenly aware of unusual behavior. A growing number of big-city police departments and other law enforcement agencies across the country are embracing a new system to report suspicious activities that officials say could uncover terrorism plots but that civil-liberties groups contend might violate individual rights. In Los Angeles, Boston, Chicago, Miami, and several other cities, officers are filling out terror tip sheets if they run across activities that seem out of place, like someone buying police or firefighter uniforms, taking photographs of a power plant, or espousing extremist views.

Ultimately, state and federal officials intend to have a nationwide reporting system in place by 2014, using a standardized system of codes for suspicious behaviors. It is the most ambitious effort since the September 11 attacks to put in place a network of databases to comb for clues that might foretell acts of terrorism. "We have to enlist literally state and local and community people to be part of the eyes and ears about what is brewing," Chertoff said. "It is going to be in this kind of an environment the beat policemen who see something funny or unusual that is likely to be able to detect one of the threads of a plot."

In late 2010, Homeland Security Secretary Janet Napolitano announced a public awareness program called If You See Something, Say Something, aimed at encouraging millions of Americans to identify and report suspicious activities. The campaign, which started on the New York and Washington subway systems, has expanded to include Walmart, the Mall of America, the sports and general aviation industries, and hotel and lodging associations. This type of campaign makes sense, as long as civil liberties are not abused. But the emphasis on the program now raises questions why such an obvious program had not already been in place.

Vulnerabilities exposed by the Zazi plot and by the terrorist attacks in Mumbai, India, in November 2008 have prompted the Homeland Security Department to retool many of the training programs it provides to government specialists as well as to industry groups. Homeland Security's office of bomb prevention conducts training courses not only on how to defuse homemade bombs but also on how to identify and report people who try to buy large quantities of commonly used beauty supplies, such as acetone and hydrogen peroxide, which are also the main ingredients used to make triacetone tiperoxide, or TAPT, the explosive of choice for many terrorists, including Zazi. Homeland Security has also been running training exercises with the hotel and shopping mall industries. In December 2010, for example, the department gathered hotel and mall security officials at a location in northern Virginia where they participated in a mock terrorist attack to test their responses.

Muslim community leaders in the United States have denounced the rise in homegrown radicalization. Law enforcement officials say that a growing number of Muslim leaders who are angry and embarrassed at a tiny minority of violent extremists are providing authorities with information about individuals who are espousing violence in the name of Islam. Steven L. Gomez, special agent in charge of counterterrorism in the FBI's Los Angeles field office, said that as a result of community meetings he has held, one individual came forward with a tip about a man who was becoming radicalized. "That person said, 'I am telling you this because I trust you,'" Gomez said. "That is a success right there."

Looking back over the decade since 9/11, Michael Leiter acknowledged that putting counterradicalization plans in place both at home and abroad much earlier could have helped blunt the threat sooner. Now, as Al Qaeda and its affiliates increasingly aim to encourage and exploit self-radicalized Americans, Leiter knew that he could defend against the inevitable only so long. "We are going to see the trend you see in the short term continue," Leiter said in November 2010. "Our job is to make sure no one gets killed, all the time knowing that we can't do that."

9

"IS AL QAEDA JUST KLEENEX?"

On a Tuesday morning in the spring of 2010 President Obama's top national security aides rushed into the Oval Office with an alarming report: Credible intelligence warned of a new terror plot to strike the United States with an unconventional weapon. This warning came just as the administration and its counterterrorism council were recovering from the intelligence failure that allowed the Christmas bombing attempt in Detroit four months earlier to come far too close to success. And the source of the new plot was the same: Yemen, the sanctuary for Al Qaeda in the Arabian Peninsula (AQAP). Formed in 2009 through the merger of Osama bin Laden's Yemeni and Saudi affiliates, AQAP had become the region's most active and alarming terrorist organization.

American intelligence assets, aided by Saudi Arabia's clandestine service, had picked up the chatter and had spotted the faint signs. AQAP operatives were attempting to acquire significant quantities of castor beans, which are used in cooking and in food production; they also offer some medicinal benefits. But inside the castor bean itself is something else: ricin, a toxin so potent that even harvesting the bean in its natural state is dangerous without proper precautions.

AQAP, like many other Al Qaeda affiliates, remained determined to strike at the United States with a weapon of mass destruction, but for the moment it focused on the less ambitious goal of using toxins. "Brothers with less experience in the fields of microbiology or chemistry, as long as they possess basic scientific knowledge, would be able to develop other poisons such as ricin or cyanide," the AQAP propaganda arm would post to its online English-language journal, *Inspire*, in the fall of 2010, in an article headlined "Tips for Our Brothers in the United States in America." Administration and intelligence officers would see this as another piece of evidence, public proof, of the AQAP threat stream. In the past, such articles had been dismissed as largely inspirational rather than operational.

This time, though, American intelligence believed the threat was real.

Connect the dots.

That's what you do to fight terrorism. The picture is never sharp. The information is never precise. What's the threat? How capable are the would-be actors? From where and how soon? You build the assessment bit by bit until a recognizable pattern emerges, one that can be subjected to analysis supplemented by experience, gut instinct—and luck. If this doesn't come together you have a failure of predictive intelligence.

The April 2010 intelligence reports warned that AQAP operatives in Sana'a, the capital of Yemen, were attempting to contract out for large quantities of castor beans. The operatives planned to move the castor beans and other precursor agents to a hideaway in Shabwa Province, in one of Yemen's rugged, nearly unapproachable tribal areas, where they would concoct their supplies of potent toxins. "The assumption was they were attempting to weaponize them," said a senior administration official. How would they do it? Most likely packed around an explosive, and most likely in a contained space, like a shopping mall or a subway system.

The precedent was a 1995 attack in the Tokyo subway, when the Aum Shinrikyo cult released sarin nerve gas on underground trains, killing twelve, injuring more than five thousand, and nearly paralyzing one of the world's leading economies for weeks. AQAP had come up with an even more deadly plan. A speck of pure ricin the size of the period at the end of this sentence can kill if injected into the bloodstream; a minute amount of it, if inhaled or swallowed, will cause death within thirty-six hours. There is no antidote or cure. Several countries, including the United States, have tried unsuccessfully to convert ricin into a weapon causing mass casualties, but that hasn't stopped terrorists from trying. In 2003, British and French operatives broke up Al Qaeda cells that possessed components and manuals for making ricin bombs and maps of the London Underground.

Intelligence officers considered this latest threat "significant" and an indication of the evolution of the new enemy. A ricin dispersing bomb detonated in the New York subway or the Washington Metro or San Francisco's BART would not result in mass destruction on a 9/11 scale, but as one counterterrorism expert pointed out, "The actual casualties of a given isolated attack might be small, but the psychological impact on people who ride transportation systems around the world would be significant. Do I have to now worry about getting poisoned on the way to work, each time I step on the metro?"

Gathered in the White House Situation Room, senior national security and intelligence aides debated whether AQAP had the sophistication to pull off the attack, even as the intelligence picture became clearer. They noted that a ricin bomb requires more chemical and engineering sophistication than just wrapping the toxin around an explosive. In the course of the debate, intelligence officials argued that the questionable capacity of the plot might be an indication of a larger American success against Osama bin Laden and Al Qaeda's senior leadership hiding in Pakistan. The intelligence was clear that any attacks against the United States would more likely come from outside Pakistan's tribal areas, the officials pointed out, and that meant the terror network was splintered. Any new attacks would be smaller bore, and, while deadly, would be indicative of Al Qaeda's diminished capability and ambition.

Other officials insisted that this was a misreading of the emerging tactical directives among the Al Qaeda offshoots. It was true, one official said, that AQAP could not mount a 9/11 type of attack, "but that is not their approach. They are trying to find targeted ways to do limited attacks that have big psychological impact and/or show that they can."

In February 2011, Michael Leiter of the National Counterterrorism Center told Congress that he considered AQAP "probably the most significant risk to the U.S. homeland." Leiter had reason to be especially sensitive to AQAP's growing threat. The failed Christmas Day plot in 2009 showed that the NCTC missed clear warning signs that Umar Farouk Abdulmutallab, the Nigerian man trained by AQAP, was plotting to blow up the airliner. The lesson was noted throughout the American intelligence community. "After Christmas, a discussion that had been out there, but sort of on the low burn, suddenly became a bigger issue," said the DIA's John Tyson. "What about the non-CT data? When you get CT data, you have to bang it up against this non-CT data—this travel data and customs and visa data and all of this information that, quite frankly, we don't need to know until we have a need to know."

This is the new face of terror. While Al Qaeda persists in its efforts to obtain weapons of mass destruction, its affiliates are concentrating on "niche terrorism"—a fairly low bar for tactical sophistication but a disproportionately high level of psychological and economic impact. And the face of small-bore terrorism is Anwar al-Awlaki, an American born in New Mexico, who has Yemeni and American citizenship and is one of the leaders of AQAP. He speaks idiomatic American in his outreach to extremists and potential future followers in the West. His online propaganda employs four-color visuals and impeccable English. "AQAP now provides its online community with a compelling, comic book experience, one that equips individuals with the tools they need while demystifying the path they must take to become their own Al Qaeda superhero," said Jarret Brachman, the author of *Global Jihadism* and a terrorism consultant to several government agencies.

Given Awlaki's shrewd analysis of the West, he is convinced that the creative use of toxins like ricin will inflict massive psychological and economic damage. "AQAP seems satisfied with disruptive attacks, even if less destructive, and they are very creative," said one senior counterterrorism official. "Awlaki is a very savvy analyst of the West, and he knows that a poison-type attack, even if not mass-casualty, would have a mass effect. He is asking, 'How can I get into their heads? How can I fuck with them?' "

AQAP's strategy forced the Obama administration to rethink its own. On issues of counterterrorism, the handoff from Bush to Obama had been one of change as well as of continuity. Predator strikes? Endorsed and expanded. Defenses on the home front and aboard airliners? Yes. Harsh language, harsh detention techniques? Cancelled. Intelligence briefings to the president? Where Bush had been eager for detailed updates about every threat, Obama understood that the commander in chief should watch trends and should be told of significant operations but should not get distracted by the details, no matter how fascinating—a sensible approach for senior decision makers.

"I think part of the reason for some of the far-reaching measures that were taken after 9/11 was the feeling of extraordinary inadequacy of our information," said Defense Secretary Gates. "After 9/11, all the filters came off information. So anybody anywhere in the world who made some comment about bombing the

United States or getting a weapon of mass destruction—all those reports came straight into the leadership of the country and I think it scared the hell out of them. I mean, they really didn't know whether there might not be a nuclear weapon of mass destruction set off in New York or in Washington within weeks of 9/11. And because all the filters were off, any comment anywhere in the world that we picked up, shot right to the top. I think there was just overload." The resulting policy decisions were understandable in a nation traumatized by the death, casualties, and loss of 9/11, Gates said. "A lot of the measures, including the renditions, Guantánamo, the enhanced interrogation techniques—all were out of a sense of desperation to get information because we had so little," he added.

But history has cast its judgment, and so has Gates. He was the first member of the Bush cabinet to secretly lobby to shut down the prison at Guantánamo Bay. Its value as a source of actionable intelligence on future attacks had diminished over time, because all information has an expiration date stamped to the minute of capture, and that was certainly true of those detainees who had spent years behind bars at Camp X-Ray. But the downside, Gates pointed out, was that Guantánamo gave a powerful boost to Al Qaeda's global effort to recruit potential jihadists and put American troops at increased risk everywhere they deployed in the Muslim world.

Another challenge to the American counterterrorism effort in the later years of the Bush administration was that the growing number of intelligence and law enforcement agencies in Washington remained in conflict with one another and with the military. Policy makers were unable to impose a unity of effort on all the arms of government power. "In the early days, we were like a drunken octopus trying to solve a Rubik's cube," said a seasoned commander of one of the Pentagon's most secret counterterrorism units. But a measure of control and coordination had been imposed by the time Obama was sworn in. In fact, and for a time, the government was feeling pretty confident.

Then came the Christmas Day attack in December 2009, in which the poorly trained bomber, who had left plenty of clues in his wake, slipped through the system and almost blew up a passenger plane. In the final weeks of the year, American intelligence officials, using spy satellites and communication intercepts, were intently focused on pinpointing the location of Al Qaeda fighters so the Yemeni military could strike them. By doing so, they hoped to prevent attacks on the U.S. Embassy in Yemen, or other targets in the region with American ties. But they had unwittingly left themselves vulnerable to an attack on the homeland itself, for they had assumed that the militants were not sophisticated or ambitious enough to get operatives into the United States. Intelligence analysts had enough information in those days before Christmas to stop the suicide bomber from getting on his flight, yet they did not act. "We didn't know they had progressed to the point of actually launching individuals here," John Brennan said at a White House briefing two weeks after the failed attack. "Had that plane gone down, that would have been their version of 9/11," said a senior American intelligence officer who regularly attends counterterrorism strategy sessions with the president in the White House Situation Room. "Obviously not in scope—but they had to deal with the shock of a potential event. They had to turn at that point, and recognized that there was a different face on the war on terror."

Obama, celebrating the holiday with his family in Hawaii, was furious at the lapses. Perhaps not surprising, given his cerebral nature, the president did not assign blame to individuals but demanded that the system not fail again. He also sought advice from his senior aides as to what he, as commander in chief, needed to do to make the bureaucracy more effective, more responsive, and more accountable. "He has been much more interested in figuring out analytically what happened, what potentially went amiss, fix whatever went wrong, to close whatever gap or address the lack of capability," said one senior White House adviser. "So he'll often ask, 'What do you need that you don't have? Is it a resource issue, is it an authority issue, are you doing all you can or is there something you could be doing if you had a policy decision that allowed you to do more?' "

The president had begun a series of weekly sessions on countering violent extremism, and these took on a new focus, a fresh discipline, and a palpable urgency as 2010 began. There had never been a lack of attention to the threat, the president's advisers maintained. But the sessions often had the air of a tutorial, introducing a new concept, a new capability, or a new legal tool. That changed after the Christmas bombing attempt. One participant recalled a lengthy discussion in the supercharged atmosphere of early 2010 on whether the role of bin Laden and Al Qaeda's central leadership hiding in Pakistan actually had diminished and was less capable of executing a catastrophic attack or whether they were just as dangerous in their role as the most recognizable terrorist brand name and as an inspiration to other potential jihadists. "Is Al Qaeda just Kleenex?" the president asked, provocatively. And, if Al Qaeda is only a trademark, how should American counterterrorism efforts adapt to the new "business model"?

The newly energized sessions, which earned a nickname among White House staff as Terror Tuesdays, would last up to an hour and were held in the Oval Office or, if too many principals or deputies attended, the meeting was moved to the Situation Room. Participants would begin each week with an overview of counterterrorism intelligence that focused on the homeland and then moved on to risks to American interests around the globe. "The president is very clear in setting expectations and making sure when something is a high priority and that he wants a report back on what actions have been taken," said one senior official with a seat at the table.

Other Tuesday sessions were more succinct: "He gives homework assignments," according to one of those participating. "He grades our work at the next session. You know, 'What did we do about this, did we follow up on that?' So, in that sense, it is a very good mechanism in ensuring high-level visibility on these threats, but not just for the president but also for the principals. Many times their bureaucracies are working these issues hard day in and day out, but having the principals briefed up and joining the president on these issues ensures that the departments and agencies bring their best to the table."

The same sense of discipline and focus was brought to the intelligence side of the president's briefings as well. "There is a conscious effort now to give him a structured brief on the nature of the threat, near, medium, long-term for radicalization," said a senior intelligence official. While Bush showed an appetite for tactical and operational details—the number of spies working against Al Qaeda in Pakistan or which missions had been carried out in the previous twenty-four hours—Obama wanted to understand the strategic nature of the threat and demanded to know when his personal orders were required to break through resistance across the intelligence and security community to make things work at the tactical and operational level.

One veteran counterterrorism official said that Obama often prods officials to break down the barriers to sharing information between departments, called "stovepipes" in Washington vernacular: "That is a very familiar point that he makes as he is faced with the problems we are facing on a daily basis, that we are not sitting in stove-pipes, that we are not underresourced in a time of fiscal austerity."

A case in point: Before heading off for the holidays in the hours before the Christmas Day attack, Dennis Blair, the director of national intelligence, was running down a checklist with the National Counterterrorism Center's Michael Leiter. One item was how the national security bureaucracy could help manage the looming budget crisis by trimming $35 million from the counterterrorism center's budget. After Christmas, their first conversation was all about how to spend an extra $100 million that the White House budget office suddenly found to finance the center's operations.

■ ■ ■

Prior to the Christmas Day attack, the Obama administration had been too many steps behind Al Qaeda in the Arabian Peninsula. In tracking the ricin plot, it felt it was a step ahead, and officials would continue to monitor it throughout 2010. And in dealing with the threat posed by homegrown extremists who have allegiances to Muslim lands overseas, administration terror fighters pledged to be ahead even of leading indicators. Clearly, the rise of AQAP underscored the increasing importance of Al Qaeda's affiliates around the world and the impact they and Al Qaeda itself were having on Americans heeding the siren call of extremism. But what was actually happening at home?

Another Terror Tuesday in the White House. This time the agenda was al-Shabab, a terror cell based in Somalia that was loyal to Al Qaeda. In July 2010 it carried out its first attack outside Somalia's borders, claiming credit for the suicide bombings at two popular nightspots in Kampala, Uganda, where soccer fans had gathered to watch the final match of the World Cup. With a large population of Somali Americans in the United States, Obama and his advisers knew that the recruitment of some of them was a matter of grave concern. The problem had two prongs: Disrupt any terror plotting by Shabab that could threaten the United States and its allies but do it in a way that gave Somali Americans no fuel for radicalization.

"Part of the way is just messaging," said one senior official who attended the session. "Showing that we don't necessarily seek to dictate the outcome of events in Somalia beyond what the democratic process has for Somalia. So, we don't seek to destroy you, we don't have any plan to destroy the entirety of the Shabab movement."

The debate took a dark turn when some around the table lobbied for bombing Shabab training camps, given that intelligence had identified the locations, with GPS coordinates ready for the cruise missiles. Some argued that killing or incapacitating two hundred Shabab extremists would be a good thing for America's counterterrorism efforts. Others argued that such a strike would serve to inflame a new and wider circle of Somalis at home and in the United States.

A compromise was struck: An execute order would be considered only if a high-value target—a senior Shabab leader, a visiting emissary of Al Qaeda, or a member of a cell who was training for a credible attack on the West—was present in the camp inside Somalia. But the debate revealed an enduring contradiction of American counterterrorism policy: Cruise missiles are easy; preventing radicalization is hard. There is no magic bullet for the latter task, and outreach programs, such as an effort by the Department of Education to train teachers in the urban Midwest about how to watch for radicalization among Somali American youth, have to be handled with great sensitivity. But such efforts can only mitigate the problem of radicalism, especially when impressionable young men see or hear about innocent people who have been killed by American operations in Muslim countries.

"Collateral damage" is a powerful fuel for radicalization, and U.S. officials are well aware of the risk inherent in each mission when innocent people are killed or wounded. "When we kill somebody, there is going to be someone else to take their place," said Leiter. "And it is relatively easy to take someone off the battlefield. But there is something that is less satisfying about starting a program that engages young Somalis to prevent radicalization; that is softer and mushier, and to many it is a less interesting conversation." He described how, in interagency meetings, a discussion of hunting terrorists is immediately relevant and exciting for many participants. Bureaucratic battles and lack of progress on the concepts of preventing terrorism are less exciting; the results are hard to discern and quantify. Officials celebrate the elimination of each terrorist even though he may be rapidly replaced, but those are the victories you can measure.

"Here we are, it is 2010, and it is the first time that the Department of Education has been brought in to do a roundtable and talk to professional educators about radicalization and the role they might play in helping to prevent it," Leiter said. "I think it is great that we are doing it. But you have to have a lot more of these sorts of programs to see real progress."

At the White House and Pentagon, and across the broad spectrum of intelligence agencies, senior officials concede that they underestimated the capabilities of AQAP prior to the Christmas Day attack. "We are not underestimating them today," said Michele A. Flournoy, the undersecretary of defense for policy. "No. I think they are under the microscope." No plot better illustrated AQAP's ability to shift tactics to try to avoid this heightened scrutiny than the group's scheme in late October 2010, in which toner cartridges packed with explosives were sent from Yemen to out-of-date addresses for two Chicago synagogues. A tip from Saudi intelligence thwarted the plot, and the packages were intercepted in Dubai and Britain. Though the attack failed, AQAP took great delight in mocking the West, claiming that the operation had cost only $4,200 to carry out and had wholly disrupted global air cargo systems—an example of low-cost attacks designed to inflict huge economic damage. In its online magazine, *Inspire*, AQAP crowed, "Two Nokia mobiles, $150 each, two HP printers, $300 each, plus shipping, transportation and other miscellaneous expenses add up to a total bill of $4,200. That is all what Operation Hemorrhage cost us."

Even though the plot failed, AQAP had also proudly claimed credit for the Christmas Day attack, seeing it not as a defeat but a victory. "Al Qaeda in the Arabian Peninsula is now the most operationally active node of the Al Qaeda network," said John Brennan, just days before the first-year anniversary of the airliner plots. "Their definition of 'success'—stoking fear, even if their attacks fail—portends more such attempts."

By the first months of 2011, Awlaki and AQAP had not been able to mount a ricin attack, either because of a lack of technical skill or because the plot was knocked off course by continued pressure from the U.S.-backed police and military troops in Yemen, who were carrying out attacks against suspected AQAP fighters. Despite this success, however, President Obama's senior advisers still feared that a ricin plot remained a live option for AQAP. "We continue to treat it as worthy of serious concern," said a senior administration official. "It is not just the narrow effect a ricin or other unconventional attack would have. It is what it might strike in the way of fear or concern across a whole host of dimensions if that might happen." If that threat wasn't cause enough for worry, Saudi intelligence sources later uncovered a diabolical twist to the ricin plot: Terrorists were attempting to place the toxin in bottles of perfume, especially a popular local fragrance made from the resin of agar wood, and then to send those bottles as gifts to assassinate government officials, law enforcement and military officers, religious scholars, and journalists.

So the devil is indeed in the details—underwear, shoes, perfume, cell phone chatter—all of which are dots that need to be connected in a global effort unlike any that the United States has ever before undertaken. It is an old saw that the military always prepares for the last war. When it comes to combating global terrorism, there *is* no last war. The administration and a great part of the American government are making it up as it goes along. The plots reflect AQAP's ingenuity and resourcefulness, qualities not lost on Michael Leiter as the NCTC and the rest of the government try to prevent every attack, knowing that eventually the terrorists will succeed. "In this era of this more complicated threat and a more diverse threat and lower-scale attacks," Leiter said in a December 2010 speech, "stopping all attacks has become that much harder."

"We have to be honest that some things will get through," he added. "Innocent lives will be lost."

10

THE OBAMA STRATEGY

The air in the Roosevelt Room was filled with tension as more than a dozen senior Pakistani and American government officials gathered for negotiations on October 20, 2010. The discussions were animated; the frustration on each side palpable.

The Americans warned that unless Pakistan cracked down on militants hiding in the tribal areas of North Waziristan who were attacking and killing American soldiers in Afghanistan, the administration might be unable to persuade Congress to keep writing the checks for more than $2 billion a year in assistance to Pakistan. But the guests from Islamabad shot back that their forces were stretched thin. Trust us, they said: The Pakistani Army would carry out an offensive on its own timetable.

In a relationship suffused with tension and flare-ups—at that moment, over a NATO helicopter gunship that had accidentally killed three Pakistani border guards, which prompted Pakistan to retaliate by closing down a supply route for fuel and food to NATO troops into Afghanistan—the meeting had been expected to serve as a lubricant to keep the allies talking.

The Roosevelt Room is just a few steps from the Oval Office, in the West Wing of the White House. So not long after the meeting began, President Obama made a dramatic and unannounced entrance. The president had a message he wanted to deliver personally. Earlier in the day, he had convened the National Security Council for its monthly meeting on Afghanistan and Pakistan. The administration was in the midst of a midcourse review of a strategy that Obama had set out in a speech at West Point nearly a year earlier, on December 1, 2009, to reverse Taliban gains in large parts of Afghanistan, better protect the Afghan people, and step up attacks on Al Qaeda and other Islamic extremist groups in Pakistan. It was the Pakistan piece of the strategy that worried Obama that October afternoon.

There was nothing impromptu about the president's dropping in unannounced. The main focus of his attention during the thirty-five-minute session was Pakistan's army chief, General Ashfaq Parvez Kayani, who was viewed as the most powerful man in Pakistan. Obama opened his comments by seeking to dispel Pakistan's fears that the United States would abandon the region as it had after the Soviet withdrawal from Afghanistan in 1989. He even went as far as dismissing a standard ploy of Pakistani propaganda: that the Pentagon had a secret plan to steal Pakistan's nuclear arsenal, its main strategic deterrent against its archrival, India.

As the discussion moved toward Pakistan's role in combating extremists, Obama fixed his gaze on Kayani. In measured tones more solemn than threatening, the president said that he was not interested in weakening Pakistan's security. But he warned that Pakistan's security strategy could not include supporting "murderous groups" such as the Taliban and the Haqqani network. If there was an attack against the United States that was found to have originated from the tribal areas, he, as commander in chief, would do whatever was necessary to protect the United States and its citizens. "Americans would expect no less of me," Obama told Kayani and the rest of the delegation. "My first duty is to protect American citizens. I know Pakistan would feel the same way."

He left unsaid the specific steps the American military would take in retaliation against such a terrorist attack. But Obama's implicit warning that he would order a major military response—most likely massive air strikes on Pakistani territory well beyond the now-familiar CIA drone attacks and commando raids—left no doubt that he was serious, one Pakistani official and one American official recalled. The foreign minister, Shah Mahmood Qureshi, and the other civilian Pakistani ministers nodded silently in agreement at the president's position. Kayani, sphinxlike as always, betrayed no hint of what he was thinking.

This was a significant escalation of a similar message that General James L. Jones, the national security adviser, and Leon E. Panetta, the CIA director, had delivered to Pakistani officials in Islamabad in May. That meeting had come two weeks after Faisal Shahzad's unsuccessful attempt to explode a crude car bomb in Times Square. But hearing the same blunt words from Obama himself, in the White House, well, "that got Kayani's attention," said the Pakistani official.

Obama's warning to Kayani that his military needed to clamp down on the Islamic fighters who were using safe havens inside his country, or pay the price of devastating American air strikes, was yet another example of how the U.S. government was adopting classic Cold War notions of deterrence to protect the United States against terrorists. The message was clear: If we are attacked, you will be attacked. But the difference today was that the threat of punishment was sometimes invoked against nominal allies, with the president himself offering a national blood oath to hold Pakistan, an ally, responsible for acts of terrorism against the United States launched from its territory and to punish it.

But unlike Cold War deterrence, when the weapons were held in ready reserve, now, in the age of terror, the United States was not just threatening but already was on the attack, using armed Predator drones for constant strikes on terror targets inside the sovereign territory of Pakistan. The drone strikes had two complementary goals, one tactical and one strategic. The immediate, tactical goal was to bring about the death of Al Qaeda leaders, other militant commanders, and their operatives. But when looked at from a longer perspective, the fear of the remotely piloted, heavily armed drones overhead had proved to be a deterrent in itself, pushing Al Qaeda senior leaders deeper into hiding, preventing their gathering together, and keeping them constantly on alert, in motion, and off balance.

At the NSC meeting earlier in the day, the discussion had focused on the effectiveness of the drone strikes. While American officials acknowledged the limitations of the strikes and the fact that they could not substitute for troops clearing and holding ground, they had become the tactic of choice against Pakistani militants in Obama's first two years in office. Pakistani Army operations in six of the seven tribal areas near the border with Afghanistan have helped drive fighters from Al Qaeda, the Pakistani Taliban, the Haqqani network, and other militant groups into the seventh tribal area, North Waziristan, where the insurgents run a virtual ministate the size of Rhode Island. By bunching up there, insurgents are ultimately making it easier for American drone strikes to hit them from afar. American officials are loath to talk about this silver lining to the storm cloud they have long described building up in the tribal area of North Waziristan. This is because they do not want to undermine the Obama administration's urgent public pleas for Pakistan to order troops into the area or to give Pakistan an excuse for inaction.

While the overall effectiveness of the strikes is impossible to ascertain, there are many accounts to confirm that a significant number of insurgent fighters and leaders have been killed. Indeed, the drone strikes have been a signature weapon of the Obama administration. The outlines of this preference grew out of Obama's presidential campaign, which hinged on his opposition to the Iraq War and his support for more and smarter efforts against Al Qaeda.

As the campaign reached its peak in the fall of 2008, both

Obama and his Republican rival, Senator John McCain, began receiving classified intelligence briefings designed to prepare them for taking office. On September 2, Mike McConnell, the director of national intelligence, flew to Chicago to brief Obama on the most pressing national intelligence. In scheduling the meeting, Obama made clear that he only wanted to discuss terrorism. He was serious. As McConnell recalled, "They gave us an hour and we spent fifty-five minutes on terrorism." The discussion focused on the safe havens in Pakistan and the Bush administration's frustrations in getting the Pakistani leadership to undertake large-scale operations against Al Qaeda and the other militants in the tribal areas.

As president-elect, Obama immediately embraced the aggressive campaign against Al Qaeda in Pakistan. And soon after taking office, he rapidly escalated the pace of the CIA's attacks against Al Qaeda and its affiliates in the tribal areas. Increasing the number of strikes to a total of 53 in 2009, the new administration conducted more attacks in its first year than in the entire eight years under President Bush, and their number more than doubled to 118 in 2010. The drone strikes were coordinated to target specific leaders and areas deemed most critical to America's counterterrorism efforts. Notably, in 2009 the CIA began targeting the Pakistani Taliban in South Waziristan. The air campaign intensely took aim at its leader, Baitullah Mehsud, and his inner circle, launching 17 strikes against him alone that year. On August 5, the CIA finally found him. Predator drones launched a barrage of missiles at Mehsud as he received dialysis on the roof of a home in South Waziristan, killing him and his family instantly. That next month, the Pakistani Army launched a major clearing operation against the Pakistani Taliban and its allies in South Waziristan. The operation sought to eliminate the Taliban sanctuary and establish a command post in Mehsud's former headquarters. In support of these operations, the CIA targeted militant groups fleeing into North

Waziristan, the traditional home of the Haqqani network and a major base of Al Qaeda's training camps.

In an effort to stifle the expanding drone strikes, Al Qaeda and its allies sought to attack the program and the American spy network using whatever means possible. On December 30, 2009, Al Qaeda deployed a double agent named Abu Dujanah al-Khorasani to Forward Operating Base Chapman, a secret intelligence base in the remote mountains of eastern Afghanistan. He was known to the CIA as Humam Khalil Abu-Mulal al-Balawi, and on this day he was determined to achieve martyrdom by detonating himself in the midst of a group of senior CIA personnel running the intelligence program for which he was an informant. Beneath Khorasani's Afghan National Army uniform was a vest of explosives. The ensuing blast killed fourteen people, including seven CIA officers and a senior Jordanian intelligence official. The strike, orchestrated by senior Al Qaeda figures such as Ayman al-Zawahri and Hakimullah Mehsud, a member of Baitullah's tribe (but not a close relative) who succeeded him as head of the Pakistani Taliban, dealt a painful blow to the CIA's elite counterterrorism program. The bombing also triggered a brutal CIA counterattack against Al Qaeda, the Pakistani Taliban, and the Haqqani network. In the year following the attack, nearly every member of the terrorist network responsible for the bombing was targeted and killed, removing more than half of Khorasani's fellow operatives, according to Flashpoint Global Partners, a New York–based security consultant. Hakimullah Mehsud himself narrowly survived a drone strike against him on January 13, 2010.

Through early June 2011, there had been thirty-four drone strikes in the tribal areas, and many top Al Qaeda and other militant leaders had gone deeper into hiding. The target list for the drones had been expanded to include lower-level militant commanders and clusters of fighters. Expanding the scope of the attacks was designed not only to kill more subcommanders but also to sow fear and dissent within the militants' ranks. After each strike, Al Qaeda and Pakistani Taliban leaders typically round up several suspected informants and execute them, creating a cycle of fear that American and Pakistani intelligence officers say tears apart the terrorist cells from within.

The drone strikes are only part of the CIA's secret war inside Pakistan that President Obama has approved. The arrest and detention in early 2011 of Raymond Davis, a former Special Forces soldier turned CIA security contractor, for fatally shooting two Pakistani men after what American officials have described as a botched robbery attempt, inadvertently pulled back the curtain on a web of covert American operations inside the country. A third Pakistani man on a bicycle was killed by an American team in an SUV rushing to help Davis. The CIA team with which Davis worked in Lahore, Pakistan, was tasked with tracking the movements of various Pakistani militant groups, including Lashkar-e-Taiba. For the Pakistanis, such spying inside their country is an extremely delicate issue, particularly since Lashkar has longstanding ties to the ISI, Pakistan's main spy service. Davis was released in March 2011 after weeks of secret negotiations between American and Pakistani officials, a pledge of about $2.3 million in "blood money" to the families of the men who were killed, and quiet political pressure by Pakistani officials on the courts. Nonetheless, the episode worsened already frayed relations between the CIA and the ISI, created a political dilemma for the weak, pro-American Pakistani government, and further threatened the stability of the country, which has the world's fastest-growing nuclear arsenal.

The campaign in Pakistan underscores the blurring of lines between soldiers and spies in secret American missions abroad since 9/11. President Obama's decision in late April 2011 to nominate Leon Panetta to succeed Robert Gates as secretary of defense and General David Petraeus to take Panetta's job at the CIA marked the latest evidence in this trend. As CIA director, Panetta hastened the transformation of the spy agency into a paramilitary organization, overseeing the sharp escalation of CIA drone strikes in Pakistan and an increase in the number of secret bases and covert operatives in remote parts of Afghanistan. General Petraeus, meanwhile, aggressively pushed the military deeper into the CIA's turf, using Special Operations troops and private security contractors to conduct secret intelligence missions. As commander of the military's Central Command in September 2009, Petraeus also signed a classified order authorizing American Special Operations troops to collect intelligence in Saudi Arabia, Jordan, Iran, and other places outside of traditional war zones. The result is that American military and intelligence operatives are at times virtually indistinguishable from each other as they carry out classified operations in the Middle East and Central Asia.

Having taken office during a time of war, President Obama gave a simple initial order to his national security team: First, do no harm to successful plans. But the new administration also launched a top-to-bottom review of the highly classified "Execute Orders," or ExOrds, an undisclosed reassessment of Bush policy conducted by Obama's top advisers to continue, cancel, or reshape the standing priorities and powers granted the military for operations against global terrorist targets outside the official war zones of Iraq and Afghanistan. It was partly an exercise in good governance to ask which military operations had been teed up and to analyze the rules of engagement under which military actions could be taken to achieve which counterterrorism objectives. But most of all, the new commander in chief wanted to know who was responsible at each step of the way with the authority to say go or halt.

Senior Defense Department and military officials involved in the effort stressed that many, even most, of the ExOrds inherited from the Bush administration were adopted without editing. But there was one significant change: Defense Secretary Gates, retained in his post from the previous administration, had privately expressed concerns even when serving under President Bush that a number of high-priority counterterrorist operations could be launched on the say-so of the global combatant commanders, the four-star generals and admirals who control American military forces and military action in separate regions of the world. Although the logic made sense—high-value targets are fleeting, the intelligence quick to expire—Gates was deeply concerned about the delegation of launch authority solely to regional four-stars, despite the prestige of those commands and the experience of those commanders.

"It has been my practice since I took this job that I would not allow any kind of lethal action by U.S. military forces without first informing the president or getting his approval," Gates said. "I can't imagine an American president who would like to be surprised that his forces were carrying out an attack someplace around the world without him knowing about it. So I decided that we should change all of the ExOrds to make them conform in policy with my practice—that, in essence, before the use of military force, presidential approval would be sought." Cognizant that some high-profile terrorists might pop up only briefly and then vanish, Gates created a system where options for potential types of missions were discussed with the president in advance so that the commander in chief could delegate authority beforehand to strike specific fleeting targets.

Revising the ExOrds was just the first step in reshaping American counterterrorism strategy by the new president and his team. It was, to be sure, an effort that included both continuity and change, and its architect was the National Security Council's John Brennan. While a staunch defender of the CIA drone strikes, Brennan also understood that it would take much more than killing or capturing Al Qaeda fighters to defeat Islamic extremists. As he told an audience at the Carnegie Endowment for International Peace in Washington in December 2010, "A counterterrorism strategy that focuses on the immediate threat to the exclusion of the more comprehensive political, economic and development-oriented approach is not only short-sighted but also doomed to fail."

Brennan was clearly indicating the shape of strategy to come: an official review of American counterterrorism policy. The new document was expected to be released on September 11, 2010, to mark the ninth anniversary of the 9/11 attacks, but pressing government business and the standard interagency negotiations over language pushed the release into 2011.

Though it may seem like an academic exercise, a national strategy document does serve a purpose, focusing the government's resources and attention, and clearly defining priorities in a way understandable to the nation. The Obama document seeks to be the U.S. government's most detailed articulation of a national counterterrorism strategy in five years.

Rather than define terrorism as a global threat, it describes which regions of the world most warranted American attention as the source of the greatest risk. It focuses aggressively on the central leadership of Al Qaeda and its more violent affiliates, but it pauses before authorizing the use of military force against other extremist organizations if they are not a direct threat to the United States and its allies. It also pauses if striking those targets would actually inflame more tensions rather than create security. It elevates to the level of presidential policy the reality that all of government must unite to combat terrorism, and that tactical successes would nonetheless bring only stalemate if the United States continues its program of serially attacking terror leaders without also building up the security capacity of those nations at risk of hosting extremist cells. As a first principle, it states that counterterrorism objectives should not be the driver of American policy in the Middle East, the Horn of Africa, or North Africa, but should be just one part of a comprehensive foreign policy and national security plan. Perhaps most important, while labeling Al Qaeda as

the number-one extremist threat, the Obama administration carefully lowers the Bush administration's lingering rhetoric that terrorism is a truly existential threat to the nation.

Many European allies had accused the Bush White House of fear-
mongering. While counterterrorism cooperation between American
spy agencies and their European counterparts remained strong in
the Bush era, the political chill hindered broader efforts to win
public support for the programs. Once in office, Obama made
mending those political ties a priority and put his top European
policy aide, Elizabeth Sherwood-Randall, in charge of the effort.
By the spring of 2011, the deepening political relationships had
helped boost the efforts of counterterrorism officials on both sides
of the Atlantic. "The more the political friction was lifted out of
that environment, the easier it was to have those conversations,"
said Nick Rasmussen, a holdover from the Bush White House who
is John Brennan's top counterterrorism deputy.

The administration's new strategy also expressed the belief that
any hope for success requires the government and people of the
United States to have, both physically and emotionally, the resilience to absorb the next attack and to recover and move on.
That truly would minimize any gain terrorists would hope for in
attacking.

"In the immediate aftermath of 9/11, I remember it very vividly,
we didn't know what we were facing," Brennan said. "There was
a palpable fear about WMD attacks in the national capital region.
It was the second wave that was amply reported; there was good
intelligence it was going to happen. So people were talking about
an existential threat because the magnitude of the threat—what Al
Qaeda had put into place—was an unknown. I think over time we
have come to understand better what Al Qaeda's capabilities are
and what its limitations are. Al Qaeda certainly would like to
carry out an attack that could have the consequences equal to a
9/11, which is why they would like to get their hands on some
kind of nuclear device. But I think one of the things we have rec-

ognized as a nation is that we can't just guard against 9/11 type of attacks. It has become a multidimensional challenge to us, because it really spans the spectrum from potentially existential threats that could have devastating consequences, all the way down to an individual shooter who could also have a powerful psychological impact on the nation."

The new counterterrorism strategy, Brennan maintained, would seek to take into account that range and would require the government to focus beyond one part of the threat. "We have to be prepared," Brennan said. "I think that is what we are trying to do, whether it be the physical defenses, the security measures we put in place, or engagement with our partners. We are trying to minimize the prospects. The prospect of any one of these types of attacks along this spectrum is going to be diminished because of these actions."

In cabinet-level meetings to chart the administration's counterterrorism strategy, Gates shared his concerns that the nation's political leadership must redefine how it thinks about and talks about another attack. "We've created an environment in which politicians are just waiting to jump on each other if there's a failure," said Gates, who has served eight presidents of both parties. "The idea of perfect security is completely contrary to the real world. And yet we've got an environment in which even a failed attempt becomes the subject of criticism, so that the government is willing to throw countless dollars at this problem in order not to look like they're slacking off." This is an issue, he said, that requires elected officials of both parties to, in essence, watch each other's backs. "It almost has to be a bipartisan initiative in both the executive and the legislative branches to say, in effect, 'We will not be afraid,'" Gates added. "We will do everything humanly possible. We will not distort our values. We will not let them claim victory by changing our way of life and the way we look at the world."

The American public needs to change its mind-set, as well, Gates argued. "We appear as a people to be afraid all the time," he said.

"Americans in the past have always been resilient. I think this is a change for us. And I wish we could get back to where we were. We are not a fearful people."

Since 2009, federal officials have braced for the threat of home-made bombs against civilian targets in the United States. In response, the Department of Homeland Security under President Obama began working closely if quietly with a wide spectrum of private businesses to guard against what were perceived as the most likely attacks. In December 2009, the department gathered dozens of security directors from the hotel and shopping mall industries at an undisclosed site in northern Virginia for an all-day exercise to test their responses to a simulated terrorist threat and series of attacks in a major American city. In one of four domestic and international scenarios, a resident called in a report of a suspicious package in a hotel's underground parking garage. The city's bomb squad quickly evacuated the area, found the package, and disarmed it. But just an hour later across town, a car bomb exploded next to a major hotel and shopping mall, killing or injuring dozens of people. About fifteen minutes after that, another bomb detonated sixty feet away from a staging area police were using to respond to the initial attack, injuring four officers and wounding seven other people.

With each piece of new information or each new event, the security officials responded as if they were facing a real attack, taking steps to secure their buildings and customers, and sharing information with federal, state, and local authorities. In doing so, they identified potential gaps in protective measures and infor-mation sharing, including which specific news items should be released to the public and how they ought to be disseminated. "These are all security officers so they're not novices at this," said Rand Beers, the Homeland Security Department's senior counter-terrorism official. "In some ways, we are showing the progression of sophistication on the part of the terrorist groups" by focusing on sequential attacks.

While American national security officers remained unwavering in their belief that Al Qaeda remained just as unwavering in its desire to mount another 9/11-style, mass-casualty attack, they also began acknowledging that the more likely style of terrorist mission was to replicate in the United States an offensive that had claimed the lives and limbs of more American military personnel in Iraq and Afghanistan than any other: improvised explosive devices (IEDs) planted in roadways. It made sense, and it worried Michael Vickers at the Pentagon. "If the signature weapon for us is the Predator, then the signature weapon for them is the IED," he said. Vickers was analyzing those trends as he was being promoted from assistant secretary for special operations to undersecretary for intelligence, joining the inner circle of government intelligence chieftains. He had also recently completed his dissertation, earning a Ph.D. at Johns Hopkins University, a goal long delayed by the tempo of his public service. The dissertation is massive: 1,013 pages, printed in three volumes. Titled "The Structure of Military Revolutions," the work examines significant changes in war fighting across the core military capabilities: firepower, mobility, protection, sustainment, and the realm of command-and-control, communications, and intelligence.

Vickers was applying military analysis dating back to Clausewitz not only to earn his Ph.D. but also to understand the adaptability of today's militants and a new weapon of choice: the IED. Explosives can be bought, stolen, or mixed with relative ease in basement laboratories, and there is little in the way of defense. In the case of Faisal Shahzad, it was only an observant street vendor— and the incompetence of the bomber—that prevented an explosive-packed SUV from detonating in Times Square.

Senior commanders agreed. "One of the questions I asked myself back then is, 'When do they show up here?'" said Admiral Mullen. "The fact that it hasn't happened, I think, is certainly due to the dramatically improved effort in the interagency, in the government, between governments, among governments on the one hand and, quite frankly, a little bit of luck that one of these hasn't been pulled off. But we recognized that potential a long time ago, and certainly we think about it."

The military keeps internal statistics on the spread of IEDs out of Iraq and Afghanistan, and have tracked how they now appear in the thousands, and with devastating effect, in Pakistan and India but also with less notice in Thailand, Sri Lanka, the Philippines, Colombia, Somalia, and parts of North Africa. Even Russian security forces have faced the devices in the republics of Ingushetia and Dagestan. Jonathan M. George, of HMS Inc., a private company that analyzes IED attacks and advises on countermeasures, maintains a database gathered from public documents and media accounts. He said the number of improvised explosive devices that detonated or were disarmed outside of Iraq and Afghanistan totaled more than 3,000 in 2006, more than 4,000 in 2007, again more than 4,000 in 2008, and dipped to about 2,000 in 2009. They rose again to over 3,000 in 2010. Something else rose, as well: the number of casualties from those attacks, owing to the increasing lethality of each blast. Pakistan had the most improvised explosive attacks outside the war zones, followed by India, Russia, and Thailand. But officials are certain the United States, with its vast, open roadways, will become a target.

"Certainly, it's a real threat in our country, as well," Admiral Mullen said.

In his repeat tours as chairman of the Joint Chiefs of Staff, Admiral Mullen has served as the senior military adviser to President Bush and President Obama. He acknowledged that he came to the top military job as agnostic, even skeptical, that the lessons of Cold War deterrence had much to offer in the new age of terror. "This is an area that we sort of put on the shelf for twenty-plus years so we are really at the beginning of trying to understand it again," he said early in his tenure as chairman. "Deterring them, individuals who will kill themselves, who have no moral boundaries, who just have such a different view of life and what it means—it is not insurmountable, but I haven't figured out how to do it."

And so it was notable when Admiral Mullen traveled in the fall of 2010 to Stanford University to address a Hoover Institution conference on deterrence. He declared that traditional strategies to credibly impose costs on adversaries through combinations of threatened punishment and sustained denial had new relevance in counterterrorism. "While not all extremist groups share the same goals or ideology," he said, "they do retain sufficient autonomy to make their own strategic choices, which in my mind makes them vulnerable to some form of coercion, and perhaps even deterrence." He underscored the reality that several terrorist organizations— such as Hezbollah and Hamas—had begun the transformation from shadowy, stateless cells to take on attributes of nation-state powers. "The closer aligned the group is to a state, or the more governing responsibilities it assumes, the more susceptible it is to influence," he said.

To be sure, Osama bin Laden was beyond personal deterrence and, at the other end of the terror cycle, likewise are suicide bombers by the time they strap on a vest of explosives and ball bearings. "To really deter terrorism at that level, the conditions that lead a person to that decision point must be addressed," Mullen said. "We can continue to hunt and kill their leaders, and we will. But when a person learns to read, he enters a gateway toward independent education and thought. He becomes more capable, more employable, and enjoys a sense of purpose in his life. These accomplishments delegitimize the terrorists' ideology, replacing the fear they hope to engender with the hope they fear to encounter. Now that is a deterrence of truly strategic nature."

After his address, Mullen acknowledged that the concepts of the "new deterrence" were not fully formed, but he said it was taking the shape of a strategy and was not simply a slogan sought for adoption by administration officials. "There isn't a fight that I'm in that I'm not asking the question, 'What could we have done to avoid this? Or, what can we do to avoid this in the future in terms of the kinds of things that we see?' " he said. "And so many of them these days are network-based, so if you look at who's in the network and how did it get created—when you look at the structures that are in a network, how is it financed? Who are the people? Where are they coming from? Where do they get their training? What's their background? And then I think maybe even some of the conventional deterrence theory starts to apply. How do you bring pressure on them, on every aspect of the organization from a deterrence standpoint? How do I raise the ante, how do I raise the price just in simple cost-benefit terms to every aspect of this network? You pick the number: 25 percent of them—the irreconcilables that are the ones that are going to die for what they believe in. And yet they can't be functional without the 75 percent of their organization that isn't idealistic but that doesn't have much of a future."

Despite the tactical successes, despite efforts to create a new strategy for countering terrorism, Admiral Mullen acknowledged a grim truth: "Everybody believes we're going to get hit again."

11

COUNTERSTRIKE IN ABBOTTABAD

When it was over, President Obama called it one of the greatest military and intelligence operations in American history. Yet it was nothing more than the logical culmination of nearly a decade of missteps, mistakes, trial and error under fire, and ultimately lessons not only learned but taken to heart. So it was that the United States succeeded in tracking and killing the man who inspired and planned the terror attacks of 9/11.

The raid on the compound in Abbottabad, Pakistan, produced an outcome beyond the president's most optimistic forecast: Osama bin Laden dead, all of the American assaulters safely returned to base with an intelligence bonanza in their rucksacks, and even their bomb-sniffing dog extracted without a scratch. Yet as cabinet secretaries, senior intelligence officers, law enforcement and homeland security chiefs, national security advisers, and media counselors gathered in the White House Situation Room on Sunday, May 1, 2011, in the final hours before the attack, uncertainty reigned. There was no guarantee that the tall man whose every movement in the courtyard of his compound had been logged by CIA watchers in a nearby safe house was truly bin Laden. What would the orders be if Pakistan learned of the raid or heard the operation under way, and rushed police and military forces to confront the American commandos? Were there tunnels for escape or deadly booby-traps? Previous failures haunted this meeting, too: the 1980 Desert One operation that had failed to rescue the American hostages from Iran and the 1993 Black Hawk Down tragedy that had cost the lives of eighteen American soldiers in Mogadishu, Somalia. In fact, in the mission's opening minutes, a super-secret stealth helicopter went down hard in the bin Laden compound and was so damaged that it had to be blown up and left behind, all because the temperature was seventeen degrees warmer than expected, degrading the pilot's ability to control his descent with a full load of commandos. But, unlike Desert One three decades earlier, this time a backup helicopter was hovering nearby and flew to the compound.

Advance planning for the raid attempted to anticipate, even divine, all of the possible outcomes, from spectacular success to catastrophic failure. Each option presented to the president was accompanied by a list of numerous potential outcomes, each demanding a different response. All of the contingencies were collected in a three-ring binder two inches thick, called the Playbook. The national security, intelligence, and military officials who had spent months gaming out the raid had "red teamed" the scenarios for flaws, drawing up what are called "branches" and "sequels" that attempted to predict and then plan for a rapidly expanding set of potential results. Early that Sunday, as President Obama's war council convened in the Situation Room, all members had the Playbook in front of them, which meant anything could happen.

When the operation was over, and everyone in the Situation Room was breathing again, Defense Secretary Robert M. Gates uttered his ultimate judgment on the complex operation. He noted the many moving parts, assembled across many months, requiring the seamless integration of so many agencies across the entire government, and contrasted it with the capabilities of the intelligence and military communities he had helped manage during his service to eight presidents over the previous four decades. His verdict was straightforward: "This mission simply would not have been possible before."

Osama bin Laden's trail had gone cold, at least since 2007, until the summer of 2010, when a team of Pakistanis working with the CIA spotted a white sport-utility vehicle in Peshawar, Pakistan, that they had been seeking. After years of detainee interrogations, document analyses, and electronic signals intercepts, the U.S. government knew the driver only by a nickname, but as the operatives jotted down the SUV's license-plate number, the CIA launched a process to identify the suspect by name. He was a courier who was believed to be bin Laden's only link to Al Qaeda and the outside world. In the weeks that followed, intelligence agents conducted an arm's-length tracking of the man, until he led them to a surprisingly large and well-protected compound in Abbottabad, a well-to-do small city not far from Islamabad, where Pakistan's prestigious military academy is located and where many retired Pakistani military officers live.

A decade of counterterrorism campaigns had built up the muscles of the vast network of American agencies responsible for intelligence, surveillance, and reconnaissance. So when the order went out to develop an "ISR soak" on the walled compound, the system knew how to bring on a brute-force yet almost invisible effort. In addition to the CIA safe house quietly rented to keep direct watch on the compound, the intelligence community turned its electronic eyes and ears on the site, scooping up minute-by-minute information to build a pattern-of-life model on the compound and its residents. Photographs and video from aircraft and satellites were analyzed by specialists who had been trained to assess covert construction in North Korea or Iran. (They usually look for nuclear sites or ballistic missile launchers.) In advance of this mission, the analysts were able to draw up detailed blueprints of the buildings and walls, bringing order to the images of construction and terrain.

The CIA and Special Operations officers in charge of the mission would repeatedly say that the "situational awareness" they were given about the compound gave them confidence.

It was obvious, too, that the high-value target inside the compound was operating on trusted experience, apparently enhanced by years of hiding. He had good operational security of his own. The human footprint was small, almost unnoticeable. There was no legion of Arab guards in SUVs with tinted windows, as might have been expected. The compound was far larger than its neighbors, but it had no Internet or telephone connections. And the occupants never turned on their cell phones; in fact, the electronic signals captured from the compound were so faint that it seemed those inside not only turned off their cell phones but even removed the batteries and SIM cards long before entering.

It was a network fighting a network. And, in the end, it was bin Laden's operational requirement to have a human courier connecting him to his terror network—someone to physically transfer thumb drives with treatises, orders, demands, and videos and to receive feedback from the field—that led the United States to where he was hiding in plain sight.

American intelligence officials had increasing confidence that they were finally closing in on bin Laden. In February 2011, CIA director Leon Panetta summoned Vice Admiral William H. McRaven, the commander of the Joint Special Operations Command, to CIA headquarters in Langley, Virginia, to share what the agency knew about the mysterious compound and to begin planning a military strike. Even a few years earlier, it would have been almost unfathomable that such a conversation would take place. Special Operations zealously guarded its turf, and the CIA's covert operatives viewed the commandos suspiciously.

That had to change. It happened first on the ground in Afghanistan immediately after 9/11, when small detachments of Army Special Forces soldiers, working closely with CIA officers, backed the Afghan Northern Alliance and a militia force loyal to Hamid Karzai in the south and routed Al Qaeda and the Taliban. This tactical cooperation grew over the years and was expanded and refined under General Stanley McChrystal, whose hunter-killer-exploitation teams in Iraq were supported by analysts from the CIA, DIA, NSA, and FBI. McChrystal employed the same strategy when he assumed command of the allied mission in Afghanistan in 2009. Within a year, the pace of intelligence-driven operations, the so-called night raids against the Taliban and other militants, skyrocketed. More than a dozen times each night, teams of American and allied Special Operations forces and Afghan troops, supported by CIA and DIA analysts, swooped in on houses or compounds across the country. The raids targeted Taliban shadow governors, midlevel insurgent commanders, and individuals who handled finances and logistics for the Taliban.

That kind of seamless operational cooperation became common on a smaller scale in Yemen, Pakistan, and other shadowy battlegrounds. "One of the things we have seen since 9/11 is an extraordinary coming together, particularly of CIA and the military, in working together and fusing intelligence and operations in a way that just, I think, is unique in anybody's history," Secretary Gates said five days after bin Laden was killed.

In Washington, however, the marriage of the military and intelligence worlds had faced a bumpier ride. Gates's predecessor, Donald Rumsfeld, was openly disdainful of the CIA's abilities and worried that the agency's relatively small cadre of case officers was unable to support major military operations in Afghanistan and Iraq. Rumsfeld set out to improve the Pentagon's own human intelligence network, including dispatching small intelligence teams abroad. But sometimes the teams were sent in without the knowledge of the ambassadors and CIA station chiefs in various countries, causing turf battles. Rumsfeld's departure in late 2006 and his replacement by Gates, a former CIA director, salved the bureaucratic wounds. President Obama's decision in April 2011 to nominate Panetta to succeed Gates as defense secretary, and General

David Petraeus to follow Panetta at the CIA, further reinforced the blurring of lines between soldiers and spies in secret American missions abroad.

It was into this environment that Admiral McRaven began drawing up military options for capturing or killing bin Laden.

At the same time, a high-level team of administration officials headed by John Brennan and Denis McDonough, the deputy national security adviser, began developing the Playbook, a mind-bending series of what-ifs and negative scenarios. The group marched through a range of issues to be worked out in advance of any presidential decision. What were the implications of military action on civilians in or near the compound? How would the U.S. government manage the backlash from the Muslim world if an attack failed? What would be the political blowback at home? The possible fate of bin Laden was debated almost endlessly. "It was looked at from the standpoint of if we captured him, what will we do with him? Where would he go? If he was killed, what will we do with him, and where would he go?" Brennan said.

The Playbook grew even thicker after Admiral McRaven presented his options to Panetta, who in turn presented them to the president on March 14. By then, evidence was growing that bin Laden was living in the compound in Abbottabad. Intelligence analysts had noticed a tall man strolling in the compound's dirt courtyard for one or two hours a day. Increasingly, they became convinced that the "Pacer," as they called him, was bin Laden. Intelligence officials were reluctant to get a closer look through informants or technical surveillance for fear of tipping off the Al Qaeda leader.

One option proposed by Admiral McRaven was to blast the "Pacer" with missiles from a CIA Predator drone while he was out for one of his daily walks. The agency had carried out about 240 drone attacks in Pakistan over the preceding seven years. But the strategists were concerned that the Predator might not pack enough punch to finish off bin Laden with certainty.

Gates directed military officials to examine the option of a massive aerial bombardment, much like the planned B-2 assault in August 2007 on the Tora Bora cave complex, where some intelligence analysts had believed bin Laden would join a war council of top Taliban and Al Qaeda commanders. For the Abbottabad mission, military officials estimated that striking bin Laden's compound would require thirty-two bombs of two thousand pounds each. An airstrike that size would destroy the compound and anything in it, but another question arose: How could American officials be certain that bin Laden had been there if his remains were obliterated? White House officials worried that any strategic blow to Al Qaeda from the killing of its leader would be delayed, perhaps indefinitely, if bin Laden's death could not be confirmed. And dropping that much ordnance in a well-to-do community of a nation with which America was not at war risked a high civilian death toll and severe diplomatic damage.

A joint raid with Pakistani operatives was briefly considered and then rejected, especially as concerns mounted about who within Pakistan's military or security services may have known about bin Laden's suspected hideaway. "It was decided that any effort to work with the Pakistanis could jeopardize the mission," Panetta said. "They might alert the targets."

Another leading option was a helicopter assault. Just as they did in the planning for the possible raid in early 2002 against Al Qaeda leaders in Chalus, Iran, the Navy SEALs carried out mission rehearsals using mock-ups designed to resemble bin Laden's compound. This time, however, the intelligence provided by the CIA safehouse in Abbottabad, as well as satellite photos and intercepted cell-phone calls, gave the SEAL team a much clearer picture of their target.

But, as with the proposed Iranian mission nearly a decade earlier, the bin Laden operation carried huge political and diplomatic risks for the military and for the White House. Admiral McRaven's planning unfolded at the same time relations with Pakistan had soured dramatically over the arrest of Raymond Davis, the CIA contractor imprisoned for shooting two Pakistanis on a crowded street in Lahore in January. Some administration officials feared that an American operation against the Abbottabad compound could trigger a backlash from Pakistan's government, and Davis could wind up dead in his jail cell. Davis was ultimately freed on March 16, clearing away an obstacle for the military and intelligence planners. But President Obama directed McRaven to build a "fight your way out" option into the plan, with two helicopters following the two main assault copters as backup in case of trouble and attack aircraft standing by if needed.

On Thursday, April 28, at the fifth National Security Council meeting held on the mission planning since mid-March, three options remained on the table: the helicopter assault, the Predator strike, and a decision to wait for more intelligence to develop on the compound's inhabitants. Obama ended the meeting and said he wanted to weigh the options. Sixteen hours later, the president had made up his mind. The helicopter assault would go forward. He summoned aides to the White House Diplomatic Room, told them the mission was "a go," and directed them to start drafting the military orders.

"The president was trying to balance competing objectives," said Nick Rasmussen, the White House's deputy counterterrorism adviser. "On the one hand, he was trying to keep the U.S. military footprint small and to avoid a confrontation with the Pakistanis. But he also had to weigh how to remove bin Laden from the battlefield in a way that did not leave uncertainty, which could potentially undermine the impact of the entire mission."

On Saturday, President Obama took a break from rehearsing for the annual White House Correspondents Dinner to speak to the mission commander one last time. He then called Admiral McRaven at his headquarters in Afghanistan to wish him luck.

The parallel efforts to harvest intelligence on the Abbottabad compound and build options for a mission to get bin Laden were among the government's most tightly compartmentalized secrets. "There were people inside the intelligence community witting of the effort to develop a picture on this target, and on who might be there, but they had no involvement up until the end on possible courses of action," said one official involved from the start. Membership in the top-level group actively focused on plotting options for a raid was kept extremely small: fewer than two dozen people across the entire United States government. The number of those who were "read in" to the intelligence expanded substantially as the president made his decision, which came on Friday, April 29.

All those in the know were required to maintain a façade of business as usual. In private, it might be easy to mask one's anticipation for a raid on the most wanted man in the world. But Saturday night was the annual White House Correspondents Dinner, broadcast live on C-SPAN. Among the guests were the president himself, who delivered the traditional comic monologue, as well as Secretary Gates and the Pentagon's Michael Vickers, the undersecretary of defense for intelligence, whom Gates had designated as his point man for the operation. But their attendance that night at a gala dinner, wearing black tie and poker faces, was nothing compared to the social obligations facing Michael Leiter, the director of the National Counterterrorism Center. He got married that Saturday night.

The imperative of operational security continued into Sunday morning as the principal players positioned themselves without public notice at CIA headquarters and in the White House Situation Room. All public tours of the West Wing were cancelled so that tourists would not see, and wonder at, the entire war council arriving at the White House on an otherwise quiet spring Sunday. Michael Vickers, whose tradecraft spanned decades as a Green Beret and CIA agent, knew that the simple act of calling in a driver or secretary would be a noticeable change in the battle rhythm of a day off. So he drove himself to the Pentagon to gather the files, folders, and background material required for a day that would see him crisscrossing Washington from the Pentagon to the White House to the CIA and back to the White House.

As Vickers left his office, his inner compass guided him on a brief detour. He walked a perimeter line toward the southwest edge of the Pentagon, arriving at a two-acre, gently landscaped park organized around 184 illuminated benches, each bearing the name and age of a victim of 9/11, the innocents who died aboard American Airlines Flight 77 and those who perished by force of blast and flame inside the Pentagon building. He stood quietly, alone, in the early morning light. Only then did he walk to his car and drive himself across the Potomac River for his first White House meeting on what would become a historic day.

Their names may never be known, their faces may remain unseen, but the strike package that flew by helicopter out of Jalalabad, Afghanistan, for the bin Laden compound numbered seventy-nine: Navy SEALs, intelligence specialists, medical corpsmen, translators, and the bomb-sniffing dog. Little is known of the strike team commander, other than that he had scores of successful raids under his belt and that McRaven described him to White House officials as "absolutely the single guy I would choose for this mission."

For the operation, bin Laden was assigned the code name Geronimo. Inside the White House Situation Room, the president and his war council followed the mission via video link narrated by Leon Panetta at CIA headquarters. Soon after Panetta announced, "They've reached the target," one of the four helicopters carrying the assault team lost lift and descended faster than anticipated owing to unexpectedly warm temperatures. Its tail snapped off against a wall, but there were no injuries. The SEAL team commander adjusted his plans, and the unit executed its well-trained art of improvisation. A second helicopter, which had been tasked to hover over the main building while the commandos fast-roped onto the roof, instead landed on the ground inside the compound.

A third flew in from reserve. The SEALs set explosive charges to blow open a door to the main house and a brick wall behind it, which some said was a false door disguised as a ruse. Abu Ahmed al-Kuwaiti, the courier whose SUV had led American intelligence to the compound, began shooting at the strike team, which returned fire, killing him and his wife. A second man—al-Kuwaiti's brother— was spotted and believed readying to shoot; he too was killed. As the commandos made their way up a stairwell, bin Laden's son Khalid rushed toward them and he was killed as well. Smashing into the third-floor rooms atop the guest house, the commandos came face-to-face with bin Laden himself. "We have a visual on Geronimo," Panetta told the officials gathered in the Situation Room. An AK-47 and a Russian-made Makarov 9-mm automatic pistol were said to be within the Al Qaeda leader's reach. One of bin Laden's wives charged at the strike team; she was shot in the leg but not killed. A few minutes later came the message, "Geron-imo EKIA"—Enemy Killed in Action—with the trademark close-quarters sharpshooting of American Special Operations forces, the deadly efficient "double-tap." One bullet to the head and one to the chest.

Only then did the president speak. "We got him," he said.

If it was said that the JSOC raid on the Iraqi border town of Sinjar in September 2007 had produced the Al Qaeda Rolodex, the strike on bin Laden's safe house produced Al Qaeda's data bank. Even bin Laden's clothes gave up tantalizing pocket litter: several hundred euros—and two telephone numbers. "This collection represents the most significant amount of intelligence ever collected from a senior terrorist," said one American official. "It includes digi-tal, audio, and video files of varying sizes, printed materials, computer equipment, recording devices, and handwritten documents." The cache was said to include documents, computer discs, DVDs, ten computer hard drives, and one hundred thumb drives.

In a sign of the cooperative focus on unlocking the trove, a multiagency task force led by the CIA was assembled to triage, catalogue, and analyze this intelligence, all building on the lessons of sensitive-site exploitation learned across Afghanistan and Iraq. As if to prove the enhanced aura of cooperation, government officials repeated the list of those involved in exploiting the intelligence: the Department of Homeland Security, the Defense Intelligence Agency, the Office of the Director of National Intelligence, the Federal Bureau of Investigation, the National Media Exploitation Center, the National Counterterrorism Center, the National Geospatial-Intelligence Agency, the National Security Agency, and the Treasury Department.

The first priority was to search for clues on planned or pending attacks, real and aspirational, and to learn Al Qaeda's assessment of the gaps in America's defenses. Within hours of bin Laden's death, security was stepped up along rail lines, since threats to U.S. transportation networks were among the first translated from the documents. A handwritten notebook from February 2010 discussed tampering with tracks to derail a train on a bridge, possibly on Christmas, New Year's Day, the day of the State of the Union address, or the tenth anniversary of the September 11 attacks. But the government said there was no evidence of a specific imminent plot.

The task force also sought clues to identify and locate the surviving members of Al Qaeda's senior leadership. Within hours of the raid, the United States would launch a fresh wave of drone strikes into the tribal areas of Pakistan and into the deserts of Yemen. "This was the ultimate raid of its kind, which has been evolving over the past decade," Michael Vickers said just days after the mission, as the intelligence community was unlocking the secrets of bin Laden's files. "It was the combination of human skill, technical capabilities, and organizational coordination. All of that came together. It was the fusion of those things. None of those things by themselves would have gotten you there."

■ ■ ■

The death of bin Laden marked a major victory for the American military and intelligence agencies. But it also offered the Obama administration a rare opportunity to undercut the terrorist group's narrative and brand-name appeal.

In the weeks leading up to the raid, White House aides prepared messages and counterarguments to Al Qaeda's narrative to be used by senior American officials in briefings and interviews in the event bin Laden was killed or captured. They also devised strategies for getting America's message across on Twitter, Facebook, and other social media sites. "We essentially prepared a messaging strategy for every possible circumstance to include a good outcome as well as for more difficult, messy situations, even catastrophic ones," said Ben Rhodes, the deputy national security adviser for strategic communications.

At the State Department, Richard LeBaron's strategic communications center worked with public affairs officers at U.S. embassies around the world on Arabic and Urdu translations of President Obama's speech to the nation announcing bin Laden's death. Arabic speakers at State Department media centers in London and Dubai disseminated the themes in Obama's address. LeBaron's office produced talking points for American embassies and consulates on how to address accusations that bin Laden wasn't really dead or that the Pentagon had violated Islamic law by burying him at sea.

Unlike the military command in Iraq in 2006, which failed to fully exploit the public relations value of the captured video produced by Abu Musab al-Zarqawi, the leader of Al Qaeda in Iraq, the Obama administration sought to pounce on the propaganda windfall from bin Laden's death.

The day after bin Laden was killed, White House officials gleefully pointed out that he was living in comfort with his family in a walled, fortresslike house far from the rugged war zones of Pakistan's tribal areas or southern Afghanistan. "Here is bin Laden, who has been calling for these attacks, living in this million-dollar-plus compound, living in an area that is far removed from the front, hiding behind women who were put in front of him as a shield," Brennan told reporters. "I think it really just speaks to just how false his narrative has been over the years."

But there were several mistakes in Brennan's statements, which underscored the continued weakness of the American countermessaging strategy. Within twenty-four hours, the White House was forced to correct the fact there were no women shielding bin Laden when he was shot and killed. A further correction, about whether bin Laden was armed and participated in a firefight with the Navy SEALs (he wasn't and he didn't), also had to be made. First accounts of complicated military missions are almost always incomplete or inaccurate. But in his haste to trumpet the mission's operational success, Brennan heralded details about bin Laden that turned out to be wrong, undermining the credibility of the rest of his message in the Muslim world and elsewhere in the world.

White House officials dismissed the missteps as the normal discrepancies of early combat accounts and said that their broader themes would be more enduring. Bin Laden died, they argued, at a time when Al Qaeda was already struggling to remain relevant in the surging democratic current of popular revolutions that had toppled dictators in Tunisia and Egypt and that had roiled the Arab world from Libya to Syria to Bahrain. They noted that Ayman al-Zawahri, bin Laden's Egyptian deputy, was an unlikely figure to take up the leader's mantle, pointing out that he was an irascible micromanager who lacked bin Laden's charisma and religious stature and did not enjoy the respect of the wealthy Persian Gulf Arabs who are among Al Qaeda's biggest financial donors. American officials made no secret about trying to sow dissent among senior Al Qaeda leaders as they scrambled to pick a successor to their fallen leader.

The CIA's release of five videos of bin Laden on May 7, just days after they were recovered from his hideout, illustrated the Obama administration's efforts to minimize the Al Qaeda leader's mystique, even among mainstream Muslims who admired him for standing up to the West. The selected outtakes from bin Laden's recorded messages to his followers appeared to be part of an American effort to underscore bin Laden's vanity. In one video, bin Laden is shown watching himself on television in his house, and his beard is mostly white. In the other four videos, in which bin Laden addresses the Muslim world, his beard is black. U.S. intelligence officials openly speculated that the Al Qaeda leader had dyed his beard black in those videos in order to appear younger.

In the wake of the raid, American officials were convinced bin Laden's death offered them a unique opportunity to unnerve other Al Qaeda fighters and commanders. "It demonstrates no terrorist is safe," Rhodes said. But in light of the fact that the United States was so ineffective in combating Al Qaeda's narrative while bin Laden was alive, many doubts remained as to how well it will succeed now that he is dead.

As difficult as combating Al Qaeda's message has proved for American officials, another source of frustration has been to manage the often contentious relationships with pivotal counterterrorism allies. When the Navy SEAL team helicoptered into Osama bin Laden's compound, relations between the United States and Pakistan were already plummeting to their lowest levels since 9/11.

Bin Laden's residence—for more than five years—in a house less than a mile from Pakistan's equivalent of West Point, in Abbottabad, a city seventy-five miles from Islamabad, prompted angry American demands that Pakistan's powerful military and spy agency, the ISI, investigate its ranks for Al Qaeda confederates. A month after bin Laden's death, U.S. officials said they had no proof of official Pakistani government complicity in sheltering the Al Qaeda leader. But in a country where the lines blur quickly between active and retired ISI officers, many Americans suspected that bin

Laden enjoyed at least quasi-official support while in hiding in Abbottabad. "It's inconceivable that bin Laden did not have a support system in the country that allowed him to remain there for an extended period of time," said Brennan.

Within days, some members of Congress began calling for slashing all or part of the $3 billion in economic and military aid the United States sends to Pakistan each year and sharply scaling back ties with Islamabad. While neither of these outcomes is likely, the United States has no choice but to recalibrate its security relationship with Pakistan. The stakes are simply too high. The nightmare scenario for Pakistan is that Islamic radicals infiltrate and seize control of the country's nuclear weapons. Though Pakistan's arsenal of deployed weapons (estimated in 2011 as at least ninety bombs and warheads) is considered secure, senior American officials remain deeply concerned that weapons-usable fuel, which is kept in laboratories and storage centers, is more vulnerable and could be diverted to terrorists or other radical groups by insiders in Pakistan's vast nuclear complex.

Moreover, the United States relies on Pakistan for supply routes into Afghanistan to sustain the nearly one hundred thousand American troops in that country. Despite the deteriorating relations between the CIA and ISI, tactical cooperation among U.S., Afghan, and Pakistani troops in the tribal regions of both countries had actually improved in the year prior to the raid. "Simply wishing away Al Qaeda isn't going to happen," Nick Rasmussen said. "We're going to need Pakistan's help to complete the fight against terrorist networks."

Without its longtime leader, Al Qaeda is at a crossroads. "What bound the organization together more than anything else was the persona of Osama bin Laden," said Michael Leiter. "There was an attraction, an aura, a gravitas that only bin Laden had. With bin Laden's death, a great measure of Al Qaeda's cohesiveness is destroyed." Who will lead the organization based in Pakistan? What role will affiliates and like-minded groups in Yemen, North Africa, and Somalia play? How can the United States and embattled allies like Pakistan and Yemen move to exploit vulnerabilities in the organization's hierarchy and operations? The weeks and months following bin Laden's death gave the United States and its allies a window of opportunity, as terrorist networks tried to regroup, making them more vulnerable to counterstrikes. "This is not the time to take our foot off the gas," Obama told his top national security advisers just hours after the Abbottabad mission concluded.

Michael Vickers, reflecting on the mission's impact, envisioned a difficult battle against a determined foe. "Bin Laden's death is a tremendous strategic blow to Al Qaeda," he said. "The top structure, particularly bin Laden, but also Zawahri, are critically important to the strategic defeat of Al Qaeda. But so is taking apart the network so they can no longer function as an organization, taking away their sanctuary and preventing their ability to come back. We are well along that path."

"TELL ME HOW THIS ENDS"

It will be impossible to end terrorism.

It will be impossible to eradicate the root causes of terrorist action: poverty or lack of education or hope; the humiliating corruption in public life across the developing world; a false-prophet interpretation of American foreign policy as a twenty-first-century crusade to occupy sacred Muslim lands. Nor will it be possible to silence everywhere and forever the caustic voices of the misguided minority calling for violence against innocents in the aspiration of creating a better world. Even the task that is far simpler by comparison—to find and finish off terror cells—will never be fully achieved. As uplifting as was the prospect of populist revolts pressing for democracy across the Muslim world, political upheaval in the region risks disorder—and opportunities for terrorist cells to find new safe havens.

"There is a fundamental tension in seeking a counterterrorism 'grand strategy,'" said the Pentagon's Michael Vickers. "How do you get at the long-term strategic defeat of these groups? One model that was put forward was that they spring from an unhealthy political and social system. I need to remake that system if I am going to get at the root causes of these problems. We promote democracy, we promote development—we do that no matter what, but are they critical instruments? Is this the only way I can defeat the enemy in counterterrorism? The counter approach is to work with what you have, while not abandoning your long-term goals. Shore up the security institutions. Work with intelligence—more near-term things—but to try and tamp down this threat and drive it to low levels in lots of critical places."

You can destroy the people in Al Qaeda, including bin Laden himself, but you can't destroy the idea of Al Qaeda. And as for the brand name of Al Qaeda—an inspiration to a rising tide of terror affiliates across the Islamic world as well as to self-radicalized, individual, lone-wolf extremists in the West—it has barely been dented. American forces are racking and stacking terrorists like cordwood. But America has not killed terrorism.

So, how does this end?

Americans face a challenge, and the nation must alter its thinking about terrorism and terrorist attack. America must adopt a culture of resilience. Yes, every effort must be made to disrupt, dismantle, and defeat Al Qaeda and its affiliates. Yes, defenses must be erected to prevent attack and deny terrorists tactical successes that might be trumpeted as strategic victories. Yes, the nation must encourage economic progress in the developing world and seek to empower those who feel powerless. But a demand by the American people for perfection against terrorist attacks, a zero tolerance for error, hands extremists victory anytime they even get close. The Christmas Day bomber failed to set off his bomb. The plane didn't crash. The printer-package bombs from Yemen were intercepted. Yet it was the nationwide recrimination in the wake of those failed terror attacks that created a sense of terror.

Al Qaeda has adopted a dual-track strategy. It still seeks a weapon of mass destruction to create mass casualties for mass cost or at least for mass public effect. And along with these efforts at mounting a major attack, Al Qaeda inspires affiliates and disaffected, loner jihadists to take fists of pebbles and throw them repeatedly into the cogs of American life and industry. The inevitable calculus is that a few will get through. Do that enough times, and it has the impact of a major attack. A terror operation that costs a few thousand dollars, even if it fails, can prompt the government and industry to spend billions in response. And these repeated tiny assaults are exceedingly difficult to thwart. America has learned a lot and has been fortunate. But the American military, law enforcement, and intelligence communities cannot be lucky and good all the time. The terrorists have learned, too. They only have to be lucky, and good, occasionally.

The nation's top terrorism watchers express a concern that the United States will come under growing attack from the inside. Much as street gang and organized crime problems crest and fall but are never flat for long, so the best efforts by law enforcement may be unable to prevent homegrown extremism unless communities step up their efforts to police and care for their own. Short of that, officials expect the terrorist tool of choice in overseas combat zones—the IED—to migrate to the United States, as it already has with the attempted Times Square car bombing. Officials have quietly tightened rules on the domestic purchase of explosives and a number of other critical ingredients for homemade bombs, like the ammonium nitrate used by Timothy McVeigh to bring down a federal office building in Oklahoma City.

So when the terrorists do get through, the nation must deal with it and return to normal that day, as has been the practice in Israel and Britain. Within hours after the transit system attacks in July 2005, the London Underground was packed with commuters. The United States must emulate and have in place a robust system of rapid response and a plan for immediate recovery. America must learn to offer a shrug to terror attack that denies the effect being sought. That should be front and center in every major speech by the nation's leadership on national security, but it is politically risky, as any president's opponents will charge that the government is offering an implicit acceptance of inevitable attack.

A fundamental message in the battle against violent extremism is that the United States cannot lose sight of its values, as no doubt there will be a growing tension between credible calls for greater surveillance and profiling on one hand, and full-throated defense for privacy and civil liberties on the other.

"In the months before Fort Hood, I was testifying on behalf of the intelligence community, advocating for the extension of certain aspects of the Patriot Act," recalled Michael Leiter of the National Counterterrorism Center. "For very good reasons, people had some concerns. And I got a lot of, Why should we allow you to continue to spy on Americans? Several weeks later in the wake of Fort Hood, I was back up on the Hill. And I will tell you that a whole lot fewer people were complaining about me spying on Americans and a whole lot more people were complaining that I wasn't spying enough. That is a tough line to walk. So these are the sorts of tensions that we have. Being whipsawed between these two extremes can be extremely problematic and very difficult to maintain, either security or protection of civil liberties."

In June 2011, the White House announced that Leiter was stepping down after nearly four years as director of the National Counterterrorism Center. He had contributed a lot of work to the updated counterterrorism strategy that the Obama administration was preparing to unveil in the coming weeks, but now he wanted to spend more time with his new bride. Leiter also believed it was time for someone else to take the helm to "bring fresh eyes to the problems we face." He felt proud of the progress that the center, and the government overall, had made in combating terrorism, but he also sounded a familiar warning to the nation to remain resilient in the face of a future attack. "We'll do more to defeat the enemy," he said, "by not overreacting to the inevitable act of terrorism."

The nation is without a doubt moving ever closer toward the dangerous precipice of another attack. The length of the journey to that next mass-casualty strike has been extended by years of successful counterstrikes. And it is possible, but not certain, that the severity of the attack—the drop off the cliff—has been diminished. But the attack is coming. The most important thing the nation can do is be resilient. That denies terrorists the strategic victory they seek.

Thomas Schelling's successors have spoken. Deterrence—updated, expanded, even redefined—is now official American policy for countering Al Qaeda and its affiliated terrorist organizations. As the Obama administration prepared for the tenth anniversary of the 9/11 attacks in September 2011, the White House and the Pentagon announced that they were adapting the principles of Cold War deterrence in their effort to combat extremists. "Though terrorists are difficult to deter directly, they make cost/benefit calculations and are dependent on states and other stakeholders we are capable of influencing," declared the National Military Strategy of the United States for 2011. "When directed, we will provide capabilities to hold accountable any government or entity complicit in attacks against the United States or allies to raise the cost of their support. And we must take further steps to deny terrorists the benefits they seek through their attacks." The United States, the strategy declared, stands ready to retaliate for any attack across the entire spectrum of military, economic, and diplomatic capabilities—and at a time and place of the president's choosing.

Is that enough?

With the lessons of an Afghanistan tour still fresh in his mind, Jeff Schloesser voiced concerns that the United States had failed to keep pace with the shifting tactics and strategies of Al Qaeda and the Taliban. "They have been able to innovate faster than we have, and we have been relatively unsuccessful in stemming the recruitment of new terrorist wannabes," he said. "You now actually have a larger number of Americans who want to be revolutionaries against their own country. We have not done a good job about that." In August 2010 Schloesser retired from active-duty service. He did so in the aftermath of an Army investigation into the conduct of three of his subordinates during a controversial battle at Wanat,

Afghanistan, in July 2008 that left nine American soldiers dead and twenty-seven wounded. Though the Army cast no blame on him and exonerated the subordinates, Schloesser chose to retire after thirty-four years of service rather than pursue a promotion to lieutenant general. He left to become president of an aviation services company.

Since leaving government at the end of the Bush administration in January 2009, Juan Zarate has served as senior national security adviser to CBS News and as a senior adviser to the Center for Strategic and International Studies, where he is directing a major study of the future of Al Qaeda and its affiliates. "Though we are safer now than after 9/11, we still face an adapting terrorist Hydra," Zarate said in the winter of 2011. "AQ remains a serious threat, but the greatest danger we may face now from terrorism is the ability of a small group of individuals to spark geopolitical crises or the renting of societies with a singular terrorist flashpoint."

John Tyson, the DIA's terrorism expert, has been tracking Al Qaeda since Osama bin Laden was just a loudmouth with a large bank account. As the nation approached 9/11's tenth anniversary, he conceded that he remained pessimistic that the United States will ever be able to declare victory in the campaign against violent extremism. The enemy today, he said, is not the enemy of 9/11. It has spread. It has transformed. It has metastasized. The interlocking global network of Al Qaeda is based on pledges of affiliation as well as on sympathetic action. Terrorism inspired by Al Qaeda cannot be defeated as it is defined today. The task, he said, is to push the threat to a lower level, and manage—and accept—a degree of risk. Even though an American commando raid into Pakistan decapitated Al Qaeda, killing its charismatic founder and strategic leader, the terror network and its affiliates will seek to regroup, adapt, and strike again. The scenes of Americans rallying and cheering outside the White House, at the World Trade Center site, and in Times Square to express national relief and jubilation at the death of bin

Laden might have resonated like images from the end of World War II. But, unlike Nazi Germany and imperial Japan in 1945, religious militancy has not been defeated.

"There is not going to be a V-J Day, there is not going to be a Wall coming down," Tyson said. "Hopefully it will go out with a whimper and not a roar. But it is not something we can defeat. It is something that is going to have to defeat itself. It is something that is going to have to implode on itself, in terms of its widespread popularity, like how communism imploded on itself."

He paused, collecting his thoughts. "I would consider it a success if we get back to the point where it is still considered a national security issue but it is far down the totem pole, like it was pre–East Africa embassy bombings, where you had generals saying, 'Why should I care about terrorism?' "

NOTES

This book is drawn from more than two hundred interviews that we conducted with current and former military personnel, diplomats, and intelligence officers, as well as law enforcement, Pentagon, and White House officials who participated in the operations, intelligence analysis, and policy making in the decade following the terrorist attacks on Washington, D.C., and New York City on September 11, 2001. Our reporting for this book led us to sources throughout the United States and in more than a dozen foreign countries, including Iraq, Afghanistan, Pakistan, Djibouti, Saudi Arabia, Mali, and the Philippines. When possible, we have named the sources who were interviewed in the notes that follow. However, because of the nature of reporting on sensitive military, intelligence, and law enforcement operations and policies, oftentimes involving classified information, many of our sources spoke to us on the condition that they remain anonymous. In each case where we used anonymous sources, we carefully weighed the trade-offs between the need for transparency in reporting this book and the important information that confidential sources could provide.

PROLOGUE: IN THE BEGINNING . . .

1   "One of the lamentable principles": Thomas C. Schelling, *Arms and Influence* (New Haven: Yale University Press, 1966), p. xi.

4   "traditional concepts of deterrence will not work": White
         House, National Security Strategy of the United States, 2002.

4   "I don't believe that. I just don't believe that": Author interview
         with Thomas C. Schelling, Bethesda, Md., December 2009.

5   "A new deterrence calculus combines": White House, National
         Strategy for Combating Terrorism, 2006.

6   "The single biggest threat to U.S. security": President Barack
         Obama, "Remarks by President Obama and President Zuma of
         South Africa Before Bilateral Meeting," Blair House, Washing-
         ton, D.C., April 11, 2010.

6   "First, it is not easy to smuggle out of the country": Author inter-
         view with Thomas C. Schelling, Bethesda, Md., December 2009.

7   "There have been numerous reports over the years": John Bren-
         nan, Washington Convention Center, Washington, D.C., April
         12, 2010.

8   "I don't think anybody would argue": Author interview with
         John Tyson, Washington, D.C., May 19, 2010.

8   "My hunch is that by the time they have a bomb": Author inter-
         view with Thomas C. Schelling, Bethesda, Md., December 2009.

1. KNOW THINE ENEMY

11   At the U.S. Embassy in Kuwait City: The description of Jeffrey
         Schloesser on September 11, 2001, is from author interview
         with Major General Jeffrey Schloesser, USA (Ret.), Arlington,
         Va., February 25, 2010.

12   Juan Zarate stood at the window: The description of Juan
         Zarate on September 11, 2001, is from author interview with
         Juan Zarate, Washington, D.C., August 17, 2010.

15   "His operational experience spans covert action": Official
         Department of Defense Biography of Acting Undersecretary of
         Defense for Intelligence and Assistant Secretary of Defense (SO/
         LIC&IC), http://www.defense.gov/bios/biographydetail.aspx
         ?biographyid=178.

17   Vickers was featured in the book Charlie Wilson's War: George
         Crile, Charlie Wilson's War: The Extraordinary Story of How
         the Wildest Man in Congress and a Rogue CIA Agent Changed
         the History of Our Times (New York: Grove Press, 2003).

17   "My view of terrorism was shaped by my experiences in the
        '80s": Author interview with Michael Vickers, Arlington, Va.,
        August 26, 2010.

19   "The *Cole* attack, where they tried to kill our guys": Author
        interview with John Tyson, Washington, D.C., September 17,
        2010.

21   Bush, who had begun the day in Florida: The description of Air
        Force One's journey on September 11, 2001, is drawn from
        an e-mail exchange with Mark Knoller, CBS News, April 17,
        2010.

22   "We are not under pretend attack": Author interview with
        Admiral Richard W. Mies, USN (Ret.), Arlington, Va., April 21,
        2010.

22   Even as Stratcom was rehearsing: Author interview with former
        senior military officer, Spring 2010.

24   "Forget Europe": The discussion of Schloesser's Joint Staff
        assignment is from author interviews with General John Abi-
        zaid, USA (Ret.), at the United States Military Academy, West
        Point, N.Y., January 12, 2010, and with Major General Jeffrey
        Schloesser, USA (Ret.), Arlington, Va., February 25 and April
        13, 2010.

25   "There were people up and down the hallways who couldn't
        spell Al Qaeda": Author interview with a senior U.S. intelli-
        gence official, Northern Virginia, Spring 2010.

25   "Pretend it's a box": Author interview with a senior U.S. intel-
        ligence official, northern Virginia, Spring 2010.

26   "We in no way thought we were giving them leads": Author
        interview with former director of Central Intelligence and
        director of the National Security Agency Michael Hayden,
        Arlington, Va., April 8, 2010.

27   "In those early days, believe me, we saw them all": Author
        interview with a former staff member, National Security Coun-
        cil, Washington, D.C., April 2010.

27   "George, Bob, get together and sort this out": Author interview
        with a former senior administration official, 2010.

28   "Just nuts": Author interview with a former Defense Depart-
        ment official, 2010.

29   "When we would go up and do an early conceptual brief":

Author interview with Major General Jeffrey Schloesser, USA (Ret.), Arlington, Va., March 10, 2010.

30 "We thought we could take our counterterrorist forces": Author interview with General John Abizaid, USA (Ret.), at the United States Military Academy, West Point, N.Y., January 12, 2010.

31 The plan called for hunting: Author interview with a former senior military officer, Summer 2010.

33 "You learn very quickly that most insurgencies are not brought to heel": Author interview with General Richard Myers at National Defense University, Fort McNair, Washington, D.C., Summer 2009.

33 "Two + Seven was pretty crude": Ibid.

34 "If you get these guys simultaneously or in quick order": Author interview with John Tyson, Washington, D.C., September 17, 2010.

35 "In the end, it was asking for pre-approval": Author interview with Major General Jeffrey Schloesser, USA (Ret.), Arlington, Va., March 10, 2010.

37 "Who was in charge of the war on terror from 9/11 to now?": Author interview with General Richard Myers at National Defense University, Fort McNair, Washington, D.C., Summer 2009.

38 "to shake the trees hard": Author interview with a senior FBI counterterrorism official, Washington, D.C., 2010.

38 "What we began to realize pretty rapidly": Author interview with Arthur M. Cummings II, Washington, D.C., April 9, 2010.

40 "Before, it would be that": Author interview with Robert S. Mueller III, Washington, D.C., March 11, 2011.

40 "We made a very visible presence there": Author interview with Paul J. Browne, New York Police Department, Summer 2009.

42 "He doesn't have much patience for the battle of ideas": Author interview with a senior military official, Arlington, Va., Spring 2010.

43 "Despite remarkable victories, the fight against terrorism is far from over": General John Abizaid, USA, Testimony Before the Senate Armed Services Committee, September 25, 2003.

44 "Are we capturing, killing or deterring and dissuading more ter-

rorists every day": Secretary of Defense Donald Rumsfeld, October 16, 2003.

2. THE NEW DETERRENCE

46 "really neck down the number of words": Author interview with Barry Pavel, Arlington, Va., September 28, 2010.

48 "I said, 'Mr. President, you never have a meeting on the war on terrorism,' ": Author interview with Douglas Feith, Washington, D.C., June 30, 2009.

48 "It came from my head": Author interview with Barry Pavel, Arlington, Va., September 28, 2010.

51 "People at the time thought that terrorists weren't deterrable": Author interview with Matthew Kroenig, Washington, D.C., Summer 2009.

52 "Isn't anyone . . . thinking about deterring terrorists?": Ibid.

52 "I just remember it intellectually being a very good piece of work": Author interview with Douglas Feith, Washington, D.C., June 30, 2009.

52 "a perverse form of religious hope": Undersecretary of Defense Douglas Feith, Speech at American Israel Public Affairs Committee, April 21, 2002.

55 "If you can remove a certainty of success": Author interview with General James Cartwright, Arlington, Va., February 21, 2011.

55 "Don't define deterrence so narrowly": Author interview with Matthew Kroenig, Washington, D.C., Summer 2009.

56 "A new deterrence calculus combines the need to deter terrorists": White House, National Strategy for Combating Terrorism, 2006.

56 "We will selectively be able to enhance our deterrence": Ryan Henry, Arlington, Va., February 3, 2006.

58 "We decided that wouldn't change him one bit": Author interview with Major General Jeffrey Schloesser, USA (Ret.), Arlington, Va., March 10, 2010.

60 a brief statement by President Bush: President George W. Bush, Statement on North Korea Nuclear Test, White House, Washington, D.C., October 9, 2006.

61   "Today we also make clear that the United States": Secretary of
        Defense Robert Gates, Carnegie Endowment for International
        Peace, Washington, D.C., October 28, 2008.

62   "The artful presentation of Al Qaeda": Author e-mail interview
        with Richard Barrett, February 22, 2011.

63   "What we've developed since 9/11 is a better understanding":
        Author interview with Michael Leiter, director of the National
        Counterterrorism Center, McLean, Va., January 15, 2008.

63   "It hit very close to home for me": Quoted in Sheryl Gay Stol-
        berg, "For Antiterror Chief, a Rough Week Ahead as Hearings
        Begin," *New York Times*, January 17, 2010.

64   "Someone asked me what I thought about going to work":
        Michael Leiter, comments to Intelligence and National Security
        Alliance, Washington, D.C., February 24, 2010.

3. THE EXPLOITATION OF INTELLIGENCE

66   "The epitome of the word 'cavalry'?": Author interview with
        Lieutenant Garry Owen Flanders, USA, 2010.

70   "They did an initial triage": Author interview with a Department
        of Defense intelligence officer, Washington, D.C., May 2010.

71   "These guys wanted results": Quoted in Eric Schmitt and Caro-
        lyn Marshall, "Task Force 626: Inside Camp Nana," *New York
        Times*, March 19, 2006.

72   "That was a situation where we were building the airplane":
        Author interview with John Tyson, Washington, D.C., 2010.

72   "Literally you were talking to the guys who were going to be
        knocking down doors": Author interview with John Tyson,
        Arlington, Va., 2010.

74   "It gave us their whole game plan for Baghdad": Author inter-
        view with a defense intelligence officer, Tampa, Fla., 2010.

75   "Once that stuff started coming back": Author interview with
        Major General John Campbell, USA, Afghanistan, 2010.

76   "What we found in those documents": Author interview with
        General Raymond Odierno, USA, Arlington, Va., 2010.

78   "If you don't lock your door, you can't complain about bur-
        glars": Author interview with a former Marine Corps officer,
        Washington, D.C., 2010.

78   "We were getting our asses kicked by suicide bombers": Author
        interview with a senior military officer, 2010.

79   "It was the kind of thing done a thousand times before": Author
        interview with a senior military operations officer, Tampa, Fla.,
        April 29, 2010.

80   "These Al Qaeda were as—what's the right word?—as anal":
        Author interview with a senior U.S. counterterrorism official,
        Washington, D.C., 2010.

80   "They videotape everything, like Pamela and Tommy Lee":
        Author interview with a military intelligence analyst, Tampa,
        Fla., December 2009.

81   "From Vietnam to 9/11": Author interview with a Special
        Operations community veteran, 2010.

81   "If you can learn something about whatever is on those hard
        drives": Author interview with Major General Mark O. Schissler,
        Arlington, Va., January 11, 2008.

82   It was first disclosed in the *New York Times*: Thom Shanker
        and Eric Schmitt, "Pentagon Says a Covert Force Hunts Hus-
        sein," *New York Times*, November 7, 2003.

83   "Every operation is a fight for intelligence": Author interview
        with General Stanley A. McChrystal, USA, Arlington, Va., June
        10, 2009.

84   "I remember when we first started taking this stuff": Author
        interview with a Department of Defense intelligence analyst,
        Washington, D.C., May 19, 2010.

85   "more atomized—the individual guy who is bombing you every
        day": Author interview with Michael Vickers, Arlington, Va.,
        March 16, 2010.

88   "from the bow and arrow to the rifle": Author interview with
        Lieutenant General Gary North, USAF, Persian Gulf region, July
        2008.

89   "The fighters' overall youth suggests": Joseph Felter and Brian
        Fishman, *Al-Qa'ida's Foreign Fighters in Iraq: A First Look at
        the Sinjar Records* (West Point, N.Y.: Combating Terrorism Cen-
        ter at the U.S. Military Academy, no date), p. 16.

90   "The Sinjar records reinforce anecdotal accounts": Ibid., p. 27.

91   "For example in Libya": Author interview with a U.S. counter-
        terrorism expert involved in the Sinjar process, 2010.

91   "Whoever finds the intel, owns the intel": Author interview with a senior military operations officer, Tampa, Fla., April 2010.

91   "McChrystal said this is not something that should stay in the intelligence world": Author interview with a senior U.S. defense official, Arlington, Va., 2010.

92   "To do it, it involved dragging the shooters kicking and screaming": Author interview with a military intelligence analyst, Tampa, Fla., April 2010.

94   "I can't walk into a country and say, 'Stop foreign fighters'": Author interview with a senior national security official, 2010.

95   "This guy named Dailey would come in from the State Department": Author interview with a senior U.S. national security official involved in Dailey effort, undated.

97   "They can't cross-check names on databases or anything": Author interview with a senior national security official, 2010.

97   "Before Sinjar, we sort of 'soccer-Mom'ed' it": Author interview with a former Marine Corps officer, Washington, D.C., May 11, 2010.

98   "You can see you have to work with other countries": Speech by General David H. Petraeus to Association of the U.S. Army, Washington, D.C., October 7, 2008.

4. THE PROBLEM OF PAKISTAN

100   "This is the epicenter of terrorism in the world": Author interview with a senior U.S. military officer, Arlington, Va., Summer 2010.

101   "We kept building and building the case of the safe havens": Author interview with General Michael Hayden, USAF (Ret.), former director of Central Intelligence and National Security Agency, Arlington, Va., April 8, 2010.

102   "It wasn't just increase the Predator campaign": Author interview with a senior Bush administration official, Washington, D.C., April 2010.

104   Dame Eliza Manningham-Buller . . . said in an unusual public statement: See Alan Cowell, "Blair Says Homegrown Terrorism Is Generation-Long Struggle," *New York Times*, November 11, 2006.

105 "I saw my role as coordinator, organizer, and gadfly to the inter-agency process": Author interview with Juan Zarate, Washington, D.C., August 17, 2010.

106 "If we weren't concerned about what was happening": Thom Shanker, "In Pakistan, U.S. Defense Secretary Seeks Support to Counter Taliban," *New York Times*, February 13, 2007.

108 "There was just a lot of chatter": Author interview with former National Security Adviser Stephen Hadley, Washington, D.C., April 28, 2010.

108 "Al Qaeda was bringing more and more people": Author interview with General Michael Hayden, former director of Central Intelligence and National Security Agency, Arlington, Va., April 8, 2010.

108 "Pakistan was Job One from the beginning": Author interview with Michael Vickers, Arlington, Va., August 26, 2010.

108 "When you are looking for indications": Author interview with Frances Fragos Townsend, Washington, D.C., January 8, 2010.

109 On July 10, Homeland Security Secretary Michael Chertoff said in an interview: "Chertoff's Gut," *Chicago Tribune*, July 12, 2007.

109 "It is the same intuition people use in medicine": Author interview with Michael Chertoff, Washington, D.C., October 28, 2009.

110 "It hasn't worked for Pakistan": Mark Mazzetti and David Sanger, "Bush Aides See Failure in Fight with al Qaeda in Pakistan," *New York Times*, July 18, 2007.

111 "In 2007, we're in a period where we were especially worried": Author interview with Michael Leiter, McLean, Va., November 4, 2010.

112 "What it enabled you to do was say": Author interview with Michael Chertoff, Washington, D.C., October 28, 2009.

113 "We were running and gunning": Author interview with Frances Fragos Townsend, Washington, D.C., January 8, 2010.

113 But the fears seem justified when authorities in Germany and Denmark: Nicholas Kulish, "New Terrorism Case Confirms that Denmark Is a Target," *New York Times*, September 17, 2007.

114 a "monstrous blood bath": Mark Landler, "German Police Arrest 3 in Terrorist Plot," *New York Times*, September 6, 2007.

115   "This looked to be bigger than Anaconda": Author interview with a senior U.S. military officer, Washington, D.C., 2011.

115   "It was a big deal": Author interview with a senior U.S. military officer, Washington, D.C., 2011.

116   "The threat stream was viable": Author interview with a senior national security official, 2010.

116   "If UBL had been there": Author interview with a senior national security official, 2010.

117   "Fallon's view was you're swatting a fly": Author phone interview with a former senior U.S. military officer, February 2011.

117   "There was a lot of concern about how much ordnance": Author interview with a senior U.S. military officer, January 2011.

117   "This was carpet bombing, pure and simple": Author interview with a senior national security official, Washington, D.C., February 2010.

118   "It went from being a salad to a stew": Author interview with General Michael Hayden, former director of Central Intelligence and National Security Agency, Arlington, Va., April 8, 2010.

119   the "trip from hell": Ibid.

119   "Mr. President, we've seen a merger": Ibid.

121   The roller-coaster relations between the CIA and the ISI hit a new low: Mark Mazzetti and Eric Schmitt, "Pakistanis Aided Attack in Kabul, U.S. Officials Say," *New York Times*, August 1, 2008.

122   "I saw it in longer terms than I think others did": Author interview with Major General Jeffrey Schloesser, USA (Ret.), Arlington, Va., March 10, 2010.

123   "The operation made a lot more noise on the ground": Author interview with a senior national security official, Washington, D.C., 2010.

5. TERROR 2.0

128   "That AQ 'ExOrd' was the first designed against an enemy": Author interview with a Bush administration national security official, 2010.

129   "Just like if I want to go to Iraq with the Fourth Division": Author interview with a Bush administration national security official, 2010.

129   "A fortress mentality will not work in cyber": Author interview
        with Deputy Secretary of Defense William Lynn, Arlington, Va.,
        January 2010.

130   "You don't just deter with costs, but also with benefits": Gen-
        eral Larry D. Welch, USAF (Ret.), U.S. Strategic Command
        Deterrence Symposium, Omaha, Neb., August 12, 2010.

130   "Deterrence has been a fundamental part": Author interview
        with a White House official working on cybersecurity, Washing-
        ton, D.C., 2010.

131   "We are looking beyond just the pure military might": Author
        interview with General Kevin Chilton, USAF, Omaha, Neb., Feb-
        ruary 19, 2010.

131   "States, terrorists and those who would act as their proxies":
        Mark Landler, "Clinton Urges Global Response to Internet
        Attacks," *New York Times*, January 21, 2010.

132   "We knew we could pull it off": Author interview with a senior
        Pentagon official, 2009.

133   "The Internet forum is the connective tissue of the global Jihad":
        Author interview with a U.S. intelligence officer, 2010.

134   "General Abizaid was the Centcom commander": Author inter-
        view with a U.S. counterterrorism official, Arlington, Va., 2010.

135   "this country, over its two-hundred-plus years of history": Author
        interview with General John Abizaid, USA (Ret.), U.S. Military
        Academy, West Point, N.Y., January 12, 2010.

136   "We invited everybody and their brother": Author interview
        with a senior administration official, Washington, D.C., August
        2010.

137   "It is a Sufi sect": Author interview with a U.S. military intelli-
        gence officer, Arlington, Va., 2010.

138   "When you're working against terrorists": Author interview
        with a senior military officer, Baghdad, 2010.

138   "Now, if there is a honey pot like that": Author interview with
        a former National Security Council official, Washington, D.C.,
        2010.

140   "We chased them all over the globe": Author interview with a
        senior Pentagon official, Arlington, Va., 2010.

140   "a knock-down, drag-out interagency battle": Author interview
        with an administration official, Washington, D.C., 2010.

141   "The community is split": Author interview with Arthur Cum-
        mings, Washington, D.C., April 9, 2010.

143   "There's your decision space": Author interview with General
        Keith Alexander, Fort Meade, Md., September 22, 2010.

146   "We can take them down for a brief time": Author interview
        with a U.S. military planner, Tampa, Fla., April 29, 2010.

147   "All Al Qaeda products appear to go through": Author inter-
        view with a U.S. operations officer, Tampa, Fla., April 28, 2010.

147   "We had the ability to hack into their phones": Author inter-
        view with a U.S. intelligence officer, 2010.

148   "They go into open forums": Author interview with a U.S. State
        Department official, Washington, D.C., 2010.

148   "With the decrease in online postings": Author interview with a
        senior military officer, Arlington, Va., 2010.

150   "They were substantially radicalized on the Internet": Author
        interview with Arthur Cummings, Washington, D.C., April 9,
        2010.

150   "There are tens of millions of people playing at one time":
        Author interview with a U.S. counterterrorism official, April 29,
        2010.

151   "You know, I could put up filters for every single one of those
        people": Author interview with a senior U.S. counterterrorism
        official, Washington, D.C., February 23, 2010.

6. COUNTERING AL QAEDA'S MESSAGE

152   "We will, however, relentlessly confront violent extremists":
        President Barack Obama, "A New Beginning," Cairo, Egypt, June
        4, 2009.

155   A study by the West Point Center for Combating Terrorism:
        Scott Helfstein, Nassir Abdullah, and Muhammad al-Obaidi,
        *Deadly Vanguards: A Study of al-Qa'ida's Violence Against Mus-
        lims* (West Point, N.Y.: Center for Combating Terrorism, U.S.
        Military Academy, December 2009).

155   "Our view of the speech was pretty simple": Author interview
        with Ben Rhodes, Washington, D.C., September 27, 2010.

157   "Roughly one year since Obama's Cairo address": Pew Global
        Survey, June 2010.

157   An Arab Public Opinion Poll: "Arab Majority Backs Nuclear Iran," Zogby International, August 6, 2010.

157   "The Cairo speech, initially at least, was very important": Author interview with a senior State Department official, Washington, D.C., August 27, 2010.

158   "What I think we got after that speech": Author interview with Ben Rhodes, Washington, D.C., September 27, 2010.

159   "It's a discrediting": John Brennan, New York University Law School, March 18, 2011.

160   But when the *New York Times* disclosed in February 2002: Eric Schmitt and James Dao, "Bush Seals Fate of Office of Influence in Pentagon," *New York Times*, February 26, 2002.

160   "You can destroy the people in Al Qaeda": Author interview with General John Abizaid, USA (Ret.), U.S. Military Academy, West Point, N.Y., January 12, 2010.

160   "You're putting your finger in the dike": Author interview with Philip Mudd, Washington, D.C., February 23, 2010.

161   "We haven't killed the innocents": Ayman al-Zawahri, April 2, 2008.

162   a growing number of extremist forums are now using password-protected sites: Author interview with Evan F. Kohlmann, Riyadh, Saudi Arabia, January 24, 2011.

162   "Fallujah was a festering cancer": Author interview with Lieutenant General Thomas F. Metz, USA (Ret.), Arlington, Va., September 27, 2010.

165   "It was just a missed opportunity": Author interview with Michele Davis, Washington, D.C., Spring 2010.

166   "We were struggling with, what does a messaging and ideological battle look like": Author interview with Juan Zarate, Washington, D.C., March 8, 2010.

166   "I had the authority to drop a bomb": Author interview with a senior military officer, Arlington, Va., 2010.

167   "The main goal was to create a constant drumbeat": Author interview with Mark Pfeifle, Washington, D.C., March 4, 2010.

168   In other locations, the messaging was integrated more seamlessly: Eric Schmitt, "U.S. Training in Africa Aims to Deter Extremists," *New York Times*, December 13, 2008.

168   "Young men in the north are looking for jobs": Author interview
           with Alexander D. Newton, Bamako, Mali, November 2008.

168   a report issued in October 2003: Steven R. Weisman, "U.S.
           Must Counteract Image in Muslim World, Panel Says," *New
           York Times*, October 1, 2003.

169   "What terrorists want to do with young people": Author inter-
           view with James Glassman, Washington, D.C., February 15,
           2010.

171   "We were losing the battle": Author interview with Gonzalo Gal-
           legos, Washington, D.C., Spring 2010.

172   "This is not a propaganda contest—it is a relationship race":
           Judith McHale, "Striking a Balance: A New American Security,"
           Center for a New American Security, June 11, 2009.

172   "It's both microphones and drones": Author interview with a
           senior Pentagon official, Arlington, Va., 2010.

174   "I thought I asked for this a year ago": Author interview with a
           senior administration official, Summer 2010.

174   "I got my butt chewed in that meeting pretty hard": Author
           interview with Denis McDonough, Washington, D.C., January
           13, 2011.

174   "If this were easy, people would have done it a long time ago":
           Author interview with Ambassador Richard LeBaron, Washing-
           ton, D.C., February 18, 2011.

176   "The goal is fuzzing out the militants' radio broadcasts": Author
           interview with a U.S. government official, Washington, D.C.,
           2010.

177   "We can either play into Al Qaeda's narrative": Denis
           McDonough, Adams Center, Sterling, Va., March 6, 2011.

177   "We have come to a realization": Author interview with John
           Tyson, Arlington, Va., September 18, 2010.

178   "This is not about getting them to love us": Author interview
           with a senior Department of Defense official, Arlington, Va., 2010.

179   "It is not always best for us to hammer the counterterrorism
           drum": Michael Leiter, speech to the Center for Strategic and
           International Affairs, Washington, D.C., December 1, 2010.

179   "The U.S. government clearly has a challenge in terms of mes-
           saging": Michael Leiter, comments from Aspen Strategy Group,
           Aspen, Colo., June 30, 2010.

179   "we are farther behind than I would like": Author interview with Michael Leiter, McLean, Va., November 4, 2010.

179   "We help make our own luck": Michael Leiter, speech to the Center for Strategic and International Affairs, Washington, D.C., December 1, 2010.

7. THE NEW NETWORK WARFARE

181   "But once we showed that slide": Author interview with Barry Pavel, Arlington, Va., September 28, 2010.

182   "Obviously, hard-core terrorists will be the hardest to deter": Author interview with Michael Vickers, Arlington, Va., August 26, 2010.

183   "It doesn't take a lot of money to be a terrorist": Author interviews with intelligence analysts at MacDill Air Force Base, Tampa, Fla., April 2010.

183   "If it's not job number one, then it's number one-A": Author interview with a senior military officer, Tampa, Fla., April 29, 2010.

183   "There are these terror web sites": Author interview with a Central Command intelligence officer, Tampa, Fla., April 2010.

184   "Many Hawala buildings have three-hundred-plus separate family businesses": Author interview with a Central Command intelligence officer, Tampa, Fla., April 2010.

184   "At Treasury, we used financial information": Author interview with Juan Zarate, Washington, D.C., August 17, 2010.

184   "The important person in this chain is the one with the relationships": Author interview with a Central Command intelligence officer, Tampa, Fla., April 2010.

185   "More than anyone else, Yazid possessed links": Stuart Levey, "Loss of Moneyman a Big Blow for Al-Qaeda," *Washington Post*, June 6, 2010.

188   "The guys who are doing the weapons transfers?": Author interview with a U.S. military officer, 2010.

188   "Take him out, and suicide bombings from that network": Author interview with a U.S. military officer, 2010.

189   "They are very proud": Author interview with a Central Command intelligence officer, Tampa, Fla., April 2010.

189   "When a person moves, that's when we can get them": Author interview with a Special Operations officer, 2010.

189   "You have to take the people with specialized experience off the battlefield": Author interview with Michael Leiter, McLean, Va., November 4, 2010.

191   "We by ourselves don't really pursue the threat of terrorism": Author interview with Major General Samuel T. Helland, USMC, Camp Lemonier, Djibouti, December 2004.

192   "is a model of how we can deter terrorists": Author interview with Lieutenant General Douglas E. Lute, USA, Washington, D.C., 2005.

194   "It is a deterrent mission": Author interview with a senior Pentagon planner, Arlington, Va., 2005.

195   "The successes we enjoy, and the gains": Author telephone interview with Admiral Timothy J. Keating, USN, August 2009.

195   "In general, the Joint Special Operations Task Force–Philippines": Quoted in Thom Shanker, "U.S. Military to Stay in Philippines," *New York Times*, August 20, 2009.

195   "Help the Philippines security forces": Quoted in ibid.

197   "We are determined to stay until we finish this menace": Author interview with Major Shazad Saleem, South Waziristan, Pakistan, June 2010.

198   "We want to keep a low signature": Author interview with a senior Pakistani military officer, Pakistan, 2010.

199   "This is the most complex operating environment I've ever dealt with": Author interview with Colonel Kurt Sonntag, USA, Peshawar, Pakistan, June 2010.

200   "settling down and maturing": Author interview with Lieutenant General Tariq Khan of the Pakistani Army, Peshawar, Pakistan, June 2010.

201   "the bombers often had been child brides of terrorists": Author interview with Lieutenant General Mark P. Hertling, Arlington, Va., June 21, 2010.

205   "It's a brute-force effort": Author interview with a defense intelligence officer, Arlington, Va., September 2010.

205   "We can unravel that": Author interview with a U.S. military officer, April 29, 2010.

205   "Another major breakthrough": Author interview with a U.S. intelligence officer, April 29, 2010.

206   "We can go into an interrogation": Author interview with a U.S. military officer, April 29, 2010.

206   "Knowing about a missing toe": Author interview with a U.S. intelligence analyst, April 29, 2010.

207   "The bad news is, we don't know how to manage all of the information yet": Author interview with Major General James O. Poss, USAF, Arlington, Va., 2010.

208   "Today, an analyst sits there and stares at 'Death TV' ": Speech by General James E. Cartwright, New Orleans, La., November 2010.

208   "If you look at it from a network standpoint": Author interview with John Tyson, Arlington, Va., May 19, 2010.

8. THE RISE OF HOME-GROWN EXTREMISM

209   "He's not Jack Bauer": Juan Zarate, remarks at the Center for Strategic and International Studies, "The Changing Terrorist Threat and NCTC's Response," Washington, D.C., December 1, 2010.

210   "We have to be honest that some things will get through": Michael Leiter, "The Changing Terrorist Threat and NCTC's Response," Center for Strategic and International Studies, Washington, D.C., December 1, 2010.

211   "Since I was fifteen": Quoted in Colin Miner, Liz Robbins, and Erik Eckholm, "Bomb Plot Foiled at Holiday Event in Portland, Ore.," *New York Times*, November 28, 2010.

212   American Muslims were better assimilated culturally and economically: Mark A. Randol and Jerome P. Bjelopera, "American Jihadist Terrorism: Combating a Complex Threat," Congressional Research Service, December 7, 2010.

213   a wide-ranging report issued in August 2007: Al Baker, "New York City Police Report Explores Homegrown Threat," *New York Times*, August 16, 2007.

213   "I have a better understanding of radicals in London": Remarks by Michael Leiter, Washington, D.C., February 24, 2010.

214   "It is difficult to understand": Author interview with Homeland
         Security Secretary Janet Napolitano, Washington, D.C., March
         21, 2011.

214   "We have a good capability to detect and disrupt": Dennis
         Blair, director of national intelligence, Testimony Before the
         Senate Homeland Security Committee, January 20, 2010.

214   "Counterterrorism in newspapers is about plots": Philip Mudd,
         comments on panel on "Domestic Intelligence," hosted by
         Bipartisan Policy Council, Willard Hotel, Washington, D.C.,
         October 6, 2010.

215   "There was no doubt in my mind": Author interview with Jim
         Davis, Federal Bureau of Investigation, Denver, Colo., 2010.

217   "He thought he could talk his way out of this": Author inter-
         view with Steve Olson, Federal Bureau of Investigation, Denver,
         Colo., 2010.

218   "He felt somewhat of a misfit": Author interview with Eric
         Jergenson, Federal Bureau of Investigation, Denver, Colo.,
         2010.

219   In a 2007 PowerPoint demonstration: Scott Shane, "Wars
         Fought and Wars Googled," New York Times, June 27, 2010.

220   "Can you tell me a way to save the oppressed?": Andrea Elliott,
         Sabrina Tavernise, and Anne Bernard, "For Times Sq. Suspect,
         Long Roots of Discontent," New York Times, May 16, 2010.

221   "sheikhs are in the field": Ibid.

221   "Brace yourselves, because the war with Muslims has just
         begun": Michael Wilson, "Judgment Day in Two High-Profile
         Cases: Times Square's Would-Be Bomber Is Defiant as He Gets a
         Life Term," New York Times, October 6, 2010.

222   "As the pace of mobilization increases": Author interview with
         Michael Leiter, McLean, Va., November 4, 2010.

222   "What we have seen is that the distance": Michael Chertoff,
         Q-and-A response at panel hosted by Bipartisan Policy Council,
         Willard Hotel, Washington, D.C., October 6, 2010.

224   "That person said, 'I am telling you this' ": Author interview
         with Steven L. Gomez, FBI, Washington, D.C., October 20, 2010.

224   "We are going to see the trend": Author interview with Michael
         Leiter, McLean, Va., November 4, 2010.

9. "IS AL QAEDA JUST KLEENEX?"

226 "Brothers with less experience": Al Qaeda in the Arabian Peninsula, *Inspire* 4 (Fall 2010): 57.

226 "The assumption was they were attempting to weaponize them": Author interview with a senior Obama administration official, Washington, D.C., Winter 2011.

227 "The actual casualties of a given isolated attack": Ibid.

228 "but that is not their approach": Ibid.

228 "probably the most significant risk to the U.S. homeland": Michael Leiter, House Homeland Security Committee, February 9, 2011.

228 "After Christmas, a discussion that had been out there": Author interview with John Tyson, Arlington, Va., May 2010.

229 "AQAP now provides": Jarret Brachman, House Homeland Security Committee, March 2, 2011.

229 "AQAP seems satisfied with disruptive attacks": Author interview with senior intelligence official, Washington, D.C., 2010.

229 "I think part of the reason for some of the far-reaching measures": Author interview with Secretary of Defense Robert Gates, Arlington, Va., January 11, 2010.

230 "In the early days, we were like a drunken octopus": Author interview with senior military officer, Washington, D.C., 2011.

231 "We didn't know they had progressed to the point": John Brennan, White House briefing, Washington, D.C., January 7, 2010.

231 "Had that plane gone down": Author interview with a senior American intelligence officer, 2010.

231 "He has been much more interested in figuring out analytically what happened": Author interview with a White House adviser, Washington, D.C., 2010.

232 "Is Al Qaeda just Kleenex?": Interview with an Obama administration national security official, Washington, D.C., 2010.

232 "The president is very clear in setting expectations": Author interview with senior administration official, Washington, D.C., 2010.

232 "He gives homework assignments": Author interview with a senior Obama administration official, Arlington, Va., January 2011.

233   "There is a conscious effort now to give him a structured brief":
        Author interview with a senior U.S. intelligence officer, 2010.

233   "That is a very familiar point that he makes": Author interview
        with senior administration official, Washington, D.C., 2010.

234   "Part of the way is just messaging": Author interview with a senior
        White House adviser, Washington, D.C., 2010.

235   "When we kill somebody, there is going to be someone else to
        take their place": Author interview with Michael Leiter, McLean,
        Va., November 4, 2010.

236   "We are not underestimating them today": Author interview
        with Undersecretary of Defense for Policy Michele A. Flournoy,
        Arlington, Va., December 7, 2010.

236   "Two Nokia mobiles, $150 each": Al Qaeda in the Arabian
        Peninsula, *Inspire* 4 (Fall 2010).

236   "Al Qaeda in the Arabian Peninsula is now the most operationally
        active node": John Brennan, remarks at the Carnegie Endow-
        ment for International Peace, Washington, D.C., December 17,
        2010.

237   "We continue to treat it as worthy of serious concern": Inter-
        view with an Obama administration national security official,
        Washington, D.C., 2011.

237   "In this era of this more complicated threat": Michael Leiter,
        "The Changing Terrorist Threat and NCTC's Response," Center
        for Strategic and International Studies, Washington, D.C., Decem-
        ber 1, 2010.

10. THE OBAMA STRATEGY

239   "Americans would expect no less of me": Author interview with
        a senior U.S. official, February 2011.

240   "that got Kayani's attention": Author interview with a senior
        Pakistani official, February 2011.

242   "They gave us an hour and we spent fifty-five minutes on ter-
        rorism": Author interview with former director of national
        intelligence Mike McConnell, Reston, Va., November 3, 2010.

242   he rapidly escalated the pace of the CIA's attacks: *Long War
        Journal*, June 1, 2011, www.longwarjournal.com.

246   "It has been my practice since I took this job": Author inter-

view with Secretary of Defense Robert Gates, aboard his airplane en route from West Point to Washington, D.C., February 25, 2011.

246 "A counterterrorism strategy that focuses on the immediate threat": John Brennan, remarks to the Carnegie Endowment for International Peace, Washington, D.C., December 2010.

248 "The more the political friction": Author interview with Nick Rasmussen, Washington, D.C., March 31, 2011.

248 "In the immediate aftermath of 9/11, I remember it very vividly": Author interview with John Brennan, Washington, D.C., January 13, 2011.

249 "We've created an environment": Author interview with Secretary of Defense Robert Gates, aboard his airplane en route from West Point to Washington, D.C., February 25, 2011.

250 "These are all security officers so they're not novices at this": Author interview with Rand Beers, Washington, D.C., November 19, 2010.

251 "If the signature weapon for us is the Predator": Author interview with Michael Vickers, Arlington, Va., August 26, 2010.

251 "One of the questions I asked myself": Author interview with Admiral Michael Mullen, chairman of the Joint Chiefs of Staff, Arlington, Va., January 5, 2011.

252 "This is an area that we sort of put on the shelf": Author interview with Admiral Michael Mullen, chairman of the Joint Chiefs of Staff, Arlington, Va., January 4, 2010.

253 "While not all extremist groups share the same goals or ideology": Admiral Michael Mullen, Hoover Institution conference, Stanford University, November 12, 2010.

254 "Everybody believes we're going to get hit again": Author interview with Admiral Michael Mullen, chairman of the Joint Chiefs of Staff, Arlington, Va., January 5, 2011.

11. COUNTERSTRIKE IN ABBOTTABAD

256 In fact, in the mission's opening minutes: Author interview with senior administration official, Washington, D.C., May 7, 2011.

257 "This mission simply would not have been possible before": A broad description of the Gates assessment in the Situation Room

was provided by a senior administration official in an author interview on May 2, 2011, and was confirmed in greater detail in an e-mail message from Gates transmitted through Geoff Morrell, the Pentagon press secretary, on May 6, 2011.

258   American intelligence officials had increasing confidence: The reconstruction of events leading up to and on the day of the Abbottabad raid is from Mark Mazzetti, Helene Cooper, and Peter Baker, "Behind the Hunt for Bin Laden," *New York Times*, May 3, 2011.

259   "One of the things we have seen since 9/11 is an extraordinary coming together": Robert M. Gates, press briefing, Seymour Johnson Air Force Base, N.C., May 6, 2011.

260   "It was looked at from the standpoint": John Brennan, press briefing, Washington, D.C., May 2, 2011.

260   Intelligence officials were reluctant to get a closer look: Bob Woodward, "Trail to bin Laden Began with One Call," *Washington Post*, May 7, 2011.

260   The agency had carried about 240 drone attacks in Pakistan: *Long War Journal*, May 2011,www.longwarjournal.org.

261   White House officials worried that any strategic blow to Al Qaeda: Author interview with senior administration official, Washington, D.C., May 7, 2011.

261   "It was decided that any effort to work with the Pakistanis": Leon Panetta, quoted in "They Might Alert the Targets," *Time*, www.time.com, May 3, 2011.

262   He summoned aides to the White House Diplomatic Room: Tom Donilon, speaking on CNN's *State of the Union*, May 8, 2011.

262   "The president was trying to balance competing objectives": Author telephone interview with Nick Rasmussen, Washington, D.C., May 7, 2011.

263   "There were people inside the intelligence community": Author interview with senior administration official, Washington, D.C., May 7, 2011.

264   "absolutely the single guy I would choose for this mission": Author interview with senior administration official, Washington, D.C., May 7, 2011.

264   "They've reached the target": The account of the strike is drawn from a detailed reconstruction by the staff of the *New York Times* in "How the Raid Unfolded," *New York Times*, May 8, 2011.

265   "We got him": Mazzetti, Cooper, and Baker, "Behind the Hunt for Bin Laden."

265   "This collection represents the most significant amount of intelligence": Senior intelligence official, news briefing, the Pentagon, Arlington, Va., May 7, 2011.

266   "This was the ultimate raid of its kind": Author interview with Michael Vickers, Arlington, Va., May 4, 2011.

267   "We essentially prepared a messaging strategy for every possible circumstance": Author telephone interview with Ben Rhodes, Washington, D.C., May 7, 2011.

267   "Here is bin Laden, who has been calling for these attacks": John Brennan, press briefing, Washington, D.C., May 2, 2011.

269   "It also demonstrates no terrorist is safe": Author telephone interview with Ben Rhodes, Washington, D.C., May 7, 2011.

270   "It's inconceivable that bin Laden did not have a support system in the country": John Brennan, press briefing, Washington, D.C., May 2, 2011.

270   "Simply wishing away Al Qaeda isn't going to happen": Author telephone interview with Nick Rasmussen, Washington, D.C., May 7, 2011.

270   "What bound the organization together": Author telephone interview with Michael Leiter, Washington, D.C., May 5, 2011.

271   "This is not the time to take our foot off the gas": Author telephone interview with Ben Rhodes, Washington, D.C., May 7, 2011.

271   "Bin Laden's death is a tremendous strategic blow to Al Qaeda": Author interview with Michael Vickers, Arlington, Va., May 4, 2011.

EPILOGUE: "TELL ME HOW THIS ENDS"

272   "There is a fundamental tension in seeking a counterterrorism 'grand strategy'": Author interview with Michael Vickers, Arlington, Va., August 26, 2010.

275   "In the months before Fort Hood": Michael Leiter, comments on panel hosted by Bipartisan Policy Council, Willard Hotel, Washington, D.C., October 6, 2010.

275   "bring fresh eyes to the problems we face": Author telephone interview with Michael Leiter, June 9, 2011.

276   "Though terrorists are difficult to deter directly": Department of Defense, National Military Strategy, 2011.

276   "They have been able to innovate faster than we have": Author interview with Major General Jeffrey Schloesser, USA (Ret.), Arlington, Va., Spring 2011.

277   "Though we are safer now than after 9/11": Author e-mail interview with Juan Zarate, March 5, 2011.

278   "There is not going to be a V-J Day": Author interview with John Tyson, Arlington, Va., 2010.

BIBLIOGRAPHY

BOOKS

Abbas, Hassan, ed. *Pakistan's Troubled Frontier*. Washington, D.C.: Jamestown Foundation, 2009.

Benjamin, Daniel, and Steven Simon. *The Age of Sacred Terror: Radical Islam's War Against America*. New York: Random House, 2002.

_____. *The Next Attack: The Failure of the War on Terror and a Strategy for Getting It Right*. New York: Times Books, 2005.

Bergen, Peter. *Holy War, Inc.: Inside the Secret World of Osama bin Laden*. New York: Free Press, 2001.

_____. *The Longest War: The Enduring Conflict Between America and Al-Qaeda*. New York: Free Press, 2011.

_____. *The Osama bin Laden I Know: An Oral History of al Qaeda's Leader*. New York: Free Press, 2006.

Byman, Daniel. *The Five Front War: The Better Way to Fight Global Jihad*. New York: Wiley, 2007.

Chertoff, Michael, and Lee Hamilton. *Homeland Security: Assessing the First Five Years*. Philadelphia: University of Pennsylvania Press, 2009.

Clarke, Richard A. *Against All Enemies: Inside America's War on Terror*. New York: Free Press, 2004.

Cloughley, Brian. *Wars, Coups and Terror: Pakistan's Army in Years of Turmoil*. New York: Skyhorse Publishing, 2008.

Cohen, Stephen Philip. *The Idea of Pakistan*. Washington, D.C.: Brookings Institution Press, 2004.

Coll, Steve. *The Bin Ladens: An Arabian Family in the American Century*. New York: Penguin Press, 2008.

_____. *Ghost Wars: The Secret History of the CIA, Afghanistan and Bin Laden, from the Soviet Invasion to September 10, 2001*. New York: Penguin Press, 2004.

Crenshaw, Martha. *The Consequences of Counterterrorism*. New York: Russell Sage Foundation Publishing, 2010.

Cronin, Audrey. *How Terrorism Ends: Understanding the Demise and Decline of Terrorism Campaigns*. Princeton: Princeton University Press, 2010.

Davis, Paul K. *Simple Models to Explore Deterrence and More General Influence in the War with al-Qaeda*. Washington, D.C.: Rand National Defense Research Institute, 2010.

Dickey, Christopher. *Securing the City: Inside America's Best Counterterror Force—The NYPD*. New York: Simon & Schuster, 2009.

Felter, Joseph, and Brian Fishman. *Al-Qa'ida's Foreign Fighters in Iraq: A First Look at the Sinjar Records*. West Point, N.Y.: Combating Terrorism Center at the United States Military Academy, no date.

Fishman, Brian, ed., and Peter Bergen, Joseph Felter, Vahid Brown, and Jacob Shapiro. *Bombers, Bank Accounts & Bleedout: Al-Qa'ida's Road In and Out of Iraq*. West Point, N.Y.: Combating Terrorism Center at the U.S. Military Academy, 2008.

Friedman, Benjamin H., Jim Harper, and Christopher A. Preble. *Terrorizing Ourselves: Why U.S. Counterterrorism Policy Is Failing and How to Fix It*. Washington, D.C.: CATO Institute, 2010.

Gallagher, John, and Eric D. Patterson. *Debating the War of Ideas*. New York: Palgrave Macmillan, 2009.

Geltzer, Joshua Alexander. *US Counter-Terrorism Strategy and al-Qaeda: Signalling and the Terrorist World View*. London and New York: Routledge, 2010.

Gul, Imtiaz. *The Most Dangerous Place: Pakistan's Lawless Frontier*. New York: Viking, 2010.

Hoffman, Bruce. *Inside Terrorism*. New York: Columbia University Press, 2006.

Hussain, Zahid. *Frontline Pakistan: The Struggle with Militant Islam*. New York: Columbia University Press, 2007.

Mayer, Jane. *The Dark Side: The Inside Story of How the War on Terror Turned into a War on American Ideals*. New York: Doubleday, 2008.

Moghadam, Assaf. *The Globalization of Martyrdom*. Baltimore: Johns Hopkins University Press, 2008.

Myers, Richard, and Malcolm McConnell. *Eyes on the Horizon: Serving on the Front Lines of National Security*. New York: Threshold Publishing, 2009.

Nasiri, Omar. *Inside the Jihad: My Life with Al Qaeda*. New York: Basic Books, 2006.

National Commission on Terrorist Attacks. *The 9/11 Commission Report: Final Report of the National Commission on Terrorist Attacks Upon the United States*. New York: W. W. Norton & Company, 2004.

Nawaz, Shuja. *Crossed Swords: Pakistan, Its Army, and the Wars Within*. Oxford, U.K.: Oxford University Press, 2008.

Pape, Robert. *Dying to Win: The Strategic Logic of Suicide Terrorism*. New York: Random House, 2006.

Rabasa, Angel, and Cheryl Bernard, Lowell H. Schwartz, and Peter Sickle. *Building Moderate Muslim Networks*. Washington: RAND, 2007.

Rashid, Ahmed. *Descent into Chaos: The United States and the Failure of Nation Building in Pakistan, Afghanistan, and Central Asia*. New York: Viking, 2008.

_____. *Jihad: The Rise of Militant Islam in Central Asia*. New York: Penguin, 2002.

_____. *Taliban: Militant Islam, Oil and Fundamentalism in Central Asia*. 2nd ed. New Haven: Yale University Press, 2010.

Riedel, Bruce. *Deadly Embrace: Pakistan, America and the Future of Global Jihad*. Washington, D.C.: Brookings Institution Press, 2011.

_____. *The Search for Al Qaeda*. Washington, D.C.: Brookings Institution Press, 2010.

Roe, Andrew M. *Waging War in Waziristan: The British Struggle in the Land of Bin Laden, 1849–1947*. Lawrence: University of Kansas Press, 2010.

Sageman, Marc. *Leaderless Jihad: Terror Networks in the Twenty-First Century*. Philadelphia: University of Pennsylvania Press, 2008.

_____. *Understanding Terror Networks*. Philadelphia: University of Pennsylvania Press, 2004.

Schelling, Thomas. *Arms and Influence*. New Haven: Yale University Press, 1966.

_____. *The Strategy of Conflict*. Cambridge, Mass.: Harvard University Press, 1960.

Scheuer, Michael. *Osama bin Laden*. New York: Oxford University Press, 2011.

Stern, Jessica. *Terror in the Name of God: Why Religious Militants Kill*. New York: Harper Perennial, 2004.

Tellis, Ashley J. *Pakistan and the War on Terror: Conflicted Goals, Compromised Performance*. Washington, D.C.: Carnegie Endowment for International Peace, 2008.

Thiessen, Marc. *Courting Disaster: How the CIA Kept America Safe and How Barack Obama Is Inviting the Next Attack*. Washington: Regnery Publishing, 2010.

Trinkuas, Harold, and Jeanne Giraldo. *Terrorism Financing and State Responses: A Comparative Perspective*. Stanford: Stanford University Press, 2007.

Woodward, Bob. *Obama's Wars*. New York: Simon & Schuster, 2010.

_____. *The War Within*. New York: Simon & Schuster, 2008.

Wright, Lawrence. *The Looming Tower: Al Qaeda and the Road to 9/11*. New York: Vintage, 2007.

Zuhur, Sherifa. *Precision in the Global War on Terror: Inciting Muslims Through the War of Ideas*. Carlisle, Pa.: Strategic Studies Institute, U.S. Army War College, 2008.

JOURNAL ARTICLES AND REPORTS

Byman, Daniel. "Remaking Alliances for the War on Terrorism." *Journal of Strategic Studies* 29, no. 5 (October 2006): 767–811.

Carpenter, J. Scott, and Matthew Levitt, Steven Simon, and Juan Zarate. "Fighting the Ideological Battle: The Missing Link in U.S. Strategy to Counter Violent Extremism." A Washington Institute Strategic Report, 2010.

D'Souza, Shanthie. "U.S.-Pakistan Counter-Terrorism Cooperation: Dynamics and Challenges." *Strategic Analyses* (July–September 2006): 525–61.

Fair, C. Christine, and Peter Chalk. "United States Internal Security Assistance to Pakistan." *Small Wars and Insurgencies* 17, no. 3 (September 2006): 333–55.

Farrall, Leah. "The Evolution of Command and Control." *Jane's Strategic Advisory Services* (November 2009): 16–20.

Gregory, Shaun. "The ISI and the War on Terrorism." *Studies in Conflict & Terrorism* 30, no. 12 (2007): 1013–31.

Kronstadt, K. Alan. "Direct Overt U.S. Aid and Military Reimbursements to Pakistan, FY2002–FY2011." Congressional Research Service, June 7, 2010.

Markey, Daniel. "Pakistani Partnerships with the United States: An Assessment." *The National Bureau of Asian Research*, November 2009.

_____. "Securing Pakistan's Tribal Belt." Council on Foreign Relations, August 2008.

Sims, Jennifer E. "Foreign Intelligence Liaison: Devils, Deals and Details." *International Journal of Intelligence and CounterIntelligence* 19 (2006): 195–217.

Task Force on Confronting the Ideology of Radical Extremism. *Rewriting the Narrative: An Integrated Strategy for Counterradicalization.* Washington Institute for Near East Policy, 2009.

Trager, Robert F., and Dessislava P. Zagorcheva. "Deterring Terrorism: It Can Be Done." *International Security* 30, no. 3 (Winter 2005/6): 87–123.

Winchell, Sean P. "Pakistan's ISI: The Invisible Government." *International Journal of Intelligence and Counterintelligence* 16 (2003): 374–88.

ACKNOWLEDGMENTS

It remains our greatest professional honor to be correspondents for the *New York Times* covering national security issues, and it was a privilege to be allowed to report and write *Counterstrike* for Times Books and Henry Holt and Company.

For their support and encouragement throughout this process, we express most heartfelt thanks to Bill Keller, the executive editor of the *New York Times*; Jill Abramson, the managing editor; and Dean Baquet, the assistant managing editor who is our Washington bureau chief. Appreciation also is owed to the other editors in the Washington bureau: Len Apcar, Rebecca Corbett, Jack Cushman, Susan Keller, and Dick Stevenson.

We are fortunate to be part of a national security team that covers the news like no other and usually keeps a sense of balance— and even a sense of humor during the most intense news crises. We thank our colleagues, comrades, and friends: Peter Baker, Elisabeth Bumiller, Helene Cooper, Michael Gordon, Mark Landler, Eric Lichtblau, Mark Mazzetti, Steven Lee Myers, James Risen, David Sanger, Charlie Savage, Scott Shane, and Ginger Thompson. John Markoff in San Francisco was a reporting partner on a range of stories on cyberwar, and Jane Perlez in Islamabad was deeply involved in our Pakistan reporting, as were Ismail Khan, Pir Zubair Shah, and Salman Masood. Andrew Lehren repeatedly performed his magic in unlocking the secrets of the WikiLeaks cables.

Paul Golob, the editorial director of Times Books, taught us how to begin transferring our skills at daily newspaper reporting to long-form, nonfiction narrative. He wielded the red pen with precision, wisdom, and patience throughout our work. Thanks, too, to Jim Wade for helping us wrestle our first full draft into shape. Alex Ward played a vital role as our ambassador between the newspaper and the publishing house. And we offer a special word of gratitude to our friend and agent, Bonnie Nadell, a tireless advocate on our behalf.

The Center for a New American Security in Washington allowed each of us to spend ninety days as a "writer in residence" to work on *Counterstrike* in an environment of intellectual challenge; it is a place where many of the sharpest thinkers on national security hang their hat or pass through for coffee and lunch. A special thanks to Nathaniel C. Fick, John A. Nagl, and Shannon O'Reilly for their encouragement and advice at critical stages of our work. We offer a special word of gratitude for the Herculean efforts of Matt Irvine, our research assistant at CNAS, who tended to the detail work and was a vital member of the team in shaping the content throughout. Maile Yeats was also a great help conducting some of the early research.

Scott D. Sagan of Stanford University and the Center for International Security and Cooperation gathered a panel of scholars and former senior government officials to review our manuscript and offer feedback in a daylong review that truly lived up to the name "murder board." For their helpful criticism and commentary, we thank Scott and a gathering of scholars that included Martha Crenshaw, Mariano-Florentino Cuéllar, Lynn Eden, James Fearon, Thomas Fingar, Michael Freedman, Elizabeth A. Gardner, and Stephen Krasner. Thanks to Jane Esberg for her organizational support of our visit. The many hours this group devoted to reading our manuscript and the daylong critique improved our book; any remaining shortcomings are our own.

We thank Geoff Morrell, Bryan Whitman, and Douglas B. Wilson in the office of the secretary of defense. We thank Captain John Kirby, Lieutenant Commander Ryan Perry, Commander Patrick McNally, Major Liz Aptekar, Major Rob Montgomery, and MC1 Chad J. McNeeley, as well as Colonel James Baker in the office of the chairman of the Joint Chiefs of Staff. We also thank Major Clifford Gilmore in the office of the vice chairman.

A special thanks goes out to those in the government public affairs community who truly believe and act on the dictum that their job is maximum disclosure with minimum delay, all to better inform the American public about how its blood and treasure are spent in defense of the nation. In the Pentagon press office, we thank Colonel David Lapan and Captain Darryn James. A team of subject-matter specialists in the press office went far beyond the call of duty in arranging interviews, checking quotes, and confirming facts. We thank in particular Commander Robert Mehal, Tara Rigler, and Colonel Jonathan Withington for their help on a range of counterterrorism policy issues and their patience. For their help in researching Air Force intelligence, surveillance, and reconnaissance developments, we thank David Moniz, Lieutenant Colonel Todd Vician, and Margaret A. McGlinn.

A special thanks also to Don Black of the Defense Intelligence Agency, Carl Kropf of the National Counterterrorism Center, Mike Birmingham of the Office of the Director of National Intelligence, and George Little of the Central Intelligence Agency.

At the White House and the National Security Council, we are grateful for the assistance of Michael Hammer, Robert Jensen, Nicholas Shapiro, and Tommy Vietor. At the Federal Bureau of Investigation, Michael Kortan and Betsy Glick. At the Department of Homeland Security, Sean Smith. And at the State Department, P. J. Crowley and Rhonda Shore. At the Justice Department, Dean Boyd.

We received strong support across the military's global combatant commands. At Special Operations Command, we thank Colonel Tim Nye, Major Wesley Ticer, and Ken McGraw; at Central Command, Rear Admiral Hal Pittman, Captain Jack Hanzlik, and Sally Donnelly; at Northern Command, Jamie Graybeal; at Strategic Command, Colonel Kathleen A. Cook, Lieutenant Commander Steve Curry, and Major John L. Morgan; and at Cyber Command, Colonel Rivers J. Johnson Jr.

A word of appreciation is owed to the men and women serving to protect U.S. national security interests at home and abroad, often in the line of fire. A large number of officers and noncommissioned officers afforded us logistical support during many reporting trips downrange to Iraq and Afghanistan and were constantly available by telephone and e-mail after we returned home safely. Our gratitude goes out to all. In Afghanistan, we thank Rear Admiral Gregory J. Smith and Colonel Erik O. Gunhus at the International Security Assistance Force, and Lieutenant Colonel Patrick R. Seiber of Regional Command East and the 101st Airborne Division. A special, if belated, thanks is offered to the officers and NCOs of Combined Joint Special Operations Task Force–Dagger, in particular the members of the 5th Special Forces Group who fought with the militia alongside Hamid Karzai and captured Kandahar in December 2001; they allowed a correspondent into their camp for a true education in the best practices of modern American military operations, lessons that have proved valuable a decade later. In Baghdad, Colonel Daniel Baggio and Lieutenant Colonel Scott Bleichwehl of Multinational Corps–Iraq proved the power of the embed in allowing correspondents to inform their readers about the war effort. And we thank Lieutenant Colonel Josslyn Aberle and Lieutenant Karen Hyland at Multinational Force–Iraq.

We also wish to thank West Point's Combating Terrorism Center, including Director of Research Scott Helfstein and a dedicated team of experts whose wisdom and publications were extremely valuable in our work.

A great number of people have given us professional and intellectual support in ways too many to mention. Among them are Rear Admiral Stephen R. Pietropaoli (USN, Ret.) of National Defense University, Rear Admiral T. McCreary (USN, Ret.) of *military.com*, Robert S. Litwak of the Woodrow Wilson International Center for Scholars, John J. Hamre of the Center for Strategic and International Studies, Kori A. Schake of the Hoover Institution, Bruce Hoffman of Georgetown University, Frank J. Cilluffo of George Washington University's Homeland Security Policy Institute, Seth Jones of RAND, Michele L. Malvesti, Torie Clarke, Jim Garamone, and Price Floyd. Mark Knoller of CBS News provided important details about the limitations of Air Force One on 9/11.

A book like this simply is not possible without the cooperation and trust of a large number of government officials and military officers. Most of them requested that they not be named, so we extend a blanket thanks to all who helped throughout this process. If we have forgotten to mention any, please accept our apologies and know that we are sincerely grateful for your support for *Counterstrike*.

Eric Schmitt and Thom Shanker
Washington, D.C.
June 1, 2011

INDEX

ABOUT THE AUTHORS

ERIC SCHMITT is a terrorism correspondent for the *New York Times* and has embedded with troops in Iraq, Somalia, and Pakistan. Schmitt has twice been a member of *Times* reporting teams that were awarded the Pulitzer Prize.

THOM SHANKER, a Pentagon correspondent for the *New York Times*, routinely spends time embedded with troops in Iraq and Afghanistan. Shanker was formerly a foreign editor and correspondent for the *Chicago Tribune*, based in Moscow, Berlin, and Sarajevo.